SURVIVAL IN JAPANESE POW CAMPS WITH CHANGKOL AND BASKET

Airman Ernest G Darch

MINERVA PRESS
LONDON
MIAMI   DELHI   SYDNEY

SURVIVAL IN JAPANESE POW CAMPS
WITH CHANGKOL AND BASKET
Copyright © Airman Ernest G Darch 2000

ISBN 0 75411 161 X

First Published 2000 by
MINERVA PRESS
315–317 Regent Street
London W1R 7YB

Printed in Great Britain for Minerva Press

SURVIVAL IN JAPANESE
POW CAMPS WITH
CHANGKOL AND BASKET

To all the POWs who died at Kuching

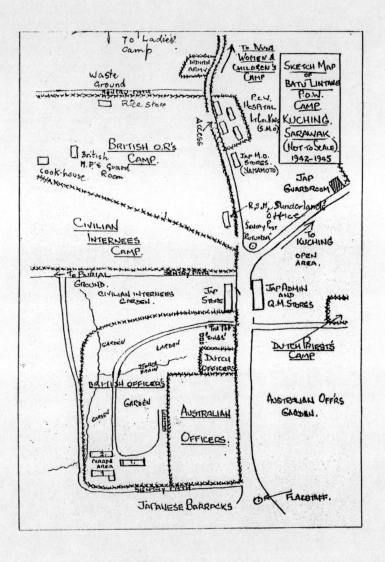

Capture

Without warning, it happened, just after midnight on 1 March 1942, while in convoy, evacuating radar equipment on the road that runs eastward from the northwest extremity of Java to its capital, Batavia. Suddenly, there was a harsh grinding of brakes as the first vehicle lurched to a stop. Then came a hullabaloo of foreign voices. What now? we asked ourselves. The crack of a rifle barked the answer, and I glanced grimly towards my mate, Freddie Pafford, who was crouched with me at the back of the leading vehicle. Without arms, there seemed only one sensible thing to do and, as though by mutual consent, we dived over the side of the lorry into a moonlit rice field.

We had received orders to evacuate our coastal radar station at Anjer, where in view was the volcano, Krakatau, and opposite the southernmost tip of Sumatra, about eleven o'clock the previous evening and, although, even before then, we had heard numerous explosions and seen the flashes that preceded them, we had never for one moment imagined that the Japanese invasion of Java, a Dutch colony, had commenced. Therefore, spreadeagled in the paddy, I thought it probable that we had blundered into a squad of Javanese soldiers who had panicked, mistaking our identity. I hardly knew a word of their language and absolutely no Japanese, so the shouting failed to enlighten me. I thought it most likely that, in a moment, our identity would be established and our evacuation continue. At the same time, it seemed wise to lie low for awhile just in case a startled Javanese fired a gun or…

I was in the act of putting on my left shoe which had come off, when there came a fusillade of shots and a blood-curdling yelp. Bullets whistled through the paddy and, quickly forcing my foot into its shoe, I ran blindly, in a crouching position like an escaping convict, away from the road. There was no longer any doubt in my mind as to what had happened. We had been introduced to the Japanese.

After a timeless few seconds, I tumbled into a ditch, sprawling flat on my stomach. Four other silent shapes joined me; besides Freddie Pafford, airmen from another lorry had escaped including

Ian Farquharson and AC Henderson.

For a while, as if just aroused from a nightmare, I could not think coherently but gradually my thoughts marshalled themselves and I realised the grave danger that still confronted us. Yet I derived some grim humour from the situation. I remembered stories that I had read of men somewhat similarly placed and I compared my feelings with theirs. Yes, it was a fact that my heart thudded so remorselessly against my ribs that I feared that it might be heard, as also my heavy breathing which vainly I tried to subdue. I knew that I was really frightened. I had never unduly dreaded the idea of being shot, but the prospect of cold steel had always sent shivers down my spine. And I had heard that the Japanese carried swords. Thus, as I lay in the ditch, I conceived horrible visions of Japanese soldiers, their long, curved, naked swords raised aloft, searching the paddy fields for an enemy whom they probably guessed was defenceless. In my mind's eye, I could see one approaching the exact spot where I was hiding and could hear his movement through the rice. He was almost on top of me – I was certain of it – and at any moment I expected him, with a heathenish whelp 'Banzai!' to plunge his weapon into my already painful body.

At the thought of all this, I make no attempt to hide the fact that I was shaking like an aspen. My teeth chattered. The prospect of death appalled me. I was too young; I was terrified of it. However, we remained unmolested, although a dreadful yell from the road heralded the fact that some poor comrade had been bayoneted. A Japanese shouted. A tank ground by. Yet, despite all this, I found that I could still be analytical, critical and cynical. Again, memories flooded in. At school, I had been told that, when faced with death, men remembered their childhood and reviewed the chief events of their life. Successive pictures of past enjoyments crossed their visions and they remembered their loved ones, with an added tenderness. So I, too, tried to gain solace by recalling all this, with a nil result. Maybe, it was because of my inability to appreciate the romance of the scene, the balance of life and death, the serene (apart from man) peacefulness of the paddy field, a half moon patching irregularly the irrigating water, the dark silhouette of coco-palms and the occasional glimpse of passing transport, black and soundless as though part of a funeral procession. There was, I suppose, a kind of poetry in the scene, a beautiful antithesis.

All I could appreciate, however, was a stationary moon which made it highly dangerous for us to move, for we were but fifty metres from the hedgeless road, having crossed the rice field in a diagonal direction. Yet, to stay put was also dangerous. What was our best course – to chance a getaway immediately or to wait until the moon had set – if it ever did? We compromised. After an eternity of time, punctuated by the grind of a passing tank and the occasional exchange of talk between two sentries who had obviously been posted, the moon dropped below a bank of cloud about fifteen degrees above the horizon. Now was our opportunity; at last, though not pitch-black, it was respectably dark.

'Now or never,' I whispered to my comrades and, hearts in our mouths, we stealthily crawled along the ditch away from the roadside. It seemed as though we crawled all night, eventually reaching cover, but my watch indicated that we had started only half an hour previously. The moon would soon be setting. I looked towards the east. There was no sign of dawn yet but the planet Venus, low down on the horizon, was splendidly bright, like the goddess that she is, and a goddess to us she would be for, by her, we would shape a rough course southwards.

'Come on,' I encouraged my comrades, a new hope surging within me. Then, like a man who, having journeyed long, by day and by night, over tractless wastes of a desert, tired of limb and parched of throat, sees at a distance an oasis, shouts and, in joyous relief bounds forward only to find a deep and broad chasm, stretching as far as the eye could see, which he must either cross or overcome by detour before he can reach his haven, so did we espy a railway line athwart our path. Immediately, I thought, 'Strategy! To what does an attacking enemy first make? Why, roads and railways! Already in command of the former, was it not logical to suppose that the Japanese would also control the latter?' So, momentarily, we halted. We were afraid to cross over, but it were no good hanging back. So, as though we were 'going over the top' in the last Great War, we at last darted across.

Our next hazard was a native kampong (village) which we

skirted cautiously, not wishing to disturb its sleeping inhabitants. Eventually, we emerged on the other side of it to see stretching southwards, a rough track. How easy it was to travel now but, once again, caution counselled us. That track seemed to be too inviting, like a particularly delectable piece of cheese placed on a nicely adjusted board, calculated on the slightest pressure to release a vicious band of metal across the neck of a mouse which had been overcome by the pangs of hunger. Better to avoid it, we thought, and veered to the right. A little further on, we stumbled across another kampong and, rather than waste time skirting it, we decided to chance it. Boldly, therefore, we walked down its one short street, finding it deserted and quiet, as though inhabited by ghosts who were now abroad haunting the souls of men. When we had drawn clear of this dreadful place, however, we discerned the first glimmerings of dawn.

Our spirits rose slowly, jerking into the stratospheres of hope, the Promised Land, El Dorado, the first sight of the Pacific! What we saw had the appearance of a low plateau, at one corner of which could dimly be observed a flagstaff with its drooping flag. Surely it was an aerodrome? Whether it was Dutch or RAF did not matter. We were not aware of a flying field thereabouts but, of course, we had all heard of the secret aerodromes in the Netherlands East Indies. Safety and refuge were at hand but, alas, it was the first of many disappointments. We rushed forward, only to discover that it had all been an illusion – the flagstaff was a palm tree with one solitary leaf hanging from its top. We plodded on again.

By now, it was light enough to spot the dark shapes of two or three aircraft circling the sky, Allied planes, of course! After a while we were not so sure. They did not conform to any of the types that we knew that the Allies possessed in the Far East. Reluctant to admit that the Japanese already had the freedom of the skies over Western Java, we, nevertheless, took care to keep under cover as much as possible.

Soon the sun rose in a welter of splendour, taking the place of Venus as our compass. Its brightness greatly heartened us, but our buoyancy was short-lived. Mounting a hill, we had a clear view towards the sea. In any other circumstances, the grandeur of the panorama towards the north would have taken our breath away. Not many miles away on the glistening waters of the Bay of Merak there rode, in the early morning sunshine, a whole Navy of about forty warships – battleships, aircraft carriers, cruisers and destroyers, together with dozens of barges further inshore. It was obviously a full-scale invasion of Java and, as we regarded the picture, our hearts plumbed the depths, for the Japanese fleet lay there as peaceful as a field of sheep on a summer's afternoon back in dear Blighty. We had no need to wonder now about the nationality of the planes that were still cruising around. Over the fleet itself, not one aircraft was to be seen. On the sea, there appeared to be no movement at all; we might have been looking at a photograph of the Home Fleet off Spithead. It was now clear that we must have been attacked near the spot where a minor road from Merak joined the road from Anjer to Serang, a town about sixty miles west of Batavia and just a few miles inland, No doubt, we had run into an advance guard, while the rear of our convoy had been subjected to the press of Japanese transport coming up from the rear. The whole position was hopeless and, for solace, I reached for my water bottle – the only one among the five of us – and allowed each man a little water, giving one of the party, who was already showing signs of weakening, a double ration.

At length, we silently turned our backs on the scene and plodded on, with added grimness. Not long afterwards, we came upon an old man working in a maze of paddy fields. Still very thirsty and rather hungry, we approached him with a view to purchasing what we required so that we could resume our journey with renewed vigour. Either the man could not, or would not, understand. I suspect the latter alternative to be correct for, although we knew very few words of Malay, we clearly asked for 'aer' (water), 'makan' (food) and 'pisanne' (banana). Grunts were the only replies. Had I known what I do now, I should have advised a much firmer line. The threat of an abrupt end to his life would, I am sure, have succeeded where cajolery had failed. But our opinion of the Javanese was then unreservedly high and we were not to know that the natives in the western province were partial to the Japanese. Unsatisfied, therefore, we continued on our way.

Our original object had been to trek southwards until we struck a road which, well to the south of the Anjer–Serang–Batavia route, I thought also led to Batavia. Once having reached the road, it would be easy to get hold of some Dutch transport, which would convey us to Batavia where we could report the loss of our equipment and have it destroyed from the air. The picture of the Japanese fleet resting so peacefully in Merak Bay had made us wonder, so that we began to debate whether, after all, our best plan was to aim at making Batavia. One man was for trekking to the southwest coast and there try to pick up a boat for Batavia. Another man was for heading straight southwards until we reached the sea from where, if the position was unhealthy, we might try to escape to Australia. On the other hand, I still maintained that the best course was to limit ourselves to the southern road, with Batavia as our objective, hoping it would still be in Allied hands. In the end my counsel prevailed partly, perhaps, because I had seemed to possess a better sense of direction and a better knowledge of the geography of Western Java. How lamentably weak I was, in at least the latter attribute, I kept to myself. For appearances' sake, I reviewed the country around us while the others waited.

Northwards, it consisted mainly of lowland, an area of rice fields and tropical vegetation, stretching as far as the sea. The road along which our convoy had travelled was invisible and no signs of the enemy could be seen, thereon. Why there should have been I don't know but, at the time, I rather expected to see troops and transports. Imagination often strangely clothes our expectations. In this instance, I looked for files of red-coated troops and groups of horsemen with standards and banners. This, no doubt, was because I had recently read a novel of Scott's based on the Jacobean period. Not a movement was to be discerned and, apart from the fleet in the bay and a few encircling aircraft, it might well have been any other morning in Java, over the past hundred years. Southwards, the scene was equally deserted but not, under the circumstances at any rate, inspiring. A line of hills, about two thousand feet in height, confronted us. The hill which we had recently climbed was low, in comparison. We were now on its southern side and between it and the next line of hills was a deep, broad valley. However, we comforted ourselves with the thought that, once over the next range of hills, we should strike the road. With this hope, we resumed our journey.

Our march was to be longer than we had anticipated. The route was also made difficult by a large area of paddy, which had to be crossed. For irrigation purposes, paddy fields were divided by low narrow banks along which we walked. These did not run in straight lines, but twisted and turned in bewildering fashion. As a result, the distance that we had to walk to traverse the rice growing area was about trebled. Not infrequently either did we slip from the bank into the water. Actually, these rice fields were very beautiful, often being terraced right up a hillside. The bright gleam of the young plants contrasted tastefully with the beautiful blue of a Java sky. However, there was little time for the contemplation of the terraced hill that we had to negotiate. Once that difficulty had been surmounted, our path led steeply upwards through rubber plantations. These, too, came to an end and, for the rest of the way, tropical vegetation was encountered.

By now, it was midday and, as we had had no food since the night before except for a few rambutans (small red coloured fruit, spiked like hedgehogs), the climb was beginning to tell. It was, therefore, with satisfaction that we spotted a small shack near the top of the hill. Inside, we discovered a small basket of rambutans, which we quickly disposed of, and some uncooked rice, a little of which we ate in its raw state. This was washed down by some of our precious water. Greatly refreshed, despite the paucity of our rations, and having left a little money as recompense to the owner of the larder, we tackled the remainder of the hill with renewed vigour. Hopes rode high once more, but they were soon to be sadly dashed. When, ultimately, we gained the summit, we beheld no road on the other side. There was a deep valley, behind which rose more hills which appeared even higher than the one that we had just ascended. There was no sign of habitation, no food, no water, other than a small drop left in my water bottle, and… no hope. Despondent, and once again feeling worn out, we merely flopped to the ground under the shade that a few bushes offered, sleep soon closing our eyes. This blissful state was of short duration. Even the elements warred against us, for we could not have slept more than an hour before being attacked by needle-like particles of rain. Not even the rain found much use for us, and the storm bustled elsewhere after tormenting us for a few minutes. Its main effect, however, was to induce us to continue our flight, with the utmost haste.

Descending the steep side of the hill was almost as fatiguing as its ascent had been. There was, too, a certain amount of danger attached to this operation, but we reached the bottom without casualty and, to our great surprise and relief, discovered a small native kampong. Stopping at what appeared to be the headman's house, we exchanged with the natives our half a dozen words of Malay and these, supplemented by movement of hand to mouth, produced the desired result. An old teakettle, filled with water, was proffered us together with two or three earthenware cups. Of the prodigious quantity of water we consumed, I will make but little mention save that we lost all restraint. I drank until I could hear the liquid rattling against the sides of my stomach. To excuse our greed, I reasoned that with only one water bottle, now refilled, between us it was best to imbibe as much liquid as possible, storing it like a camel. I only wished that we had been given the opportunity of storing up food in like manner, as we had merely been given the flesh of a few young coconuts. Perhaps, we were more refreshed by bathing in a nearby pool than by the nourishment provided for us. I don't know if we might have gained more assistance if we had been conversant with the language, but at least two facts became evident. Firstly, the natives knew of the Japanese attack and, secondly, they wanted to be rid of us. A young native, encouraged by the promise of a guilder, volunteered to lead us over a mountain track which, the natives seemed to indicate, led to the main Batavia road.

However long I live, I shall never forget that journey over those two thousand feet hills. Had we been led by a mountain goat, we could scarcely have been required to travel quicker. The young native knew no fatigue and we, not wishing to annoy him by lagging behind with the risk that by so doing we might lose his services, manfully tried to keep up with him. Despite our greatest efforts he had, at times, to await us impatiently, imparting now and then the information that it was not far to go. When at last we did crawl to the top, notwithstanding our frantic appeal and the offer of more guilders, he refused to go further. Once more, therefore, we were left to our own devices and chose a pathway that led southwards.

The trail, at length, brought us to another kampong where we not only drank but ate. Though we deemed expense no object and food was cheap, we were only given bananas and biscuits. Probably our ignorance of the language was the reason why, and as nothing else was produced I cannot overstress how important it is that members of HM Forces, no matter how humble their rank, should endeavour to pick up at least a smattering of the language of the inhabitants of the country in which they are stationed. Some may consider this unnecessary, but what if an emergency crops up such as the one we experienced and which must always be anticipated by fighting personnel? Of course, you cannot overcome everything with a knowledge of languages and, at this point, I must mention something that I might well have mentioned before. On and off, throughout the whole of our wanderings, the throb of drums could be heard. We supposed that our progress southwards was being recorded by the natives. This fact, no doubt, accounted for the reserve with which we were treated, the anxiety to get rid of us from each neighbourhood in turn and, later, other happenings of a more unpleasant nature. They knew that we were fugitives from the invading Japanese. Thus, at this kampong, too, we had no difficulty in finding a willing guide; indeed, four or five natives were quite keen, unpaid, to accompany us in the next stage of our journey, to offload us.

After travelling about a mile, and having crossed a brook by stepping stones, we saw a path obliquely joining a broad track. It was evidently of some importance in this wild terrain and looked as if it might lead somewhere, even perhaps to Batavia which, if possible, we intended reaching the next day. While crossing the brook, much to the amusement of the natives, one of our party had slipped into the water – an accident due, perhaps, more to the distracting spectacle of two or three pretty Javanese girls bathing further downstream than any lack of dexterity on his part. According to the natives, Batavia was about sixty kilometres away and, although we knew this to be an underestimate by nearly half, our spirits were nonetheless pretty high. The fact was that, having 'got somewhere' we felt absolutely tireless – supermen –we could march indefinitely, at least as far as Batavia, a feat which, buoyed up by hope and urged by fear, might not, had circumstances been favourable, have been much beyond our capabilities. The natives once again steadfastly refused to accompany us further, though there was a good deal of laughter which should have put us on our guard but did not.

We set a rapid pace, soon reaching another less rural kampong. There, we bought mineral waters and some tobacco from a native shop. Little else, indeed, was to be had. In fact, the two or three shops seemed unaccountably empty, the village almost deserted. Blissfully, however, we continued on our way. The reader must excuse me if, at this juncture, I take the opportunity of skipping a couple of days.

I was squatting in a shack. Next to me was one of my fellow prisoners, who nudged me in the ribs and said, 'I say, d'you know what? Well, I've just remembered something. When we went through that village – the one where we bought the mineral waters – over one of the buildings was the Japanese flag. I didn't realise it at the time – the red circle on a white background. They must already have been there.'

'Great heavens! Of course!' I said. 'No wonder the place was practically deserted and no wonder the natives laughed, when they saw us making in that direction!'

Once again I could have kicked myself for our blindness and, yet, I don't know. Had we realised it at the time, there was nothing that we could have done about it. Unnecessary worry would have been ours.

To resume, where I left off, somewhat refreshed, we hurried along as fast as we could. From two directions the thunder of guns could now be heard. This artillery sounded much further off to our front, northeast and southeast, than I cared to admit, but we could do nothing but hurry on. Undoubtedly, our inability to speak the language of the district was our biggest drawback. We questioned two or three natives, as best we could, but could elicit no information from them.

The Japanese were here, the Japanese were there – but where?

It was very bewildering. At last we met an apparently intelligent Indian, who told us in broken English that the Japanese had mechanised transport six miles away where the road, along which we now hurried, joined the main road, the road running to Batavia, maybe? Our hopes suffered a severe shock. Plans would have to be revised. Eventually we decided that our best course was to retrace our footsteps in the gathering darkness, look for a suitable point at which we could strike across country eastwards and leave it to the moon to guide our footsteps throughout the night. Then it came…

We heard it rushing towards us, over the tree tops, like a herd of stampeding elephants. Scrambling to the shelter of a clump of banana trees just off the roadside, we gained its protection just in time. A tropical thunderstorm, the force of which has to be experienced to be aptly appreciated, unleashed itself upon us. It was too much for the banana trees to withstand and, before long, we were wet to the skin. It was useless to remain where we were, so we regained the road and continued on our way. Imagine our disgust when, having walked about fifty metres, we spotted an attap shelter, unnoticed previously, at the side of the road. We, nevertheless, now sought its shelter and, stripping completely, wrung our clothes. This was accomplished in record time, for we were immediately attacked by mosquitoes.

The storm ended as abruptly as it had begun. The sky miraculously cleared and the moon shone from the east. We resumed our tramp. Not far past our shelter, we struck across country eastwards. In the lead, because I was the only one wearing trousers, a protection against undergrowth, I could not help feeling that, to a large extent, the safety of the party rested on me. Speed was essential, yet, caution must not be forgotten. Therefore, when stumbling across a native farmyard, I decided not to waste time by completely encircling it but, with a view to caution as well as speed, to creep quietly past. We had scarcely taken a dozen steps, when a dog yelped and continued yelping. We hesitated. Should we proceed as planned, or make a detour? The choice was decided for us. From the shadows, a man emerged with a large dog at his heels. There was no further hesitation – just one big, hurried dash down a slope at right angles to our original path. Unexpectedly, the report of a rifle was heard and, realising our danger, we sought the shelter of a tangle of undergrowth and bushes at the edge of a strip of paddy field. Hardly daring to breathe, I nevertheless decided that, if he should find us, we must kill him. This was a necessity that I sincerely hoped would not arise. My wish was gratified. After a while, the barking of the dog ceased and everything was quiet once more. We were able to emerge from our hiding place and hurry off along the edge of the rice field which, fortunately, ran from to west to east.

This part of the journey stands out in my mind more than any other. The immensity, the mystery, the changing oneness, the indestructibility of the universe were so apparent; above, the twinkling of distant worlds, beneath, the pulsating life of the water-flooded paddy fields. Rice is the lifeblood of half the population of the world. You could feel life, a throbbing part of oneself and of the universe and a thousand other forms of life, unseen yet felt, infinite, mysterious and indestructible. By contrast, there were the visible signs, thousands of tiny weaving pin points of emerald luminosity – thousands of fireflies. By contrast also were the audible sounds, throaty trumpeting from a thousand unseen mouths – thousands of bullfrogs. Yet, existing between them all, visible and invisible, audible and inaudible, tangible and intangible, between creatures other than myself and any companions, there was a mystic communion.

In this world, we travelled until after midnight when, as though by mutual assent, we stopped under some bushes, not troubling in the slightest about the soggy ground beneath and dripping leaves above. Somehow or other, I managed to snatch a couple of hours' fitful sleep, despite the continual assaults of the fiercest mosquitoes that I have ever encountered. Well before dawn, however, we were travelling eastwards once more. By now, of course, all thoughts of reaching Batavia before the afternoon had vanished. We could now only hope that we reached it at all.

With the coming of dawn, we noted a peculiar circumstance. Following us through the paddy fields, though at some distance, were two or three natives. Dressed in sarongs, according to the fashion of the East, as seen in the half light, they possessed a sinister appearance. When the sun rose, by previous association, they retained their forbidding character. Many ominous interpretations might have been inferred therefrom; at the time, however, we preferred to consider curiosity as the motive. Once, reaching a clump of jungle, we tried to shake them off but the attempt was a miserable failure and we accepted the inevitable. Not long afterwards, we encountered quite a number of Javanese and enquired of them the way. In their reply, they were very vague, but perseverance on our part had the effect of one of them undertaking to act as guide. The villain! Despite Batavia having been stated by us as our goal, he took us in the wrong direction. Dim-witted as we were, at least we knew roughly the course that we should take from the position of the sun. On remonstrating with him, he somewhat allayed our suspicions but increased our anxiety by saying that, to avoid the Japanese he would have to make a detour. Nevertheless, we decided that we'd be better off without him.

This change of front on our part resulted in a like change on the part of the natives, who came running after us. Now, they would give us refreshment and show their friendship by entertaining us. Being very hungry, we rather reluctantly followed them to a guest house nearby. Here, more natives crowded around us, trying to induce us, as we avidly ate coconuts, bananas and biscuits, to give away or sell our watches. Either hope was out of the question. All we asked for were instructions on how to get to Batavia and a quick take-off. This, at last, they seemed to comprehend and one of them indicated that he would put us on the main road nearby, but, scarcely had we reached the edge of the paddy field from where we could see the road two hundred metres away than a young Malay came rushing from the rubber plantation between us and the road. Gesticulating wildly, he gave us to understand that the Japanese were on the road and would cut our heads off if we should be unlucky enough to fall into their hands. This fact, he emphasised by vicious passes of the hand across his throat, accompanied by guttural exclamations of an exceptionally unpleasant nature. More bewildered than terrified, we allowed ourselves to be bundled into an attap shed at the verge of the rubber plantation.

'Nanti, nanti,' the natives cried.

If we would wait a minute, they said, the Japanese would be gone and we would be able to continue.

It was in this shed that my suspicious were really and truly aroused. Dog tired, I had relaxed myself on a kind of rattan platform which served as a bed and, closing my eyes, I had started to doze. Then, as though in a dream, I felt a furtive hand feel for my wristwatch and attempt to undo the strap. That did it, especially as an attempt was made to take a ring from Henderson. Jumping up with a cry of rage and feeling rather like a Gulliver in the midst of the Lilliputians, I surveyed the guilty faces, aroused my companions who had also given way to fatigue and told them what had happened. Japanese or no Japanese, we would make for the road immediately and the natives, seeing the irrevocability of our decision, made way for us, but still followed us.

We had gone barely two hundred metres when we spotted, now like a thread of doom and not our longed for objective, a tarmacadam road. Then Javanese appeared in their dozens, suddenly, unseen, as though conjured there by a rub of Aladdin's lamp. Their appearance filled us with both exasperation and apprehension. In such circumstances, boldness was called for. Accordingly, we set out resolutely, striding through the thronging natives as though they did not exist.

'Honk! Honk!' we heard. Transport, by Gad! the Japs! We thought. We scampered into a paddy field on one side of the road, but it was only a bus. Well, if public services were in operation as per usual, surely the Dutch still commanded the roads? The natives had lied, and, reassured but wet and dripping, we regained the highway. Then came the shock, though not altogether unexpected. As if by magic, parangs appeared in the hands of these villainous people. Like a tidal wave, they surged upon us. Without arms of any description, resistance was futile.

No other proof of this was needed than a severe thwack by a parang on the head of one of my comrades who dared to resist. Before we had collected our thoughts, ropes had secured us. I felt that this could not be happening to me. Only others, or fictitious characters, experienced such events. It was as though we were mesmerised into acting against our wills, but albeit accepting fatalistically. So we marched along without fear, with little sense of bitterness, with only a sort of fatalistic hopeless, helplessness. In retrospect, it was obvious that the suspicious attitude of the people of the district, their unpredictability, the way in which they had followed us, the tom-toms (which no doubt had informed each kampong in turn of our approach) had all pointed to an eventual attack. No doubt, too, our apprehension at that point had been planned. The fact was we had been misled in our appraisal of the natives of Western Java who had been reported as very much anti-Japanese whereas, in reality, the natives of these parts were the opposite. We were poor, deluded fools!

We were, of course, in a pretty perilous plight. What was to be our fate? Three courses suggested themselves to me. Number one, that the natives themselves were going to butcher us; number two, that they would hand us over to the Dutch; number three, that if the Japanese were already in control of Western Java, they would hand us over to them in the expectation of reward. The latter alternative seemed to be the most likely, for had they themselves intended to exterminate us, why bother to string us up and then to march us away from their kampong? If it were to the Dutch that they were leading us, surely they would hardly have roped us up! Besides, even though hope springs eternal, we were losing faith in the Dutch. The second alternative was indeed just a pleasing figment of the imagination.

Roped together, movement was somewhat restricted. Thus, when the natives went through our pockets, we could have resisted only with difficulty even if we had felt so inclined. My haversack was cut from my shoulders, my wristwatch removed. My fountain pen, comb and pencil were all taken, but some money I had was not found. They even went so far as to try to remove a ring from one of my comrade's fingers, but without success, the ring being too tight. Chances of being handed over to the Dutch seemed now out of the question.

We were halted after two miles. What now? I did not wonder for long. At the roadside grew a tree, its one branch stretching horizontally about nine metres above the road. We were to be the tragic heroes of the play's grim climax. They were going to hang us. That was obvious, even though I was unaware then that the Japanese had already offered the Javanese ten guilders for every allied prisoner, dead or alive. Does the murderer feel as I did as he walks to the gallows? My pulse did not beat nineteen to the dozen. Much to my surprise I was unafraid and, with grim humour, I thought of the contrast in demeanour as, shaking like a leaf, knees knocking together, I had lain in the ditch after the ambush. It was me in that ditch, but this wasn't me. By no means a man of iron nerve and indifference to death, my calmness was remarkable. No doubt it was this sense of unreality that was the cause or, maybe, after the terror of the night of the ambush, nothing could shake me or, maybe, it was because I was too tired to care.

Be that as it may, instead of fear, I felt curiosity. I was analytical – like a chemist who might study the reaction of two liquids in a test tube. I looked at the faces of my friends, studying their expressions. How would they be affected and how would I react when the noose tightened around my neck, and at the moment of my release into space? It was enthralling and I was impatient to know and almost anticipatory of the end with masochistic pleasure but, before I could learn by experience, an experience unfortunately which would never be imparted to others, two or three Javanese came running towards the group. What now? There was a hurried conference and when agreement appeared to have been reached, they jerked us away from that wise old tree and set out as before.

By their manner, I could see that they expected something to happen shortly and, although I had not understood a word of their discussions, I was pretty certain what it would be. I was right. At the next road intersection, we were unceremoniously handed over to a squad of Japanese troops, accompanied by a few bedraggled-looking white men whom, we later discovered, were American sailors. The Japanese had proved treacherous. What next?

With the Dai Nippon Gun

After we had been transferred, as though a libation to the gods, the first procedure, as might have been expected, was a thorough search. Little of value was discovered! The natives had been too thorough. This lack of personal belongings evidently aroused the suspicion of the Japanese NCO in charge, for he turned angrily upon the natives with the result that they were scared into handing over some of the loot. I noticed that my wristwatch was not among the articles that changed hands. Not that this default of the treacherous Javanese made the slightest difference to me, for the Japanese saw fit to retain all valuables surrendered by the natives save for some Dutch guilders which they magnanimously returned, probably on the assumption that Dutch money would be of no use to us, anyhow.

Of what ultimate use to the Japanese were we? If of no use, then the immediate outlook was grim indeed. Optimistically, I thought that we would be required to assist the Yanks (as we were to call the American sailors) in pulling the Japanese handcarts, to which they had so obviously been harnessed. Our captors failed to consult me. They had their own ideas. The Yanks, squatting at the roadside, were barefooted because, as we subsequently learnt, they had swum ashore from the sinking cruiser, the *Houston*. So, in accordance with the Nippon code, that we were to come to know only too well, that only men who worked should possess, our own shoes were unceremoniously removed and offered to the Yanks. Heroic refusal, not a bit of it – not even hesitation. I cannot say I blamed the sailors, though. In fact, it was the first indication of selfishness and self-preservation which, above all else, as the three and a half years of captivity wore on, became the major passion of us all, as will be seen.

Most of the Americans now being reasonably shod, the signal to proceed was given, the Americans pushing or pulling the handcarts, the Japanese either leading pack horses or weighted down themselves with equipment. We five airmen were forced to keep pace as best we could, though still roped together, as though we were highly dangerous prisoners, likely to spring upon our captors in an attempt to make a break for it at any moment. Nothing was further from our thoughts – at any rate, at that time.

I suppose our party consisted of about ten Japanese, eight Americans and we five airmen, with three pack horses. The military equipment included nothing heavier than machine guns, mostly with other equipment in haphazard fashion on the pack horses and handcarts. In a sense, the whole outfit seemed to be haphazard, with a trace of comic opera about it. Nevertheless, this mopping up or rear party, as I imagined it to be, had an air of purposeful determination about it. Had I been marching with a British Army squad, I should have exuded confidence. The NCO in charge, a cheerful little man, obviously knew exactly what job he had in hand and looked prepared to face any emergency with equanimity, while the rest of the squad, slovenly dressed, their breeches partly open at the flies or turned up at the bottom – as motley a crowd as you could wish to see – nevertheless marched with great zeal, so that I could not but be reminded of *The Mikado*.

Happier days! As I thought of the past – the worst preoccupation of a prisoner – I became overwhelmed with self-reproach. Why in the dickens had I become mixed up with these yellow men? Why! It was my own pig-headed foolhardiness – nothing more. Had I not broken that golden rule, inculcated in me by an old soldier before joining up ('never volunteer for anything'), by offering myself as one of the 512 AMES (a radar unit) for duty in Anjer? To what a pass had my first remembered violation of that rule brought me! Oh, you confounded idiot! You blundering fool – traitor to all that you love and hold dear in England, I thought. While you are in captivity, never perhaps to enjoy again freedom in this world, your erstwhile comrades – comrades true to themselves and their loved ones – are being moved to safer areas... As I thought such bitter thoughts, my sweat pricked me like a thousand needles. The sweat was not as a symptom of the tropical climate but of mortification and shame. In all my life, I had never felt so wretched. My chagrin was but a foretaste of worse things to come.

Soon there were more immediate worries. I estimated that we had commenced our trek with the Japanese at about half past ten. As the sun rose higher in the sky, the hotter the tarmac roads became until every step became a nightmare. I wondered how much longer I would be able to continue. Lashed together as we were, there was no chance of choosing the dusty spots, where less heat radiated. So feet became sorer and roads became hotter. About the time that I felt that I was nearing the end of my tether, a halt was called at a native kampong. Here, the Japanese divested themselves of their equipment, opened up their kidney-shaped dixies and scoffed their rice ration. They gave their leftovers to the Americans. Both the Americans and Japanese enjoyed some bananas requisitioned from the natives, but for us there was not a morsel, on the grounds, I suppose, that we were still drones. Our only privilege was half a dozen square metres of roadside on which uncomfortably to sprawl, while we watched the rest of the convoy satisfy their appetites. Not even water was vouchsafed us, although there were liberal allowances for all workers, both human and equine.

Yes, even the horses were fed and watered in front of our eyes. Once all those who mattered were satisfied, the Japanese relaxed themselves, smoking and indulging in idle conversation with the sycophantic villagers. Obviously, there was no hurry. We tried to sleep only to be aroused, just as our efforts were about to meet with success, by a fusillade of small stones flung at us by the delighted onlookers. Our degradation was complete – tied together, given nothing to eat and drink, spurned by all, not even allowed to lie down in peace. Fortunately, our senses, now dulled by drowsiness, prevented too close a sensitive examination of our position.

By the time that the natives had tired of their congenial pas-time, we were ordered to get up and then, to my surprise, spared a few drops of water from a glass bottle. Somewhat refreshed, we found our journey a little easier, especially as the sun was misted over and the road was less hot. Our spirits rose still further when, after leaving the southward road and striking east, we were unroped and ordered to assist with the handcarts. This task was not unduly arduous for the Japanese NCO called a brief halt every half hour or so, less for our sake than for that of his horses and his own men whom, I was surprised to discover, were, despite their air of self-sufficiency, less able to stand the pace than us half-starved prisoners. At these halts, we were given nothing to drink but the Americans, who seemed to know exactly what to do, would dart off to a native property to emerge with a glass bottle of water drawn from a well. It was not long before we learnt, uninvited, to follow the Americans to the wells.

Our worst immediate trouble, now, was blistered feet. Unused to walking barefooted, native fashion, we found travel painful even on reasonably smooth roads, while without doubt the roads were getting progressively rougher and it was almost as difficult to avoid the bad spots when pushing carts as it had been when we were roped together. In any case, any attempt to have done so would doubtless have been looked upon with great disfavour by the most distasteful of the Japanese, a veritable scoundrel, whose face blinked even more often than he swished the stick that he had provided himself with. With what pleasure did he direct this stick at us at the slightest pretext! Therefore, rather than concentrating on avoiding, undetected, the rough spots, it was far more sensible, now that we had accustomed ourselves to our predicament, to plan escape. Never for a moment did I expect the Japanese invasion of Java to result in the complete subjugation of that island in about eight days.

I thought that lines of defence would be formed, as, from what I had seen of the Dutch preparedness, a good defence was possible. For instance, from Western Java to Batavia practically all roadside trees had been holed so that they would take a charge of guncotton sufficient to fell them across the road. Bridges, too, had been mined. It seemed to me, therefore, that eventually we should reach 'the line' and that, when we neared it, a breakaway and a quick dart into the jungle – and to blazes with the consequences – was the thing to aim at. Then, in the late afternoon, an incident occurred that encouraged my hopes. During one of the rest periods, a large heron was sighted about seventy metres across the paddy, a sitting target, literally and figuratively speaking. Evidently, one of the Japanese thought so as well, for he shouldered his rifle and took careful aim. As the explosion broke the stillness of the afternoon, so the bird took off quite unconcernedly. Not a feather had been touched. This augured well for a quick dart into the jungle at a favourable moment. Alas! Forlorn hopes!

Apart from the feckless marksmanship and the sickness of one of the Americans who was left behind – as was also a sick Japanese – there was little incident. The afternoon dragged to a close and, towards sunset, after passing the conflux of two roads, lorry after lorry, packed with Japanese troops, bustled up from behind us. We must be getting somewhere, I thought, but whether this might be to our advantage or not was another matter. By now all I wanted was an opportunity to rest my blistered feet and, soon after sunset, without having 'got anywhere', my wish was granted. We were halted, the horses tethered and the captors and their captives entered a Javanese attap hut. One room was allotted to the soldiers of the Dai Nippon Gun and the other to us inferior whites. Before there was time to wash and put on a clean collar, there was unceremoniously spread on the floor of the 'kitchen hall' a large banana leaf, and a quantity of cooked rice was dumped upon it, topped off by two tins of fish. This was our evening, and one and only, meal. We had no utensils or cutlery of any description, so, crowding around, we dived in with our hands like monkeys. It was soon obvious that the main object was to eat as quickly as possible '…you, Jack; I'm all right!' as they say in the army.

Despite our circumstances, I was appalled by the ill manners of one or two of the Americans, who pushed and grabbed to obtain the lion's share and especially as much fish as they could. The servants' hall was rapidly deteriorating into the animals' cage. I had a lot to learn. I would never have thought then that, when freed with three and a half years of POW life behind me, the main impression to linger on was not the heroic and stoic behaviour of my fellow men – though much of this was in evidence – but the overpowering greed, the selfishness and the rapacity of a number of POWs. That man's primary instinct is self-preservation, and not sex or anything else is, I think, bound to be the conviction of those who have been a POW with the Japanese, or have had to struggle for existence under equally trying conditions. As time went on, this trait in us became more and more marked. We became less sensitive and more selfish until, under such circumstances, perhaps selfishness and complete disregard of the welfare of others was a virtue, but more of that later.

The primitive feast over, we flopped on to a wooden sleeping platform at the back of the hut. In crowded conditions, on hard boards, with the feeling of remorse ever present at having volunteered myself into such a mess, I would have thought sleep impossible but, not a bit of it. Hardly had my head touched the hard boards than it seemed that I was being awakened. I had enjoyed one of the soundest night's sleep of my life.

There was no fish with the rice that we received for a hurried breakfast, but I cannot remember the platter being left unclean. There is one great advantage with rice. It is easily prepared and soon eaten so that, before dawn, we were on the march again, pulling and pushing the handcarts. After half a mile, we passed what must have been a whole battalion, sprawled at the side of the road, fast asleep. As far as I could see there were no sentries, a significant fact, and in the half-darkness there was an eerie quality about the scene. Later a convoy of military vehicles passed us, crammed with grim-looking, determined Japanese soldiers, their tin helmets festooned with tropical ferns as camouflage, while the vehicles themselves bristled more with tropical creepers than with guns. Obviously the Japanese were masters of camouflage. But their aptness in this art displayed on those Javanese roads was more academic than useful, for during the whole of the morning's march not one allied plane hove in sight. This should have been disheartening to the five English prisoners, but we were far more concerned about our own discomfort.

The roads became progressively hotter and our feet, already blistered, were on fire. For the second time, I wondered how long we could stand it. With a certain amount of detachment, I came to the conclusion that I could keep going for the whole of that day and perhaps during the morning of the next day. But who could tell? One of my comrades, pushing the same cart as I did and less fit physically than the rest of us, was, I could already discern, coming to the end of his tether. I told him to pretend to push the cart while I and the two others upon it took the strain, but he still despaired. He complained of thirst. Indeed, he had good cause, for we had had no stops for water that morning. I think the reason for this was because we were not passing through any native kampongs. We had turned off from the eastward road and, as far as I could judge, were winding northwards, but what did the direction matter now? Onwards or backwards – how did it affect us? There was no sound of guns. We must be miles from any fighting, and any chance of making a break for our own lines was slender indeed. But I did not lose hope. To have done so would, at that time, have reduced our resistance to nil. Loss of hope on my friend's part was, I feared, the main reason for his feeling that he was nearing the end of his powers of endurance. His mind was no longer master of his body.

At last, however, about midday, a halt was called for no apparent reason, but, of water we were given none. My friend, unable to stand his thirst any longer, unable to watch any longer the Japanese pulling at their water bottles with equanimity, drank the water from the paddy, a highly dangerous procedure in a country with little sanitation. He could not relieve his feet and, when, soon afterwards, we restarted, going eastwards again, not far from the banks of a fairly large river, he once more gave way to his moans. It was obvious he had had enough of it and I was not altogether astonished when, about to cross the river over a bridge, at least fifty metres high, he talked wildly about flinging himself over. It took all my powers of persuasion to deter him. I told him that we would most likely reach the end of our journey soon. Little did I realise how near the truth I was. When we had negotiated the bridge, we were stopped and rested. Would that I had spoken naught! He was to struggle on bravely for three years, only to die within a few months of the end of the war.

Encamped at the bridge were a large number of Japanese troops who gazed curiously at us prisoners. This interest in us we could now observe at leisure, as our Japanese escort took their gear and left us at the side of the road. A little later we saw them again, some on the pack-horses and others on bicycles, quite a favourite means of Japanese military transport and, as they passed us, cheerfully they made motions with the flats of their hands, which suggested only too clearly that we were to be decapitated. It seemed that our fate still hung in the balance, life or death. Like the last drop of water, gathered on the edge of a window frame after a storm, quivering, seeming to grow bigger, to be on the point of dropping only to withdraw again, impossible to tell whether it will ultimately fall or be gradually absorbed into the atmosphere or the woodwork, life was thus on the scales of doubt. Yet all the same, even when we were taken over by an escort armed to the teeth, I hardly expected the worse. My optimism was justified for, instead of being marched to the place of execution, we were taken to a small hut already inhabited by prisoners who sounded a good deal more cheerful than we felt. They must have had food and drink, I thought, and was cheered immensely when, hardly had we settled ourselves than we were provided with both commodities.

The water was delicious but not the food. In all my days, I have never seen or smelt, nor hope to see or smell again, such stinking rice as we were offered. It was maggoty, gritty and tasted like brimstone. Later, we learnt that the retreating Dutch had adulterated rice supplies with sulphur to make them unpalatable, and so the Japanese, exercising their unusually developed sense of perverted humour, had thought it huge fun to give this rice to their white prisoners to eat. No matter how distasteful it was, it was better to pack in the calories because one could not tell when and where the next meal would be taken or when there might be occasion to use all one's strength. We Britishers still had no utensils but now ate – great luxury – from coconut shells borrowed from other captives.

There were now, in all, twenty-seven of us. All were Americans save for one Dutchman and us five airmen. Talk, despite the two guards stationed in the entrance to the hut, was unrestricted and we soon learnt that all the Americans were from the American cruiser, the *Houston* which, in company with the Australian cruiser, the *Perth*, had been sunk by the Japanese near Merak, the night of our evacuation from Anjer. The Dutchman had been a machine gunner in charge of a coastal squad of Javanese troops. The garrulity of the Americans and their unquenchable optimism – amounting to cocksureness – cheered us enormously, even though early escape now seemed out of the question. Even my friend with the suicidal tendencies lost some of his moroseness.

This cheerfulness was further enhanced, during the afternoon, when we were given a bath in a large shallow trough nearby. Later, there was another meal of sulphur in the hut, and that was about the climax of our activities for that day.

We were to inhabit that hut for only one night, and two incidents during that time stand out in my mind. In the first place, the incessant easy talk of one of the Americans who lay next to me. He talked about everything from American food to New York traffic, of leave in the Philippines, of the sinking of the *Houston*, of his childhood, of girls that he had had and so forth, but he did not bore.

As one of the Americans said, 'I c'd listen to that guy all day and night.'

Secondly, whenever I had to satisfy the calls of nature – and there were many of these because most of us were already suffering from diarrhoea – we were rushed to a hole in the ground, a few feet from the hut, by a Japanese soldier with his rifle at the ready, expecting from us alacrity of our bowels as well as our legs.

The next day, after the usual sulphur and water, we were formed into a working party, my first of many hundreds. Our job was to fell coconut trees, in order that an uninterrupted view might be afforded for a nearby gun site. Axes and collapsible saws were produced by way of tools and, despite the heat, we set to with a will. It was hard work and, before long, I was suffering not only from blistered feet but also blistered hands. However, as every tree dropped, we were allowed by the guards to have our fill of the sweet, cool juice of the fallen coconuts. In fact, we were on the whole reasonably treated, provided that we worked. Two Americans, who were caught slacking, received a 'beating up' from the Japanese, the first of thousands that I was to witness.

The act of beating a man is performed by the Japanese with the palm of the hand. With all the power that they can muster, they slap the culprit across the face. To duck, or visibly to ride the slap, is to court worse punishment. The victim must stand rigidly to attention and take what is coming. Should he be knocked down, it is of no use to feign unconsciousness. The human ninepin must jump to his feet immediately, once more to be knocked from a vertical to a horizontal position. I have seen prisoners who, having been felled, pretended to be more hurt than they were but they never fooled the Dai Nippon Gun and were only too eager to scramble to their feet, when kicked in the groin. The first of these beatings was not exceptionally heavy, though it gave us a foretaste of things to come. At lunchtime, when we were given a meal of decent rice topped with cubes of boiled pork, eaten from coconut shells and with shaped pieces of the same material as spoons, both of which we had now been able to fashion, a Japanese officer, the first of our acquaintance, after himself striking the two delinquents, lectured us in broken English on the futility of disobedience, and on the good treatment that we would receive if we worked hard. Actually, as far as I was concerned, it must have been a year before I did a day's really hard work again. After that, two and a half years of slavery was punctuated by yasumé (rest), due to severely ulcerated legs.

After lunch, we toiled for two more hours and were then marched back to the Japanese encampment. To our surprise, we were conducted not to our original hut but to a more solidly built one, a little way removed from the rest of the billets and near the banks of a canal that passed under a bridge nearby before it flowed into the river. At first glance, this place looked infinitely better than our previous hut but, in actual fact, it was to become a hellhouse. Not until we entered it and attempted to lie down, did we realise our misfortune. It will be remembered that we numbered twenty-seven, and the size of this hut was such that not more than ten of our number could have lain down simultaneously, in comfort. How then did we make room for nearly three times that number? The hut was oblong in shape, its internal measurements being about 2.6 x 4.6 m, with a doorway opening in the middle of one of its shorter dimensions. Therefore, we had to lie twelve to a side, that is at right angles to the longer dimensions, with three of our number wedged in the doorway. As I slept, my opposite number's legs were either under mine or on top of them. In temperate climates under normal conditions our discomfort would have been acute but, in a hot climate, despite the open door and one small window, it was unbearable, especially as most of us had tropical sores, so that the slightest movement of one's opposite number caused great pain.

This was not the end of our misfortunes. We had been in the hut for one day when an American developed what was believed to have been dysentery. He was shifted immediately. This meant, of course, a little more comfort for those prisoners wedged in the doorway, but the Japanese have an inordinate fear of disease. Therefore, we must drink no water. For three days, we lay despairingly without a drop of that precious liquid to wash down the sulphur rice which continued to turn up twice daily. All we had to drink, during that period, was the juice from eighteen coconuts obtained by two fellows who had been escorted by guards to scale coconut palms. Over a period of three days then the coconut juice, plus the moisture in the rice, was our total liquid replenishment. Some had more, some less, as the juice of one coconut was periodically shared between about six of us, it being sucked straight from a hole in the nut, so whether a fair share was received by all depended upon the judgement, and sometimes the greed, of the individual. Imagine the pitiful sight, when the evening of third day brought rain and every prisoner frantically struggled to collect the rain in cleft coconut shells as it trickled off the galvanised sheeted roof. After that day, the Japanese relaxed their precautions and we no longer went desperately thirsty.

There was, in fact, during the three or four weeks that we remained there, a gradual relaxation of discipline. At first, we were never without two grim-faced guards stationed near the entrance to the hut and, when there arose one of the frequent calls of nature, a guard always accompanied us to the latrine a few metres away. This practice was gradually discontinued, as our captors became less convinced of the likelihood of our attempting escape, an attempt which became almost inconceivable when, on 13 March, we received from the Japanese the almost incredible news of the fall of Java on 9 March. Severe though the blow was, at least I felt less annoyance with myself for having volunteered for service at Anjer, as I reasoned it almost a certainty that the comrades that I had left behind at Batavia must also be in Japanese hands. Perhaps, too, the absence of the guard's embarrassing presence at the latrine was partly due to its filthy state. It consisted of a round hole about one metre deep, with no soakaway. Across the top, two boards were laid so that, between them, there was a gap of about twenty centimetres which allowed access for the reception of filth. After a few days' use, the pit was a seething mass of maggots. Every time that I used this abomination, I had horrible visions of falling into its boiling cauldron. Not one drop of disinfectant was poured into the pit during our stay at this place which, I learnt, was called Pamarjan.

Curiously enough, I learnt the name of this kampong in connection with the use of the latrine. No toilet paper, or indeed paper of any kind, was ever issued to us, but in one corner of the hut was a shelf and, searching it for paper, I discovered some record sheets which showed that the hut had formerly been used as a dispensary, the address being Pamarjan. Just imagine such a shocking lavatory being allowed to pollute the air of a dispensary and just imagine the ridiculous mentality of the local Japanese command. Though providing such a filthy primitive convenience, no steps were taken to ensure that we boiled water as a safeguard against the spread of dysentery. Later, this disease killed many.

Another disease to be feared was malaria. At night time, the hut was invaded by hundreds of mosquitoes which gave us little rest. Without mosquito nets, we could only do our best to cover ourselves with what little else we had. Fortunately, I had been taken prisoner in KD slacks and had protection to my legs. True, my socks were no more, but the mosquitoes troubled my feet very little. It was our faces that suffered and, even when the insects were not actually biting us, there was a continual drone about our heads. After discipline was somewhat relaxed, we experimented with lighting a fire near the hut in the hope that the smoke would deter them. The only result was to make the air within the hut even more foetid so that, when darkness had fallen, we longed for the daylight. After a short spell of daylight, we prayed for darkness, because of the most persistent flies in the world. Each pest, when actually active, seemed worse than the other, and far worse than our captors! Bless 'em all, we thought.

During the three weeks spent at the Pamarjan ' nursing home', we had only one more working party, the duration of which was not for very long, neither was the work very arduous, so that we craved for working parties every day, to no avail. Besides breaking the monotony, it brought a change of diet for, when on working parties, proper rice and a mixed vegetable and meat stew could be anticipated. Normally, we received no meat.

The food did, however, gradually improve a little. With the lifting of certain restrictions came the cooking of our own food, so that we could ensure that the sulphur rice was at least thoroughly washed before being boiled. In addition to being allowed to collect water from the nearby canal, now that the dysentery scare had somewhat subsided, we were also provided with a certain amount of purer water for the brewing of tea – or at least an apology for tea because the same leaves were used over and over again – while milk and sugar were considered as unnecessary. Thus, we lived on rice and tea with the addition of one bucket of watery stew per day made from a type of seaweed, plus anything that we could persuade the Japanese to buy for us from passing natives. Few natives, however, passed by and we were not very successful though we did manage, acting through the senior NCO among us – an American CPO called Demoen – to procure a few bananas, some large flat cakes that we termed 'collision mats' and, once or twice, half a dozen duck eggs at three cents each, not much for nearly thirty hungry prisoners. Efforts to purchase meat always met with ill success. Then, after about two weeks, we had a remarkable stroke of luck. A goat – a most welcome beast! – strayed into the camp. At the time, one of our more docile guards, nicknamed Smiler, was on duty – one guard now being considered as sufficient – and he agreed that we might attempt to capture the poor animal. Imagine twenty odd, emaciated, half-naked men, chasing after one equally emaciated goat! On many occasions, we thought that we had it cornered, only to see the unfortunate beast slip from our grasping hands at the last moment. Eventually, we won and the *coup de grace* was duly administered. A butcher among the Americans, called Stone, did the rest, and we revelled in lashings of goat for supper. I thought that goat flesh tasted somewhat like mutton, but a trifle stronger. Of course, to the rejoicings of the cesspool maggots, we all ate more than our stomachs could stand and, perhaps, the psychological effect derived from the capture was more beneficial than the actual devouring of the carcass. I particularly remember Ian Farquharson tucking in with gusto!

Another diversion was organised by the Japanese. Each morning, after the first week, we were put to half an hour's PT. I think this was a good thing though, once again, more from a psychological point of view than a physical one. The calorific value of our food was scarcely great enough to warrant much physical exertion and, besides, many of us suffered from sores which movement did little to heal. I will say this much for our captors: two or three times, a Japanese medical orderly was sent to dress such sores as we suffered from. In retrospect, I feel quite an admiration for that orderly, for he worked with efficiency and precision despite the paucity of the tools of his trade. I never saw another Japanese medic giving aid to prisoners, despite future horrendous wounds.

Bathing eventually became another form of entertainment. At first, we had been allowed only to wash our feet in a dirty pond. With this privilege I was, under the circumstances, quite content until, feeling a bite and glancing down I observed a leech adhering tightly to my leg, while others were wriggling rapidly through the water in my direction. Hurriedly I beat a retreat. It was obvious, of course, that our ulcerated legs would attract every leech within the range of their smell. They caused little pain, but were the most repulsive creatures and, thereafter, I approached the pool as though Scylla had lurked there. Later, however, as I have said, we were allowed to bathe in the canal. This concession amused the Japanese as much as it pleased us for, on two or three occasions, we boasted a gallery of onlookers. One or two of the Americans were tolerably accomplished in aquatic sports and gave quite a display. Lower down the canal, the natives washed their clothes and bathed themselves and, encouraged by shouts and laughter both from us and the Japanese, a couple of boys would swim towards them, only to be called back before they reached their objective. These incidents also afforded us the opportunity to wash such garments as we had left. Already the sweat from my body had so rotted my vest that, soon, there was little left of it.

So the days dragged on, the only other diversion being talk. What I did not know about the sinking of the *Houston*, by the end of our time at Pamarjan, was not worth knowing. The Americans never tired of talking about it, so that I came to hate the very mention of the word *Houston*, but I did indulge in some very interesting 'natters' on other subjects, especially with Hampton Cray from Texas, the only marine among the Americans. He attracted a certain amount of animosity from his countrymen on the sole grounds, as far as I could gather, that he was a marine. The Americans were, in fact, a mixed lot, of Greek, German, Italian and Irish descent. Mostly regulars, there was hardly a man among them who had not contracted VD at one time or another. They thought no more of 'catching a dose' than the normal man would have of catching a cold. They were obviously as free with sex as they were tolerant and freedom-loving in all aspects, from the CPO to the AB seaman though, of course, there was the usual one unpleasant face, a lout encountered in all groups of men,

After three weeks, the dysentery patient had recovered and, on 28 March, we were told that we 'despised prisoners' were to be moved. On our last night, as a send-off, we were visited by a Japanese officer, obviously drunk but exuding warmth and comradeship. We were 'unfortunates of war' and 'could not help our present state'. He only hoped that one day we could go back to our people but, for now, we were his enemies, dependent upon his good will. Yet, he felt sorry for us so we must have these – and he distributed cigarettes among us – the first for a long time since those cadged from guards – and to our greater amazement, he passed around a partly filled bottle of whisky. It was an amazing gesture, the likes of which I only experienced once more, a week or so later but, in those early days, one came into contact with the ordinary Japanese officer and not those especially chosen for guard duties. Despite the cruelty of later guards, I hope that he saw his homeland again, as I did.

In Clink

There was little fuss or bother about our departure, the following morning. There were no boots to be cleaned, no beard to be shaved (not one razor was shared among us), no buttons to be cleaned, not even kits to be packed. We merely clambered on to the two lorries that had pulled up outside our hell-house and held tight, while the vehicles lurched and jolted for the best part of an hour over some of the byroads of tropical Java. Eventually, we drew up outside the gates of a driveway to a large house situated within its own grounds in the middle of a town that we later ascertained was called Rangkasbetoeng. Obviously this mansion was the local Japanese HQ. Without ado, we were marched into the grounds, handed brushes and receptacles and ordered to collect all the leaves and rubbish on the driveway and lawns. Once this task had been performed to the satisfaction of the Japanese, we were marched through a street of gaping natives to the local prison.

I think most of us were overcome with gloom when, having been split up into parties of nine and assigned the first three cells of one of a row of back-to-back cells numbering about sixteen, we watched the slow closing of heavy doors and heard the ominous grating of keys in metal locks. Doubtless, we should enjoy far more space in these cells than at Pamarjan, but a locked door seemed to epitomise lack of freedom. There would be, in fact, no necessity to leave the cells at all for, in the corners stood wooden tubs, their purpose being only too obvious. We were soon to learn, however, that it would be a daily routine for two men from each cell to sling their lavatory on poles for its outing around the other side of the cells to a cesspit. The empty tubs were then returned, undisinfected, to take up their normal position in the cells. Apart from the portable lavatories and the raised, bug-infested, sleeping platforms at the back of the cells, our quarters were quite bare. The one barred window to each cell looked on to a paved square, the other side of which was the entrance gate and guard room.

As far as I could judge, only one military guard was on duty at any one time. Young, inexperienced soldiers were detailed who looked quite out of place with a rifle, a sharp contrast to seasoned Japanese soldiers whose rifles seem to be part of themselves, so easily and naturally did they carry them. Inexperience often produces merriment and I remember how, one day, we had a good laugh at the antics of one of the guards. Obviously still a 'rookie', he was giving us a sort of rifle demonstration, doubtless to impress the prisoners who were gaping through the bars, when his weapon went off. The poor guard nearly jumped out of his skin and then, recovering himself, looked sheepishly towards his prisoners. Roars of encouragement greeted him, but he was not impressed, thinking, no doubt, of the punishment which would assuredly be his should his superiors learn of what had happened.

On the whole, however, we felt sorry for him because it was he who, a day or two previously, had allowed three or four very pretty Javanese girls to enter the prison precincts and to talk with us through the bars. They spoke a little English and we managed to convey to them our desire for a pack of cards. This they promised to obtain and were as good as their words for, later in the afternoon, they appeared again at the gates, but our luck did not hold good, for this time the chief native warder was about and he not only refused the girls' entrance, but refused even to accept the cards on our behalf.

Throughout our stay at the prison, this native warder was the main cause for complaint. He never smiled and always appeared to do his best to make life even more unpleasant than it then was. It was his job to supervise the division of the rations, which were twice a day eaten outside, much to our delight, and to lock us in after meals and after the daily exercise that the Japanese saw fit to impose upon us.

We had three feeds a day. The first was thrust through the window of our cells at daybreak and consisted of a small piece of cooked tara root and some unrefined sugar, both wrapped in leaves; the second, was a two-course affair of red rice, free from sulphur, and a watery green stew, eaten in the open while squatting on the ground. The rice was served in similar fashion to our breakfast, each man's rations being neatly wrapped in separate leaf receptacles, while the stew, brought to us in a bucket, was rationed into whatever containers we possessed, still mostly half-split coconut shells. The last meal, partaken of late in the afternoon, afforded further opportunity of rice sampling, augmented with neat tea and perhaps some dried fish. About once a week, we might be fortunate enough to discover a few small lumps of fat pork floating on the top of the stew drum.

There was little opportunity for supplementing our rations. Shut off from the outside world, in charge of a morose, uncooperative warder, we found chances of making purchases practically nil. We had but one working party, to the Japanese HQ, although two or three of the Americans, the fittest among us, were called for more frequently. This second visit to the Japanese HQ involved us in more scavenging. In addition, we had to clean some outbuildings. The Japanese were reasonably friendly and we were allowed to pick some limes growing in the grounds and also afforded the opportunity to trim beards. After a month of imprisonment, mine was quite lavish and to shave it off, without a preliminary clipping, with a Japanese borrowed safety razor and a discarded blade, was a rather painful process, but I felt much fresher and cleaner when the job was complete.

Fortunately, the prison boasted some rather primitive showers under which we could splash about once or twice a week. Access was also allowed twice daily to a tap in the prison courtyard. These concessions constituted about the only luxuries during our stay at the prison. Perhaps I ought to add that, after mealtimes, we were allowed to exercise ourselves by walking up and down the courtyard, this in addition to the PT, but any pleasure which might have been derived from this was more than offset by the gravelled surface of the courtyard, which cut our bare feet. As regards the compulsory PT, for those fit enough, I am afraid that our disconcerted efforts to exercise by numbers must have constituted a rather sorry spectacle.

On the whole, the days passed fairly quickly but the nights were long. Darkness fell about seven o'clock and, as there were no lights, two or three monotonous hours preceded sleep. Subjects of common interest became rather threadbare, while the Americans, and I was the only 'Limey' in the third cell, would continually harp on the sinking of the *Houston*, a ship I had come to detest even more, if possible, than I did at Pamarjan. Sleep would come at last despite the hard platform, the absence of bedclothes and the nocturnal parade of bed bugs. Mosquitoes were less in vogue.

The most disturbing element, however, was of human origin. As I have previously explained, we POWs occupied three end cells. Several of the other cells were inhabited by natives. Indeed, near the entrance was a cell which claimed two women, but the native prisoners who particularly interested us were half a dozen or so Mohammedans in the cell to one side of us. In the middle of the night, we would be awakened by their weird incantations. I felt more sorry for them than annoyed, as they were not allowed the freedom of the courtyard as we were. Indeed, a couple of prisoners in cells to the rear of ours suffered in chains. Whether our native counterparts were criminals already imprisoned before the arrival of the Japanese, or whether they were newly convicted political prisoners, I never learnt, but I should imagine that the former alternative was the most likely.

While behind bars two incidents occurred, which stand out in my mind far more clearly than any others. Number one was a most sudden and terrific bang. It broke the quiet of mid-afternoon, as we lay in the cells. For a moment, my heart stood still. For all the world, it sounded like a bomb and it was some minutes before my heart beat normally once again. Long after the commencement of a heavy thunderstorm, following quickly on the heels of the fleeting reverberations, I was thus informed that it had been nothing more than a thunderclap. I had been similarly shaken at Pamarjan when, on the second day of our imprisonment, a plane flew low overhead and I, thinking it to be an allied plane, had been badly startled. Obviously, even a month after being 'whipped into the bag' my nerves were still somewhat jangled and there was no social worker to counsel me!

The second incident was far more pleasant. Two or three days before we were released from clink, into the prison yard swaggered a Japanese officer, attired in a kimono, with a sword dangling incongruously at his side. Through the bars, we saw the native warder bustle up to bow so low that his head almost touched the ground. He straightened himself only, as the Japanese bellowed at him, to cringe like a dog caught by his master in an act of thievery. He soon thought to obey and scuttled before the officer, fumbling for his keys as he went, to the first of the cells occupied by the POWs, so that we in the third cell became unsighted. After a short interval we did, however, just catch sight of the officer and jailer reappearing, to enter the next cell. Then the key grated in our door. We smartly sprang to attention and gave the usual respectful bow as the august personage entered.

He was a middle-aged shortish officer with a classical moustache, doubtless one of the old school of Japanese officers. It was also evident that he had had a trifle too much to drink. What would we expect? Wrath or buffoonery? Our misgivings were soon quelled for his first action was to produce, from his kimono, some cigarettes which he distributed among us. From his excited talk and gesticulations, we gathered that he wept for us prisoners at Rangkasbetoeng jail through no fault of our own. He would do what he could for us. After all, were we not both peoples of civilised nations? As for these natives – pish – they were but the scum of the earth. By now, I suppose, he was properly wound up, for the time factor made it obvious that he had not unburdened his mind at such length in the other cells.

For the sake of the poor despised warder – it was just as well that our Japanese friend had not warmed up before – he whipped out his sword from its scabbard and flashed it in front of the cringing native in a threatening manner. Never had I seen such abject terror. The poor fellow sank to his knees and commenced a pitiful wailing. The officer continued to rail at him, trying to communicate to us, in the intervals between the curses that he bombarded the native with, that although this native dross was in charge of us, only due to force of circumstances, never let him consider for one moment that he was anything but our inferior.

'Get up you dog, wait at the door,' the officer bellowed, or words obviously to that effect, and the frightened creature almost crawled from the cell.

Thereupon, more cigarettes appeared from the officer's voluminous kimono. He was like a conjuror producing rabbits from a hat and a high good humour prevailed. Emboldened, one of our crowd asked if he, the officer, could let us have a bottle of whisky, as spirits, our sense of smell told us, he had been drinking excessively. 'Yes,' he said, of course, he would, certainly we should have some, and after promising still more cigarettes and a bottle of whisky, off he staggered. Despite his obviously good intentions at that time, we never saw the whisky nor, for that matter, him again, once the door had closed and he had passed through the entrance gates, watched by the frightened jailer. But whether he forgot, changed his mind, or whether a soldier sent to do his bidding confiscated the liquid, I do not know.

His visit produced one good effect. During the remaining short time at the prison, we enjoyed exceptional consideration from the warder. Morale, too, had also received a fillip, for it had pleased us to think that the natives must now realise that the Japanese did bear us respect. Anyhow, had we not vicariously had our revenge on the rotten fellow?

Then, on 14 April, more lorries arrived and we were crated elsewhere. Twenty miles was the distance that I reckoned we covered before the lorries drove through the town of Serang, which I knew, and offloaded us outside a long, low-built structure which was already occupied. Other prisoners were also incarcerated, like packed sardines, in the cinema (as it turned out to be). The conditions were atrocious and when the time came to disperse the prisoners elsewhere, many were so weak that they never regained full strength. Why had we been brought here? Rumour had it that on the morrow we were to be moved to Batavia, and this rumour was about the only one at Serang – and the place was seething with them – that bore any resemblance to the truth. Serang, in fact, was a veritable hive of rumours, and I was to hear so many optimistic yarns, that had one-tenth of them been true, our term of imprisonment would have been very short indeed. Some of the rumours were so fantastic as to merit but little consideration, although I would have been other than human had their effect not been exhilarating.

For instance, the Yanks had already re-landed in Eastern Java, the Yanks had landed in North Malaya and were sweeping all before them, the British were attacking Singapore from the sea, their armies had already joined up with the Chinese from across the Burmese border and were striking towards Saigon. The most fantastic one was that we had to give a written message for our parents to a certain Eurasian, a Mr Andrews, to have it relayed to England from a radio station near Batavia. I actually spoke to this native, presumably in the pay of the Japanese, who swore that he could do it and although hardly crediting his story, like a host of others, I gave him a message and my name and address just in case. No doubt all that was broadcast by this native was a batch of rumours. He was full of them and his tales were only cut short by an announcement that a meal was ready. It consisted of the usual boiled rice and watery green stew, served by Dutch chefs, the prisoners forming themselves into a queue with containers of all sorts and sizes.

The meal over, we found lying space back in the hut. Thereafter, I had the most enjoyable evening that I had experienced since capture. Next to me lay a young, crippled Australian officer, a survivor from the sunken cruiser *Perth*. He had been badly wounded in the leg but was supremely courageous, still full of the joys of living. He talked to me a lot about Australia and his conversation so held my attention that it was the early hours of the morning before we thought of sleep. Prior to our conversation, however, an impromptu concert was given by some of the prisoners. Small home-made oil lamps, burning coconut oil, squeezed out a certain illumination which in no way dimmed the performance of an excellent baritone, and probably even assisted a Dutch conjuror. An outsider would have found great difficulty in believing that for six weeks these men had been Japanese POWs under the most disgusting conditions. Rather than being gloomy the atmosphere was hilarious. Yet, after all is said and done, what avail to be other than cheerful?

The next morning, after a breakfast of sorts, we were taken to a yard outside the cinema where dozens of emaciated prisoners were already congregated, most of them fussing over small fires or hurrying to and from a filthy latrine. Hardly had I had the opportunity of looking about me when I was smacked by one of the biggest shocks as a POW. At first I thought my eyes were playing tricks on me, but no, approaching me was indeed my greatest wartime pal, Charlie Cleal, whom I had thought to be dead. An RAF radar operator like myself, at the time of the ambush he had been riding next to the driver in the leading convoy vehicle. After I had jumped out, I saw him no more and hardly dared to hope that he had survived. Apparently he, too, had thought little of my chances of survival. I can scarcely describe our mutual delight at our reunion. It was one of the high spots of the whole war. He had, he informed me, been trapped in the lorry, unable to move, at the time of the ambush. A bullet from a Japanese rifle had seared his side and blood had trickled down his flesh. He hadn't been sure whether he was dead or alive. All had been confusion until the hubbub had somewhat subsided and a Japanese soldier had opened the door of his cab, prodded him with a finger and then administered a fierce blow on his rump with his own tin helmet which had been lying on the seat beside him. With great presence of mind he had already decided to feign death and so still did he lie, as the Japanese poked and thumped him, that his ruse was successful. Later, the 'corpse' was to slip away to make his escape, only two days afterwards to be 'whipped into the bag', having wandered some distance towards Serang.

Apparently he and hundreds of others were to survive the crowded conditions in Serang Cinema, the Black Hole of Serang! This place and its conditions have already been so aptly described by other writers that I will dwell no further on the matter, although I heard the details from Charlie Cleal and many others. Cleal and I were later able to exchange all our experiences at leisure for, to our mutual delight, I found that we were both among the party bundled into a convoy or lorries a little later that day. We were, therefore, in high spirits as the lorries set out eastwards from Serang, obviously en route for Batavia.

The journey was completely uneventful, save for a halt at the side of the road for a meal. A few bananas, bought by those who possessed money, had to suffice us prisoners, although the Japanese slobbered over the usual rice meal from their dixies. Much of the success of the Japanese is undoubtedly due to their mobility. A far greater percentage of the Japanese Army consti-tutes fighting men than common among European and American troops. For instance, their diet is so simple that no elaborate field kitchen or a large bevy of cooks are required, when on active service. No matter whether it is breakfast, dinner or supper, it can all be carried in the dixie. This utensil, full of boiled rice, with a small tray fitted inside carrying a few lumps of meat, a little fish or pieces of cooked vegetables, and a water bottle was all that was needed. So the Japanese soldier's meal was a simple affair and I noticed, with mild surprise, that the officers' fare was no better than that of the rank and file. There was no wastage of personnel, such as batmen! Neither was time wasted for, immediately the meal was over, the transport restarted and an hour or so later we drove through familiar Batavia.

Cycle Camp – Batavia

In striking contrast to what we had been used to, all was orderliness and tidiness at the Cycle Camp. The moment we entered the gates, we noticed the difference. Our way of life would be organised here. Unfortunately, affairs had already been arranged to the advantage of the present inmates. Thus, as we alighted from the lorries, we were not shepherded by the English orderly sergeant major to one of the fairly modern blocks of army barracks, but to a wing of single-storey inferior buildings, albeit of bricks and mortar. At one end of this building, a few RAF personnel were already in residence and we airmen from the lorries were advised to find sleeping space among them. Needless to say, the best spots had already been commandeered, the small rooms into which the buildings were divided being full up. So we had to find space on the veranda. An ideal alternative, we thought, to sleep in the open – the season being the dry one – so that despite the lack of beds and the hard floor (although by now I had managed to scrounge a piece of dilapidated matting to which for some time I was determined to cling), I anticipated a good night's sleep, but, as at Pamarjan, the pest of mosquitoes ruined my hopes. On subsequent nights, I was able to protect myself by wrapping pieces of cloth around my hands and covering the lower and upper parts of my face with odd pieces of material, scrounged from here and there, leaving only my nose as the target.

We few RAF personnel were, on the whole, the beggars of the camp. Perhaps I should have used the term 'down-and-outs', for I was too proud to beg even from the most fortunate. At the Cycle Camp, we encountered a new type of POW, the soldier not captured in individual groups or in actual combat but who had, as one of an organised party, surrendered to the Japanese with the rest of his unit. They surrendered their arms and liberty, but not their clothes and personal kit. Most of the prisoners at the Cycle Camp had been taken in this way. Whole units had, at the order of the High Command, without being fired upon or without having fired a shot, turned over their arms to the Japanese and simply marched into Japanese POW camps in orderly fashion, being allowed to retain Dutch money and all their kit apart from arms, etc. It was not their fault, but it was decidedly to their advantage to commence three and a half years as Japanese POWs with kitbags full of clothes. Actually, before the end of our period of incarceration, I possessed more kit, including a safety razor with one blade, than many who at the outset of imprisonment had had an abundance, but this was due in part to the purchase of kit with money that I had managed to hang on to.

When I first walked into the Cycle Camp, all I possessed (save currency) was one pair of long KD trousers, one worn KD shirt, a badly torn sleeping mat, some old pieces of material, a halved coconut shell and a short native metal spoon that I had picked up. My vest and underpants had worn out some time ago, rotted by perspiration. None of my RAF comrades, numbering in all about twenty-five, nor the two or three Australians with whom we renewed acquaintance, had much more, so there was no one voluntarily to offer help. Either you looked after yourself or you succumbed. Throughout the whole of my period as a POW, apart from one isolated instance, I received practically no help. At not one of the camps that I stayed at, was any organised effort made to share things equally between the prisoners. There was little *esprit de corps* or co-operation from those in charge, largely perhaps because I was always attached to a camp composed of dribs and drabs of various branches of the services. In my opinion, had these privileged men possessed the courage and organising ability to have made it possible for there to have been fair shares for all, the eventual percentage of deaths among us would have been far smaller.

My shortage of kit and the fact that I was still suffering from sores on the legs had one important result, so far as I was concerned, while at the Cycle Camp. Not once was I detailed for a working party, which was demanded by the Japanese on most days. As time went on, it mattered not a whit whether one possessed head or footwear but, in those early days, lack of footwear meant no working parties. This was not altogether an advantage, for such parties broke the monotony, were not particularly arduous and often presented the opportunity of obtaining a little 'laegi' (extra) food.

The diet sheet, for the most part, was red rice and stew. Compared with what we were to receive before the end of the war, food was good and plentiful. Once a day, there was pork in the stew and there was as much reasonably clean rice as we wanted. Occasionally a little bread and fruit found their way into the camp. Then, again, there might arise an opportunity to buy. Outside the camp a road ran by and natives would sometimes risk being caught by the Japanese, bring food to the roadside and throw it to us over a high, thick hedge, but competition within the camp was keen and, as few natives would risk a bashing and being tied to a post in the full glare of the sun for a few hours, one was lucky to obtain any extra nourishment in this way. In any case, if small change was short the risk must be taken of having the correct amount returned after the five or ten guilder note, or whatever it was, had been tossed over the hedge. Altogether it was a very unsatisfactory way of doing business, but the entrepreneurial training at the Cycle Camp stood me in good stead later when one either did business or perished.

There were other ways of augmenting rations. Both pigeons and cats were numerous about the camp. Fellows would spend hours fashioning catapults and, when made, spend more hours slinging stones at the pigeons while, in some corners of the camp it was said that a cat dare not venture. On good authority, I was informed, stewed cat tasted very much like stewed rabbit, but I never had the courage to put the truth of this assertion to the test. To eat cat had always seemed to me akin to cannibalism. Then there was food to be obtained from the official canteen, which opened whenever the Japanese allowed in any extra food, which was not very often. Prices were high, of course, and with no immediate prospect of making much money, even when there was food in the canteen, it was not always a practical or attractive proposition to buy.

If the food situation was little better in its variety than at the native prison, nevertheless, we were a good deal happier at the Cycle Camp. We had freedom of movement within the camp and could wander from one part of it to another. Charlie Cleal and I palled up with two Australian radar mechanics, Brian Breillat and Douglas Potts. Both had suffered at the hands of the Japanese. Brian had been tortured and Doug had been bayoneted in the arm. They were grand fellows and had been stationed with us at Anjer. Brian, besides, was a thinker and we enjoyed many interesting conversations. We also met Archie Caswell, a compatriot of theirs who, I understand, was later to run a radio set successfully in Burma. Like us, they had little kit but had managed to scrounge a pack of cards, and we formed a bridge school. Happy memories but, alas, Doug was not to survive his imprisonment. Even in those early days, he suffered from dysentery and his arm was still very troublesome. He was so thin, that one could hardly have credited the fact that he was normally the healthy-looking specimen whom we had known six weeks earlier.

Besides the Australians from our unit at Anjer, we also met again others of the same unit, AC1 Stiven, ex-European ballroom dance champion and AC1 McGowan, in peace time, a film extra. It seemed that out of our original unit of nineteen, only ten had survived and, of those left, most suffered from stomach trouble or sores. Fortunately, there was medical treatment to be had at the Cycle Camp. Then, there was Sergeant Eric Oliver, ever an optimist, and AC Barry Paterson, masquerading while at the camp as 'Sergeant Pattison' as he had been involved with two Australians in the killing of two Japanese soldiers when on the run before capture. We soon rumbled him, but fortunately the Japanese never did.

Each day there was a sick parade. I, myself, was able to procure treatment for tropical sores. The British medical authorities in the camp still possessed their own drugs and were also allowed to purchase from the local shops. How many British lives would have been saved during the next three and a half years in that camp, had proper drugs been available throughout that period, it is impossible to say. The numbers would doubtless have been considerable, even though starvation was the major cause of death. Another big advantage in this camp, which must have tended greatly to good health, was the presence of modern latrines. Toilet paper was non-existent but native-like, I washed by backside with wet fingers dipped in water. Camp cooks probably used similar ablutional methods, ideal to discourage dysentery!

During our stay here, there were only two incidents of note. In the first place, the high-ranking officers were taken from the officers' compound and interned separately. Secondly, we received a visit from a Dutch brass band. Escorted by their Japanese captors, the bandsmen marched into the camp playing a military march and staged an excellent concert. It was also excellent Japanese propaganda. No doubt in Tokyo, cinema-goers felt almost envious of their country's POWs, stationed in exotic places.

After a month in this camp, a large part of us, all British, were detailed to move, leaving the colonial troops, including Maoris, behind. Rumour had it that we were being taken to the docks and, for about the first time at the Cycle Camp, rumour was correct. Here, as at Serang, there were the usual fantastic stories of improbable American landings. We would soon be whisked out of Java by American transport planes, but we left the camp on foot, all the same, covered by Japanese rifles. For the first time since I had entered the camp, I saw the outside world again. I was relieved, however, when we were taken to a 'covered-in' station, as I had been marching barefoot. There we were bundled into a train, joined by troops from elsewhere and eventually detrained near the docks. Outside the terminus we were, for some unaccountable reason, made to hang around for two hours. Opposite, standing by their stalls of fruit and drink, were some native vendors, obviously being badgered by some Japanese naval personnel. Never in all my life had I seen such a nondescript crowd as these sailors. They paid us little attention, although I expect we caused them as much amusement as they did us. By the time we were formed up in marching order, the sailors had lounged off towards the docks, not far off, while we were marched for two or three miles, on a road parallel to the water front, until we came to a camp already pretty full up.

Tanjoeng Priok

On the whole, my four months at Tanjoeng Priok were the least miserable of the three and a half years spent as a POW. There was plenty of organised entertainment within the camp: concerts, lectures, education classes and sport. Discipline was not particularly harsh, despite the daily roll-calls (tenkos). I, myself, did no working parties because of sore feet, but those who did had few complaints about the work at the docks, mainly unloading ships. Indeed, many would have been disappointed had the working parties ceased, because there were opportunities galore for augmenting their larders. Often, I felt quite jealous when fellows returned with tins of condensed milk stolen from the dockyards yet, broadly speaking, I preferred to stay put, doing my share of camp duties, for the leisure I had was to my liking. Most of my comrades, less lazy than I, would have been bored stiff hanging around the camp day after day, but I enjoyed the long hours reading or playing chess. There were plenty of books to be obtained and each compound possessed one or two sets of chessmen and I played a lot with airman Smith.

Basic camp rations, however, were far better than those that we were forced to exist on later. There was plenty of rice, although it was for a time strongly sulphur flavoured, albeit not in any measure as bad as that we had received at Pamarjan. Each day, there was a thin meat stew and, also, by way of a change, weekly issues of dried fish. Occasionally, too, each enclosure within the camp was allowed an issue of fruit such as pomelo or papaya and, once or twice, even bread.

In all, there were about a dozen compounds or enclosures in this camp of three or four thousand Japanese cared-for cowardly combatants. Each compound ate separately, though there was but one cookhouse, prisoners of each enclosure being detailed to fetch their rations as mealtimes came round (never too often), so that the food could be shared out in each compound under the supervision of an appointed officer.

Every compound possessed a few officers, although the one to which I, and the rest of the airmen from the Cycle Camp, had been attached, boasted by far the largest proportion, including most of the senior officers. For this reason, it also boasted the most overcrowded conditions. The elite (officers) had allotted themselves not only the best quarters but, also, plenty of space. As a result, we inferiors were pushed for room, and it was a job to find, in our attap huts, enough floor space to lie down full length at night time. As we twisted and turned uncomfortably, we often thought of the solidly built shelters that our superiors inhabited, of their wooden beds and mosquito nets. Nevertheless, some of the officers were not dictatorial, quite approachable, and doubtless magnanimously did what they considered fit to help their less unfortunate countrymen. Perhaps they reasoned that, despite their predicament, they must do their utmost to uphold the dignity, discipline and tradition of the British Army. So they still had batmen to serve their meals, to clean their quarters and wash their clothes. Class distinction must be maintained at all costs for the pukka sahibs.

There were two types of officers in the camp, those who had joined the army in England and those who had enlisted in Malaya with the entry, or the imminent entry, of the Japanese into the war. In my opinion, the former were on average by far the better type. Many of the others were definitely unfit to be in charge of the modern British soldier or, for that matter, any age of British soldier. They were too apt to treat men as coolies and showed little tact or leadership. Indeed, I would go as far as to say that two or three of them exhibited the least inspiring leadership traits that I had yet encountered. On the other hand, a few of the regular army officers were first-rate. Gifted with a flare for leadership and a love of humanity, they were the type men followed blindly, no matter how heavy the enemy's fire. One of the most outstanding of these was a Lieutenant Colonel Russell of the East Surrey Regiment. Although capable of exercising great severity when the occasion demanded it, he was, nevertheless, an understanding kindly man, one of the greatest gentlemen that I have ever met. He was humble yet, at the same time, courageous and there was hardly a man whose confidence he did not possess. Furthermore, fortunately, the Japanese regarded him highly and, although Colonel Lane was the senior officer at the camp, it was Lieutenant Colonel Russell who generally acted as mediator between us and the Japanese and it was generally known that the Japanese commandant respected him above all others.

My ability to play a reasonably fair game of chess brought me into contact with the officers in the camp a good deal and I can remember with special affection Captain Hancock, a young officer of the best type, a Lieutenant Pool of the Singapore Volunteer Corps, a Javanese ex-harbour master, a Captain Gardiner to whom I will refer later, the urbane Captain Anderson, who handled the camp concerts and his friend Captain Skee. Skee was appointed officer in charge of the small RAF contingent, until then officerless, and I think most of us thought of him with affection. At any rate, he interfered with us very little, a fact that showed a rare tact, though he was not the most energetic of men.

Besides the small RAF contingent, there was also a handful of navy men who, like us, seemed a little out of place, but they were a jolly set and doubtless did not bemoan the lack of their own naval officer when Lieutenant Colonel Russell adopted them. They probably enjoyed more privileges than any other set in the camp. A few were acting as batmen, a much sought-after post under the circumstances, while two of them struck a partnership with me, which continued until we moved from Tanjoeng Priok.

It was a peculiar partnership and arose out of the lack of proper sanitary accommodation. At first there was not one covered in lavatory in our compound and, as a temporary measure, a slit trench was excavated. To a large extent, the success of this depended upon the care with which earth was shaken over faeces straight away. Some prisoners were careless, others lacked any sense of sanitary responsibility and it was soon realised that it was useless to exhort certain backsliders to use the earth provided despite the fact that, by their failure to do so, they not only endangered their comrades' lives but their own as well. Already, there were several cases of dysentery, both bacillary and amoebic and, of course, nothing attracted the carriers of this disease, flies, more than uncovered faeces. Therefore, it was decided that the latrine must be picketed, it being the job of the picket to ensure that all excreta be properly raked over. Six rankers were detailed, three to constitute the evening watch and three the daytime watch. As I was unofficially a 'light duty' man, despite the unremitting efforts of one of the RAF sergeants to have me placed on the working party, and being still without footwear and not yet free of tropical sores, I managed to wangle myself as one of the picket, an exalted post that I held on to tooth and nail throughout the whole of my stay at Tanjoeng Priok.

Some might have found it an unbearably boring occupation, and for sure it had its dull moments but, under the circumstances, I found it quite to my liking. In the first place, I felt at last that I was doing some good; secondly, there was nothing during the daylight to prevent my reading a book or writing, provided that I appeared reasonably alert to the officers and sergeant major when the trenches were in use; finally, at night, I loved to gaze aloft at the starry sky. Night after night, the stars would shine with incredible brilliance. It was fascinating to trace the various constellations and watch them move across the sky. Celestial names such as Capella, Canopus, Aldebarran and Sagittarius possessed a magic of their own. Yet, until I joined the latrine picket, I boasted only the haziest idea of the universe beyond our own little planet, the only group of stars I knew being the Plough. With the help of a book on astronomy, I discovered a new interest and increased my knowledge of the heavens a thousandfold. Moreover, this knowledge, coupled with my nocturnal vigils, acted as a mental tonic. Did I not occasionally have glimpses of the vastness, yet oneness, of the universe, have fleeting visions of the eternal truth, of the awfulness of beauty, of God, who is universal? Was I not an integral part of all this? If so, why then be troubled? So, there were moments when, despite my predicament, I knew supreme happiness.

I had, indeed, during the evenings, ample time for philosophical contemplation as my naval friends, in keeping with their traditions, suggested four-hourly watches. The first day's watch commenced at eight o'clock in the morning and the last finished at eight o'clock in the evening. From then until eight o'clock in the morning the following morning it was the turn of the night watch. My favourite period stretched from eight o'clock in the evening to midnight. During the first two hours there was still plenty of activity in the camp, lights out not being until ten o'clock. For the next hour, some poor sleepless soul would generally keep me company, while the last hour of the watch could be spent contemplating the brilliant heavens. The watch from midnight until four o'clock in the morning was the worst. Even though dysentery and diarrhoea were rife in the camp, very few prisoners used the latrines during those hours and time would drag, despite my astronomical interests, but we soon learnt to overcome that difficulty. It was mutually agreed that, as flies foraged during the hours of daylight only, it was a waste of time to picket the latrine in the early hours.

To have pointed out this obvious fact to the camp officers would have been inviting a rebuke or risking the loss of a comfortable job. So, taking the matter into our own hands, we determined that whoever was due to take over at midnight should merely steal away to the huts for a good night's sleep. We worked a different shift each night so that, over a period of three nights, we all had a turn at each four-hourly period. Therefore the four o'clock to eight o'clock man must discipline himself to wake up not later than six o'clock in the morning so as to be on duty in time to cover over any filth before the sergeant major made his early visit to the latrines. This ruse was, to my knowledge, never discovered by the authorities, so that the week of night picketing became a regular scrounge, as we each averaged only twelve to fifteen hours' duty per week. In fact, so comfortable was the job that, when later I was issued with a pair of second-hand socks and boots, as so many other down-and-outs were, I was quite relieved to find that to wear them only aggravated my sores and was glad of the excuse to discard them, especially as one of the RAF sergeants was becoming more and more determined to rope me on to the working parties. Incidentally, this was the only official example I can recall to pool kit!

We did, of course, pray for the continued good health of the sergeant major and officers concerned with our working conditions, as a bout of chronic diarrhoea or dysentery might make known to them the non-existence of the midnight picket. I expect our game would have been played out eventually, had we remained at Tanjoeng Priok long enough, for I noticed an ever-increasing tendency on my part to oversleep on those mornings when to turn out by six o'clock was essential. Indeed, on one occasion, just before leaving Priok, I was only just in time to advertise my presence to the sergeant major, who was at the latrine before I had scampered out. By then a few concrete block latrines had been built by a gang of POWs. The contents were emptied daily, directly into the sea, by another duty party, so that one could have been unseen as a user approached, without arousing suspicion. Had the sergeant major though, been unfortunate enough to have sat on a fouled seat, then there would have been trouble, especially had the picket still been missing. Thus the primary object of the night watch was to ensure a clean seat for the sergeant major as he indulged his early morning habit.

It must not be supposed that, had the picket been caught sleeping when he was supposed to have been on duty, some light punishment would have been administered. Oh, no! In its way, a sleeping latrine picket would have been considered as culpable as a sleeping guard on duty at an army outpost. There was no special punishment at Tanjoeng Priok for such offences, in an effort to make the punishment fit the crime. Strict army discipline still prevailed. Severe punishment took the form of pack drill. Two or three times every day, British MPs marched delinquents up and down the spaces between the huts: they marched them fast and they marched them hard. Left wheel, right wheel, right about turn, right wheel, left wheel and so on – thus the orders were barked in quick succession. With a full pack on their shoulders and in the full glare of the tropical sun, these fellows were an object of pity as they must endure not only the harsh discipline of the British Army but were also subject to the rigours of ordinary Japanese prisoner of war life. Yet, the treatment meted out to these culprits was nothing compared with the brutal treatment handed out by one or two of our own MPs to their countrymen in yet another camp I stayed at later on. There, legalised murder occurred, as will be referred to later.

The Japanese treatment of prisoners at Priok was, by their own standards, reasonably humane. There were, of course, a few bashings but they were not on the grand scale. The danger period was the middle of the afternoon when all men not on working party or on camp duty were forced to take two hours' 'yasumé'. This 'siesta', of course, was not a bad thing in itself but most afternoons a couple of Japanese louts, presumably with marked inferiority complexes, would stride through the camp looking for trouble. If they caught anybody not resting, woe betide him. On the other hand, if they passed near a recumbent form that did not jump to attention with sufficient alacrity, woe betide him, too. The punishment was equally severe for him whose feet, at attention, did not form the correct angle, or whose bow was not executed with humility. The most exasperating feature of the camp was the 'tenkos'. Twice a day we had to line up (in twos, as the Japanese soldiers were incapable of counting in threes or fours) and the numbers were checked. Our captors could never accomplish this simple task without a lot of fuss and bother and often we stood in the sun for a whole hour while the check proceeded, compound by compound. On a few occasions we were also turned out in the middle of the night, in the poor artificial light available, when it was laughable to watch the Japanese trying to agree numbers.

The Japanese had good reason for these midnight checks, however, as there flourished, in the camp, an extensive black market. Some of the bolder and more enterprising spirits, especially in the enclosures not bounded by a road, were dealing with the local Javanese, and it was a fairly easy task to wriggle through the wire unobserved to contact, under cover of darkness, the natives from the nearby village. Watches, fountain pens and other valuables of that class, even clothes, were exchanged for cash or better still food, and huge profits were made. As with most such enterprises, over-indulgence crept in, so that the Japanese became suspicious and sprang a surprise roll call, whenever they had reason to suspect that prisoners were missing from the camp. I remember that, on one occasion, although the tenko revealed no discrepancy, the Japanese were convinced that one or two had ventured through the wire from our compound and they threatened us with all manner of disasters if no one owned up. No one did, but one of the Japanese noticed two badly ripped shirts, spattered with blood, caused by undue haste scrambling back under the barbed wire. The men involved were marched to the Japanese guard room, severely beaten up and detained there for two or three days. The risks were well worthwhile and the extra food that I myself obtained later, by chancing being caught bartering with the natives, probably saved my life.

The biggest racket of all, however, was the condensed milk racket. Besides the numerous tins stolen from the docks, the British authorities at Priok themselves held a large supply. Suddenly the milk disappeared. Despite all the entreaties of the camp's senior officers and exhaustive enquiries, the hiding place of the tins was never discovered, yet I bought one or two myself through another RAF officer, who had obtained them from someone else, each intermediary procuring a slice of the profit. Some of these tins actually appeared on the tables of the junior officers. The matter remained ostensibly a mystery, but it was obvious that some of the officers knew more than they were prepared to disclose and I strongly suspect that many of them nurtured a pretty shrewd idea from whence their milk supplies came. Indeed, a certain corporal's name was openly associated with the affair but the officers, being able to obtain all that they needed through their batmen, were quite content not to ask too many questions. They were at least enjoying a far greater share of the milk than they would have done normally.

There were a few other commodities on the market. Limited supplies of tinned foods could be obtained from the official canteen, provided that one had the money. A lot of prisoners possessed considerable sums, others had none. Of those who had none, some had themselves to blame, but others, and perhaps the large majority, were destitute through no fault of their own. Those with money were far less handicapped in the struggle for existence. Now the big question arises. Under such circumstances, should all monies be pooled? Should, in fact, the camp be run on socialistic lines, or should the principle be the survival of the fittest? No doubt there would be considerable difference of opinion in any argument concerning this. For my own part, however, I was, throughout my POW status, strongly in favour of pooling resources, although circumstances later forced me to act in direct opposition to my principles. I still think that such a policy of equal shares for all would have paid handsomely.

Let me make it quite clear that I did not, and do not now, advocate the expediency of this from a realisation that I was among the weaker of my fellow men. As time went on and I became more selfish and self-seeking, I found that I could live a little above the level of the average. By the exercise of a certain initiative forced upon me, I was able to augment my lawful rations considerably in later years and, definitely, consider that these extras assisted me in my fight for existence. Yet, there were numerous others who, for various reasons such as physical weakness, negative disposition, religious qualms and the like, were unable to supplement the means of their existence provided by our hosts and died through lack of nutrition, while their more enterprising comrades survived. As I have already stated, I have little doubt that had the camps been run on democratic and socialistic lines, and I am thinking mainly of Kuching camp to which later I was to be shifted, the loss of life would have been halved. 'United we stand, divided we fall' was an axiom seldom heeded in the POW camps that I had knowledge of. During the early days, the violation of this wise old saying was not so evident but it will be seen that, as time went on, the precept was disregarded.

However, when I first moved to Tanjoeng Priok, I did try to put these beliefs into practice and I have little doubt that many others attempted likewise. My closest companions were three RAF fellows, Charlie Cleal, Freddie Pafford and Norman Williams, a pleasant young man, though rather introspective, to whom Charlie Cleal and I had been attracted. Of the four of us, only Norman and I possessed money, but we decided that rather than cling to our own we should pool resources. This we did with great exactitude and neither Williams nor I spent money on commodities that we did not all share equally. We drew from our hundred guilders or so with discretion, but were generally able to augment our daily rations with a little tinned milk, or with some other tinned delicacy such as preserved meats, available in the stores. All of us gained in general fitness, despite the paucity of our belongings.

At Tanjoeng Priok there was, on the whole, a fairly high standard of fitness, although I was amazed that many of the fellows found the energy for football. Of this, there were some really first-rate games. Each enclosure boasted a team and matches were frequently played during the early evening on the camp football pitch. There were, besides some very good amateur players, a few professionals, but the most colourful personality afield was, without doubt, Wilf Wooller, the old Welsh Rugger International and Glamorgan CCC Captain. The football played was, of course, soccer, so Wilf had to adapt himself. This he managed with surprisingly good results. He figured as a centre forward, but played rather a clumsy game. However, once the ball was at his feet and his way was clear to the goal it was, look out! I have never seen a man shoot harder. At times, the ball would strike the back of the net like a cannon ball. Had he possessed nimbleness, without a shadow of a doubt he could have made as great a name for himself at soccer as at rugger.

Much as I myself would have liked to have played soccer, my sores prevented me from putting to the test my reserves of energy. My only real exercise at Priok was a walk to the sea and half an hour's bathe. Do not let it be imagined, however, that ours was a holiday camp, not a bit of it. The only prisoners allowed the privilege of seasiding were the 'ulcerated legs'. In the absence of an ample supply of drugs, the camp authorities considered that salt water constituted the best substitute. So, once a day, ulcer cases assembled outside the guard room at the camp entrance, to be marched by the guards the short distance to the water's edge. I fully enjoyed my afternoon dip, despite the fact that swimming was rather a painful process, as the water pulled at the ulcers, but at least the brine did them no harm, being, on the contrary, rather beneficial. Anyhow, there was little in the way of alternative treatment to be had as there were few drugs of any kind in the camp and, although there were daily sick parades, the British medical officer's biggest responsibilities were to place a man on a diet of rice water if suffering from dysentery or diarrhoea and to mutter 'Light duty', 'No duty', or 'Medicine and Duty', as the case might demand.

Life had its other compensations, besides bathing. As I mentioned before, a game of chess could always be had. Besides inter-compound competitions, a grand camp knockout competition was organised. Among us was an ex-youth champion of England – Orimovitch, or some such name – and it was decided that the winner of the knockout should play him in a series of exhibition matches. To my great surprise and horror, I reached the semi-final, aided by a good deal of luck, by beating two colonels on the way, a feat of which, I am not ashamed to say, I was very proud. In actual fact, I have little doubt that my run of success would have come to an abrupt end in the semi-final, as there were players left in who were better than I, one being Wilf Wooller, but the very thought of having my occasionally ill-considered moves puzzled over and ridiculed during an exhibition match, gave me the shivers. I had not, more by luck than judgement, made any howlers in the competition, but I was never put to the test as I was posted prior to the finish of the contest.

There were other means of pleasantly whiling away the time, such as debates, lectures and courses of study. The one debate that I took part in aroused much laughter, as we argued whether or not a married man has a greater chance of achieving happiness than a bachelor. I believe that the verdict went against the married man but, of course, we had little inclination for the opposite sex in those days. Food, food and more food was the greatest topic of conversation.

There were some interesting lectures, however, on subjects foreign to the delectable subject of food. Clearest of all, I remember one delivered by a lieutenant colonel who had been on secret service duties in Thailand prior to the war. He insisted that the British Secret Service had been aware of Japanese fifth column work in Thailand and had unavailingly warned the British Government of the obvious Japanese intention to invade that country. Then, there were first hand accounts of the sinking of the *Prince of Wales* and the *Repulse*, lectures on various parts of the world, on the organisation of Selfridges, on harbour master duties in Java, on the making of beer, on betting and on photography, to mention but a few. Besides these more formal affairs, there were the accounts of the early adventures of servitude.

Once again, one particular recital stands out in my memory.

Jones was one of a gang of many prisoners who, one morning, were handed shovels and herded on to a lorry which took them to some isolated spot. Having alighted, they were ordered to dig a large pit. From the well-armed appearance of their escort and their grim gesticulations, it soon became apparent, to even the most thick-headed of them, that they were digging their own communal grave.

Although an atheist by conviction, Jones said, 'I was moved to pray for deliverance.'

Meanwhile, the depth of the hole reached sinister proportions, but he never gave up hope. Quite suddenly another vehicle drew up, followed by a cackle of voices and a brisk order and the prisoners were told to stop their work and get aboard the lorry again. One can imagine their profound relief. Later, said Jones, they learnt that there had been a last minute countermanding of the order for their extermination. All the same, it had been a very unnerving experience for them but, asserted Jones, as far as he was concerned it was worth it because it brought him back to a belief in God. In fact, he most studiously attended all the religious services in the camp and read his Bible with great fervour.

Then, there was the diversion of studies. Various classes were inaugurated including shorthand, languages, maths and biology. I joined the biology and maths classes, both of which I found very interesting but, in so far as my progress in maths was concerned, it was perhaps as well that I was soon to leave the camp, as I doubt whether I should have made much headway with calculus, the branch of maths embarked upon.

Another feature of Priok were camp concerts. Under the leadership of Captain Anderson, not only variety but more serious entertainment was staged. The most ambitious undertaking was the enacting of Shakespeare's *The Merchant of Venice*. Some excellent acting was the result, and I would especially mention the part of the merchant himself played by a senior NCO (also renowned for his renderings of 'The Donkey Serenade'), and the excellent imitation of a woman given by a young soldier who was thereafter called Portia. This private's every gesture was effeminate, not only on the stage but off it as well!

For the serious-minded, including Jones, there were religious services on Sundays, conducted by a camp padre. One of the greatest achievements while I was at Priok was indeed the design and building of a small chapel within the precincts of the camp and, I think, there was hardly a man, no matter how irreligious, who did not take pride and interest in this building, erected opposite the cookhouse, just off the main camp road.

On the whole we were, for the most part, reasonably happy at Tanjoeng Priok. Although there were never the wild rumours flying around, as at Serang and at the Cycle Camp, we were receiving regular news bulletins from a radio that was in secret operation and were reasonably confident of getting out within a year or perhaps eighteen months' time. Had anyone suggested that we were to endure another three years' imprisonment, we would have laughed them to scorn. Nevertheless, thoughts of escape were not altogether absent from our minds and, for the first time since my Pamarjan days, the subject was given serious consideration.

A seaplane rode in the bay off Priok. A previously mentioned pal of mine, one Sergeant Eric Oliver, together with another air crew colleague of his, thought that they could get her airborne if given a favourable opportunity and, in my boundless optimism, I considered the notion quite possible. We could crawl through the wire one night, swim out to the flying boat and, if unmanned, board her and determine her fuel situation. If she was fully fuelled, why not take the chance of making Australia? It was, for a day or two, a pleasant dream. Then the flying boat was moved, which was just as well, for we might have attempted to make our dreams a reality. Our hosts knew only one answer to attempted escape, we were to ascertain – execution (kepala katong). Later, we learnt that four other fellows tried to escape in Eastern Java, were captured after a few days and, although the Japanese camp commandant was inclined to leniency, on reporting the affair to Japanese HQ in Java, he was ordered to execute them in full view of the rest of the camp, albeit at some distance. Apparently they died 'like men' but who, in his twenties, wanted to die 'like a man anyhow? Thousands were to be massacred before the war ended, the most horrendous atrocities occurring in British North Borneo.

I never witnessed any great atrocity at Tanjoeng Priok, although to be 'bashed up' was common enough. One awkward incident occurred about a month before the first exodus from the camp. The Dai Nippon Gun issued an edict ordering all British POWs to sign an undertaking, transferring their allegiance from King George VI to the Emperor of Japan and swearing not to attempt escape. In vain it was pointed out to the Japanese camp authorities that we could not possibly sign to that effect, as we had already sworn allegiance to our own sovereign but, it seemed, one could not argue with the Japanese Army; we had to sign. It was agreed, by the British officers that, as we should sign under duress, we could do so with a clear conscience and be sure that our signatures would not be binding. There was general concurrence, save among a small group of officers who, although generally agreeing with the theory of the invalidity of any document signed under pressure, nevertheless still refused to put pen to paper. Would there be trouble? A squad of well-armed Japanese soldiers tramped into our enclosure, which held the recalcitrant officers. Would there be a shooting? The compound buzzed with excitement. It was, however, an anticlimax as, after a short argument, the hard core of resistance disintegrated and this small group fell into line with the rest of us. I felt that it had been rather an empty gesture on their part, but, then, I was no officer or gentleman!

A month after this incident, about one thousand of us received marching orders at very short notice, before indeed I had had the opportunity of being knocked out of the chess competition! (I feel that such an important historical fact deserves mentioning!)

Hell Ships to and from Singapore

We had no idea of our ultimate destination when, after breakfast one mid-September morning, we were marched towards the railway station. Instead of ultimately being paraded on the platform, as we had expected, we were lined up alongside a dirty-looking coastal vessel at the dockside, so that it became fairly certain that we were to leave Java.

The ship did not look large enough to take us all. It was not, but not a man was left behind. Before embarking, however, there was a routine disinfestation. As each man, fully clothed, approached the ship's gangway he was sprayed with disinfectant. This was a useless procedure, I thought, because even supposing that we had been infested with lice – and few of us were in those early days – the insecticide used (DDT not yet being in use) would have failed to reach lice concealed in the seams of the clothing, etc. In any case, the residual toxic action of the insecticide would have been quite incapable of harming the embryonic louse as it emerged from the nit. Still, the performance pleased the Japanese, so there were few grumbles. They had made their point. We were no better than beasts; a fact that became abundantly clear before my release from bondage.

Aboard the luxury liner we never stopped grumbling, an Englishman's privilege, it is said, so I will refrain from describing in detail the joys of the cruise. Others have written much about Japanese hell ships, and the reader would not wish to recap. In any case, a few weeks later, we were to undergo an infinitely worse sea trip. Briefly, our two grumbles were lack of space and the shocking sanitary arrangements. The general rank and file had been allocated quarters below decks. These consisted of tiers of platforms on which there was never enough room to stretch out in comfort. Fortunately, however, on this cruise, discipline was never strict, and we were allowed to sleep on deck provided that we could find the space at our end of the ship. As regards the sanitary arrangements, these consisted of wooden boxes suspended from the taffrail. One just crept into them and what did not foul the side of the box, or the two planks forming the floor, splashed into the sea between the six-inch gap separating the two planks. As diarrhoea as ever was rife, these boxes soon became stinking abominations. Nevertheless, as I said, discipline was not strict, a fairish amount of freedom was allowed and the voyage from Batavia to Singapore – which latter city was soon learnt to be our immediate destination – was tolerable.

The food, too, although consisting of but two meals a day, was, judged by Japanese POW standards, not at all bad. Served up with the usual boiled or steamed rice, the stews were nutritious and tasty. Enriched by pork, cheese and butter (or margarine), they were a real treat to us. When considering whether or not we were ill treated by the Japanese, the difference between our standards and their standards must always be taken into consideration. For instance, the continual bashings to which POWs were subjected by their captors seem a brutal anachronism, yet it must be remembered that corporal punishment was common enough in the Japanese Army. If a Japanese soldier infringed discipline, he was quite likely to be beaten by an NCO; likewise, an NCO by an officer. The offence was then, hopefully, forgotten – there probably being no confinement to barracks. At least, such treatment had the advantage of not taking a man away from his normal duties. Therefore, when a Japanese guard 'bashed up' a prisoner, he did no more than inflict what might befall himself should he disobey regulations. Of course, prisoners were often beaten for nothing – sometimes with great brutality – on scores of occasions, but this is entirely another matter. A few Japanese guards did boast of a reputation for punishing only for a definite offence, thus implementing their own training and discipline. Now, Japanese soldiers were afforded far less comfort in troop ships than even the English rank and file and, therefore, I assert that our conditions were not incomparable to those that they themselves were used to.

The main features of the journey from Batavia to Singapore, however, were the birth, growth and spread of an almost incredible rumour. Hardly had we been aboard and learnt of our immediate destination than it was whispered that we were eventually to be repatriated. At first, such a tale appeared ridiculous but, as time went on, ridicule was silenced. Indeed, I must admit that, in common with most others on board, before we reached Singapore I, too, was convinced of imminent repatriation. The fact was that, as the rumour gathered force, every incident seemed to increase the probability. The biggest impetus was the avowed conversion to the idea of no less a person than Lieutenant Colonel Russell, who was among the officers accompanying us. To this day I cannot be certain whether he merely pandered to us, as a tonic to our morale. On the other hand, it is difficult to credit that he deliberately sought to deceive us, no matter how strongly he felt that the means justified the end. Neither can I believe that he was entirely taken in. Perhaps the truth lies somewhere between the two. Some remark or incident had induced him idly to toy with the idea of repatriation. The story circulated was that we were, after reaching Singapore, to be sent to Lorenco Marques (Portuguese East Africa) in a Japanese mercy ship, there to be exchanged for Japanese internees. Possibly therefore, there had been some allusion to this by the Japanese which had led Lieutenant Colonel Russell and others at first vaguely to daydream about such a remote possibility when certain events appeared to endorse such a theory and, in due course, possibility became a probability. We could already savour hot baths and clean crisp sheets.

Lieutenant Colonel Russell was ever an optimist so that, by the time we reached Singapore, his seeming optimism fanned by rumour had imbued us all. Imagine, therefore, the exhilarating effect aroused by the sight of the Japanese mercy ship, the *Tatuta Maru*, when on the third evening out of Batavia we sailed into Singapore Bay. Yes, we said, there was now little doubt that we were going to Lorenco Marques. Although we had to spend yet another night aboard a crowded ship, without the cooling effect of the breezes generated by the ship's movement, not a man felt anything but contentment as he gazed at the nearby mercy ship and he dreamed of the thrill of ultimately landing on English soil and thus so soon to be reunited with loved ones.

A minor shock awaited us in the morning, however. After having been lined up on the docks we were, without a word of explanation, instead of being shifted from one ship to another, unceremoniously pushed into lorries and quickly driven away. Of course, we soon remembered to believe what we wanted to believe. Obviously, we soon reassured ourselves, we could not be transferred directly from a troopship to the *Tatuta Maru*. We would have to be taken to a temporary camp, medically examined and given a certain amount of standard equipment. Besides, perhaps the mercy ship was not yet provisioned. Doubtless, many a condemned man has still hoped for a last minute reprieve, even when the noose was being swung into position.

Gradually, I let thoughts of the future slip away as we drove through the city's streets, some of which I knew so well. So far as I could see they were not much altered, except that here and there a shop was closed, there was less of a hustle and bustle than a year ago and the populace was not so clamorous. It was like the difference between an English street on an ordinary weekday and on a Sunday afternoon (of the last decade). Later we were to hear of the ill-treatment that the Japanese had meted out to vast numbers of the Chinese population of that great cosmopolitan city. Hundreds of them had been driven to the beaches, shot and left there to the whim of the tides. No wonder that business, if mainly as usual, was a good deal slacker. Then, too, there was far less to be bought and sold. In 1940, Singapore was a land of promise. Food was plentiful and forces personnel at least fed far better in Singapore than in England during the same period. Apart from the good food in some of the camps, I well remember many a delightful meal in one of the small cafés of which there were so many, in Stamford Road in particular. These were closed now.

We were soon out of the town and into the country and, after half an hour's ride, passed the famous Changi prison in which so many British internees spent some time before being sent to work on the Burma Railway. We went on past a newly formed cemetery, bristling with little wooden crosses on which, even as we hurried by in the lorries, I could read sad inscriptions, 'Private Smith aged 22; Corporal Green, aged 27; Gunner Jones, aged 20' and so on, sad reminders that already seven months' imprisonment had taken their toll.

Eventually we were unloaded on to a parade square and, after being counted and recounted, were marched away until we reached the entrance to Changi POW Camp. To our surprise, the guard on the gate was Sikh. What did it mean? Had these Indians been forced to do guard duties or had there been treachery? In any case, were they efficient or could they be bought off? Would they not be much easier than the Japanese? Later, we were to learn that they had renounced the King to whom they were sworn. This discovery came as a shock to us, as we had known nothing of this kind in Java. To our knowledge, no British or Empire troops had literally turned traitor, although we knew that many Javanese soldiers were now in the pay of the Dai Nippon Gun, for had we not seen many lorry loads of these troops armed with rifles, pass Tanjoeng Priok, having no doubt been pressed into 'home defence' duties in Java, thus releasing Japanese troops for use elsewhere, but British troops? It did not seem right. It was not cricket.

Actually, quite a large number of Sikhs in Singapore had been induced to go over to the Japanese. Poorly educated as they were, one can hardly wonder that, when assured by the Japanese (as they must have been) that the British had grossly exploited them and that the sole Japanese object in attacking the British and the Americans in the East was to liberate the country from imperialism to set up an East Asiatic Co-Prosperity Sphere and reserve Asia for the Asiatics, some gave way. Anyhow, the British were a decadent race, it was said, already the whole of their Eastern Empire had fallen, a successful landing had been made in Australia and New Zealand, and the Japanese had reached the Ganges. One can hardly wonder that under pressure – and many no doubt were given grandstand seats at some of the Chinese massacres – some gave way.

On the other hand, I later encountered many Indian soldiers who, under the most severe pressure including starvation and repeated 'bashings up', having given their oath to one Emperor, could not transfer active allegiance to another. What did surprise me, however, was to learn that the Sikhs were far more to be feared on gate duty than the Japanese and would hand out a bashing on the slightest pretext. No doubt this greatly pleased their overlords, piquing their vanity and egotism. Incidentally, all the Indian traitors, if you so called them at Changi, appeared to be Sikhs; for instance, I never saw a Gurkha co-operating with the Japanese.

However, I did not see a lot of either Japanese or Indian guards during our three weeks' stay at Changi. In September 1942, it was a well-organised camp, covering many acres, divided into separate divisions, each with a British sergeant major or other officer in command. The Japanese did not interfere much. Perhaps, they did not feel at home in Changi, as barracks were typically British Army being solidly built in three storeys, although parts of the coolie lines had also been commandeered and included in the camp. Besides being strongly constructed, the barrack blocks were well fitted out, having separate sanitary wings complete with flush lavatories and showers, so that many of the prisoners were tolerably comfortable. In fact, I would go so far as to say that could we have spent our three and a half years in these barrack blocks, despite hard labour six or seven days a week, and despite a diet of rice and stew we could, in view of our status, have survived with fortitude. Certainly there would have been a far smaller death toll.

Perhaps, the Japanese derived some grim sense of humour from contrasting the comparative ease of Changi with the grimness of impending conditions on the Burma Road, for instance. Who can plumb the depths of their sadistic minds? But even the comparative luxury of these barrack blocks for a short period was denied the airmen, for, as usual, the RAF contingent was among those detailed to the worst quarters, the coolie lines. Still, although we slept on stone floors without proper covering or mosquito nets, at least we were not cramped. The discomforts entailed by the lack of mattresses worried us little now, as the human frame soon accustoms itself to sleeping on hard, ungiving surfaces though, as the years wore on, the thickness of flesh cushioning brittle, uncompromising bones gradually lessened, so that frequent changes in position became necessary, first on the back, then on the left side, then on the right side, legs straight, knees up and so on. Similarly, as the years wore on, we found that a decent blanket or two became more essential. At night time, even in the tropics, some clothes are absolutely essential for, at all costs, one must keep the stomach warm. It was often difficult to find the wherewithal for this. By the time the Hiroshima bomb had exploded, we possessed only tattered cloth remnants.

At Changi, Charlie Cleal and I experienced a wonderful piece of good fortune. We made the acquaintance of a gallant Welsh soldier, perhaps the finest personality – certainly the most generous – whom I met as a POW. He was a complete stranger until a few days after we arrived at Changi, yet he offered my pal and me all his spare clothing – and spare meant anything of which he possessed more than two – solely on the grounds that he had been engaged on radar, as we had. Of course, we refused to take advantage of his generosity hoping, however, that he would not accept our 'No'. He did not. He insisted on making the sacrifice. How far fewer prisoners' lives would have been lost had such *esprit de corps* been fashionable! However, as I have said before, and will doubtless say again, there was never any concerted or prolonged effort made to pool resources. Bitter are my thoughts as I think of that generous Welshman who did not survive. I shall always remember him with affection and feel glad of the fact that, although he refused to accept money in return for what he gave us, on leaving Changi, we left him some of the Red Cross goods that we received there.

Yes, Red Cross parcels were distributed at Changi. During three and a half years as a POW, I participated in the contents of two parcels. Here we received one (between two of us, I believe) while later, in Sarawak, we received one between six men. We were lucky to get one in Singapore, as a supply of Red Cross parcels had been unloaded on the island about the time of our arrival there. No one but those who have for a prolonged period lived on the simplest of foods can appreciate the indescribable delicacy of such tinned foods as corned beef. Each mouthful was turned on the tongue several times, only with great reluctance being finally released to slide down the alimentary canal.

Besides Red Cross delicacies, there was a canteen available, provided that you had the money. I imagine that some of the officers were living quite well during those comparatively early days. With our meagre resources, however, we could not buy much, although I do remember, in particular, purchasing peanuts which were reasonably cheap and of high nutritive value. When chopped up and mixed with rice, they considerably increased its palatability.

Another of the amenities at Changi was a good dental service. The army had been allowed to install in the camp modern dental equipment and as there was still a fairly good supply of drugs. I was able to avail myself of the service provided, having one tooth extracted and a couple filled. Fortunately enough, throughout the remainder of my association with the Japanese, I suffered no more with my teeth, which was just as well as there were no dental facilities after leaving Singapore.

The sick bay, too, was reasonably well equipped. My tropical ulcers, which were still troubling me, were treated with iodoform. Countless others were similarly treated, but perhaps the most common complaints at Changi during that period were soreness of the lips, of the tongue and of the genital organs, and so on, due to vitamin deficiency. Two methods of treatment were being tried. Firstly, sufferers were being rationed to a little Marmite per day in an attempt to make good the vitamin deficiency. Secondly, exposure to the sun and a 'keep it dry' policy was advocated. In the following months, only the second treatment was in vogue, and it was not an elegant sight to see half a dozen fellows sitting in the sun with their legs wide open and their knees well up pointed towards the sun.

Other means devised for keeping us fit, and also maintaining discipline was, believe it or not, military drill. Each day, a typical British Army sergeant major marched us up and down an open grass-covered space, known as the parade ground or square, on which we did such complicated drills as right about turn, left turn, right turn, salute to the right and so on. The Japanese appeared to be quite unconcerned at this. They were still too cocksure of themselves and of their own ultimate victory.

Besides square bashing, there were many other diversions, For instance, as at Priok, educational classes were very popular at Changi. Then there were the concert parties, from the small banjo team to the ambitious orchestral concerts. One evening I was privileged to attend one of these latter performances. I was amazed. The rendering of some of the classical music would not have shamed a small, well-trained, municipal orchestra. Indeed, I believe that one or two of the musicians had, prior to the war, played with the large symphony orchestras. There were also a couple of excellent vocalists. It was the type of concert for which one would have cheerfully queued outside the Albert Hall.

There were, of course, working parties, although we temporary visitors were detailed for few of these. All I remember is one wood party, my most vivid recollection of this being the beating that one or two members of the party received from renegade Sikh guards presumably because of the manner in which they marched past them at the entrance gates near the main hospital, where incidentally, some really miraculous operations were carried out by British surgeons under difficult conditions.

Most working parties at the docks, and other places in the city of Singapore itself, were formed from the regular inmates. Apparently, it was worth their while to be detailed for one of these parties. Work was not exceptionally hard and the food allowed was rather better than in the camp, while there was always the chance of being able to steal foodstuffs from the docks and from various other sources. We envied those who had the opportunity of stealing. The eighth commandment never did, in the eyes of a POW, have the slightest validity provided that the goods of one's own mates were not involved. Yes, it seemed that a dock working party was the fashionable pastime in Singapore. This not too unfavourable impression of POW life was no yardstick of the brutality to come.

One heard so many tales. For instance, there was still much to be heard of the repatriation project. In fact, the rumour gathered strength. Everything still seemed to point that way. I doubt whether we really believed in this chimera, but the thought of such a possibility kept us happy. The occupants of the barracks block, mainly RAF personnel, also professed to have knowledge of the scheme. In reality, I suppose, there must have been something afoot, possibly affecting other nationalities. However, a few days before we left Changi, we experienced a damper to our hopes. One day, we marched to the square where we had been offloaded from the lorries on arrival. What now? We were not kept wondering long. During the whole of my three and a half years as a prisoner, despite the extreme privation to come, I never felt so degraded. In full view of all the hundreds on the square, we were each in turn jabbed with a needle, the usual army procedure, but also, a glass rod was thrust up each man's posterior.

Just image that you were one of a queue of 'human' animals slowly filing past a yellow doctor armed with a glass rod. As you drew nearer, you saw each man bend in turn, baring his backside while the yellow arm made an upward thrust of the rod. The nearer you got, the more it seemed to you that you were witnessing the sticking of a thousand pigs. Just before your own body drew level with the executioner, the beast in front of you bent, nearly brushing your face with his rump, upward went the yellow arm, a needle sank into his rear end, then it was indeed your turn. You bent your body, your head already bent in shame, a queer sensation was sensed from behind you and there was also a prick in your arm. It was over, but the shame lingered on. You did not care to lift your head. You did not care to glance into the eyes of the 'pig man' next to you. When at last you plucked up courage you found that you had funked an imaginary embarrassment after all, for the eyes you peered into look hurriedly away.

Needles were changed almost as infrequently as thunder storms over the Sahara Desert! After a while, the main reaction was not so much of shame but of rather worrying enquiry. Surely the Japanese would not go to the trouble of inoculating us only to ship us to Portuguese East Africa and for what purpose were the glass rods? It transpired that they were to do with dysentery tests. Why care whether or not we had dysentery if we were all to be repatriated? It was perplexing, yet, before we were bundled into lorries once again a day or so later, our cheerfulness had to some extent returned, buoyed up with the idea that, of course, no neutral country would allow the ingress of POWs, unless they had been inoculated and certified free of such diseases as dysentery. Therefore, it was not until we reached the docks that there fell the final blow to our hopes. The mercy ship was still there – oh yes – but also less worthy ships tied to the quayside, and it was into one of these, a tramp of four or five thousand tons, that we were herded, this time without disinfestation, although lice at Singapore had not been a problem. Lice infestation and scabies were for the future.

Of course, we never really believed that Lorenco Marques was our destination, did we? We knew all the time, but had been knowingly indulging in wishful thinking – the privilege of POWs. It had buoyed our spirits up and kept us amused. We had had our glimpse of paradise. We were now to endure a short period of hell. The ship we were crowded on to, a British vessel made on the Clydebank, held not only the thousand of us who had travelled from Java, including the twenty-five RAF personnel attached to the army, but also another thousand RAF personnel, all of whom had arrived at Changi some time after we had and who had for a week or so lived under canvas. A quite considerable part of the ship's quarters was already taken up by the Japanese themselves. As in our previous 'cruise ship', quarters consisted of platforms raised in tiers but, whereas from Java to Singapore we had been allowed to sleep on deck, now we were only allowed to come up to fetch meals and to use the latrines, which were sparsely designed as previously and required gymnastic prowess to use. The heat below decks was stifling and we had no room to lie down. Sleep, if sleep we had, was taken in a sitting position, with one's legs across or under another person's legs. Had we been journeying to Japan, the Lord only knows how few of us would have survived long enough to gaze in rapture as we approached that wonderful land of the Rising Sun! The barbarians! To think how they crowded us on that ship, for the sake of slave labour in Sarawak, on projects which were never the slightest of use to them.

I could have been unluckier. Thinking we should be happier if attached to the RAF, we airmen requested Lieutenant Colonel Russell to approach the Japanese authorities with a view to our transferring from the army to the RAF. The colonel did this, but met with ill-success, or so we thought. The Japanese refused to entertain the idea. How wise they were as far as twenty-five airmen were concerned! How stupid we were to have played with an unknown fate! If the Japanese had transferred us, we would have paid the penalty of attempting to alter the decreed course of events. We should, in respect of the fates, have travelled with the main RAF contingent, all of whom were transferred to British

North Borneo and wiped out by either disease, starvation or brutality, almost to a man. Indeed, after release we were incensed by the news that at San Dakan, over two and a half thousand prisoners had been force marched from San Dakan to Ranau (south of the volcanic mountain, Kinabalu) with only six survivors on the so-called 'Death March'.

During the trip, we ascertained that we were to be vouchsafed Japanese hospitality at Kuching, the capital of Sarawak, a city strange to all of us. The last evening aboard, we sighted land. I remember, too, when going to the latrine, that the lighthouse was still operational and I thought how, after all, civilisation still thrived. To be frank, I was more concerned about the food. This had been reasonably good by Japanese standards, but did not preclude us from stealing some onions stowed on board the ship. These we hid about our person as best we could, so that we spent the last evening thinking of what a nice meal could be concocted with corned beef, of which we still had a tin from the Red Cross supplies rather than of the keepers of lighthouses.

The following morning, 13 October 1942, we sailed up the River Sarawak to reach the town nearly two hours later. Would we ever sail down again? At least, we had got there! Only after captivity ended did we realise how lucky we had been when we learnt of the large number of Japanese sunken ships containing prisoners of war, many brutally slaughtered as they floundered in the sea, not to mention the projected Kuching Death March.

Arrival at Kuching

We were informed that we must march to our new camp, but that some of the kit would be allowed to go by transport. Therefore, a baggage party of about half a dozen men was formed. Sensing some personal gain, I managed to scrounge on to this party and when, later in the afternoon, the main body of the prisoners had taken to the road, we porters loaded what little kit there was on to a lorry and then scrambled up beside it. Neatly packed in one corner of the vehicle were, for the nourishment of the Japanese, a few large tins of biscuits. My presage of gain had been correct. All else was forgotten as, like vultures over a dying man, we hovered over the tins. We had no qualms in pilfering from these supplies and pleasantly passed away the time for the three or four mile journey from the docks to the camp. A still larger advantage was reaped by the baggage party. A thunderstorm burst over Kuching, and while the foot sloggers were, by the time their destination was reached, soaked to the skin, we arrived in style and in dry attire. I felt vaguely sorry for my comrades, whom we passed near the entrance to the camp, but of shame, at having scrounged on to the baggage party, there was none. Does the football fan, attending a cup match, shed tears for those unsuccessful applicants for tickets?

Both transport and the marching column were halted at an open space, about one hundred and fifty metres up the rough road from the camp entrance, flanked on its right by the guardroom. Straight on, were the Japanese offices and storeroom and from thence, two hundred metres further on, the Japanese HQ and billets. At a near hairpin bend, the road reached back to where, to the right-hand side, were some wired-off compounds and then the Japanese MO's offices and sick bay (of which more later), these all being about one hundred metres from the rear of the strategically placed guardroom, where several prisoners were to be brutally beaten.

Guards were already stationed under the rubber trees, in the apex of the triangle between the two roads. They were ill at ease. By their demeanour, an observer might have thought us a herd of wild animals, or at least dangerously disposed maniacs. One had only to move out of line to detect not only the nervous movement of rifles, but also the glimmer of fear in their almond-shaped eyes. One of my most vivid memories of Kuching is how these lads, not pure Japanese, but from occupied Japanese territory, mainly Korea, matured during our imprisonment there, from frightened pups to cocksure bullies. However, no one made a break for it, to put to the test the ability of the young Koreans to apply firm pressure on their triggers and to aim straight. I doubt whether these rookies could have. But the one or two regular Japanese soldiers around, as usual looking so at ease with their rifles, might have marred such a test.

When our numbers had been checked and rechecked, we were directed to one of the compounds opposite the hospital-cum-sick-bay and Japanese medical officers' (Yamamoto) stores. Our quarters consisted of just over twenty long wooden huts resting on dwarf concrete piers and with attap roofs. We discovered, to our amazement, that they were wired for electricity. Moreover, there was a plentiful water supply within the camp, including a 'battery' of showers. As regards the standard of accommodation, apart from overcrowding, we had, under the circumstances, little to grumble about. The bugbear was messing facilities. They were practically nil, and so the Japanese, having issued some bags of rice, very shrewdly left us to our own devices.

It was now dark and I reckoned that the chances of a meal before lights out were pretty slim. There stood, however, in one corner of the compound, an old, open-sided cookhouse used by the previous occupants of the camp, Indians, who had known the camp as Lintang barracks, prior to the Japanese invasion, The empty shell of the building was practically all that remained. Rapid improvisation solved the problem. Fireplaces were formed and empty petrol drums adapted for cooking appliances. It was little short of a miracle that, before turning in, we were dished up with the inevitable boiled rice, washed down with hot, neat tea. We slept soundly during our first night at Kuching.

Reveille awoke us early the following morning, as there was

much to be done. Cooks who had manfully toiled throughout the night produced more hot rice and tea. We felt fit for anything, even for the amazing speech that we were shortly to listen to. In fact, the most important event of the day proved to be an address to the prisoners of war by the chief of all Sarawak prisoner of war and internee camps, the great Major Suga (later promoted to Colonel). Mrs Keith, in her 1946 account of the ladies' compound, within the bounds of the same camp (of which more later), has described this gentleman in detail. I cannot hope to vie with her in this accomplishment. Certainly, I would not attempt to deny the fact that Suga was fond of children for, to my knowledge, on more than one occasion he took for a joy ride a carload of the poor mites who spent three and a half years with their mothers as Japanese internees. Yet, for all this, the general impression gained over a period of years, by the rank and file in our compound, was that Suga's word was a jolly sight sweeter than the treatment he meted out. In fact, he was something of a snake in the grass, as indeed he was often called. But then, Mrs Keith and I would disagree on many points and I feel that rather than giving an unbiased opinion of even her own compound, she brought the experienced writer's art to bear on her work, in that she left out much and invented a little to obtain a better theatrical effect. Be that as it may, I think that she could have been a little more realistic about the references to our neighbouring compound, which was detailed to provide some labour for the ladies' enclosure.

To say, for instance, that the British POWs would go to any lengths for a little tobacco, even to selling their food, was a gross misinterpretation of the facts. Of course, there were isolated instances, but in hut number 17, sheltering about fifty men, that I occupied during most of my time at Kuching, only one man would have done such a thing. Neither can I credit the fact that, passing by our compound at the conclusion of hostilities, she heard a soldier singing a Yankee song. At the time, there were only two Americans in our compound, neither of whom would probably have known Mrs Keith. It is more unlikely still that any of the British soldiers knew her to be American, without which knowledge no British soldier would have thought of chanting an

American song. However, none of us is perfect and doubtless many an ex-Kuchingite would interpret differently as we only report how we perceive matters.

Major Suga's maiden speech to us was a masterpiece of cant. He was very sorry for our predicament, brought about through no fault of our own, but, if we obeyed his orders and worked hard, no harm would befall us. For his part, he would do all in his power to lighten our load and make us happy. He said that he hoped that one day we would return safe and sound to our families. We must remain cheerful – that was most important – his favourite phrase being, 'I shimpashise wid tew', spoken in a high-pitched voice. Towards the end of his oration, and before we were marched back to our compound he spoke the classical sentence, 'I will give tew t'ree days' 'oliday, yesterday, today and tomorrow', with a rider to the effect that during today and tomorrow we could busy ourselves digging latrines and gathering firewood.

The major might well have saved himself the bother of advising us to dig latrines, for as usual they were non-existent. As a temporary measure, slit trenches were dug, the work being commenced as soon as Suga had dismissed us. I will say this for the Japanese, that we were not expected to dig the trenches with our fingers, as tools were magnanimously provided, the chief of which were changkols. We were to become very familiar, over the next three years, with this all-purpose Oriental tool. It consists of a wooden handle about 1.3 m long with a blade at right angles to it, a tool very much like the ordinary garden hoe for earthing up potatoes, but with a larger blade.

As a latrine digger, it soon proved its usefulness (and later as a grave-digging tool) and the trenches were quickly completed. Deep holes of a small diameter, situated at half a dozen points in the compound, were also excavated. Into these were thrust some old drainage pipes, so that they protruded about two feet above the ground. Gently sloping towards each pipe was fixed a V-shaped, galvanised iron or wooden trough so that its lower end emptied on to the pipe. These were the urinals which served us admirably during our habitation at Lintang barracks.

Another big task was the provision of firewood. No cut fuel

was ever provided at Kuching. We had to procure our own. A wood party was formed from the outset, and we were never able to do without it, although its constitution was to change from time to time. It was inaugurated on a more limited basis but, eventually, besides supplying wood for our own compound, it gathered wood not only for us but also for the Japanese and the ladies' compounds. The workload never decreased but gradually increased even up to July 1945, when five men were dying every day.

Our quarters were interspersed by rubber trees, so fuel resources were readily available. Green rubber wood burnt very well, on account of the inflammable nature of latex, but it needed at least four or five trees a day to keep the cookhouse supplied. In the months to come there was often panic in the cookhouse because the cooks ran out of wood before the next day's supply. Generally, there lay a way out of the difficulty. Although most of the rubber trees in our compound were felled during the early days, a few were left standing, sentinel-like, after the wood party had moved to fresh sources. In an emergency, one of these remaining trees would be felled until, when the war ended, practically every tree had disappeared.

On the whole, during the first couple of years, the wood party was a good racket. Its members were not detailed for other working parties and were in receipt of extra rations. When fuel had to be sought from further afield and carried or pushed on an old wagon for some considerable distance, the popularity of the wood party waned. The old stagers, looking after self first, gradually dropped off and big-heartedly volunteered for outside working parties, so that a wood party had to be detailed daily.

One other point must be made about rubber trees as a means of fuel. The wood was fairly soft, so that the felling and trimming of a tree was not a difficult job, despite the fact that the axes provided by the Japanese were not always of the sharpest. (They seemed to concentrate more on the sharpness of their swords – so useful for decapitation!) However, he would be an optimist indeed who would expect the best of tools in a prisoner of war camp, but we always seemed to cope.

The affairs of the camp, too, were organised early. During

these 't'ree days' 'oliday – yesterday, today and tomorrow', not only were latrines dug and wood cut, but the cookhouse properly organised, messing facilities arranged, duties assigned, a sick bay opened, and huts were properly allocated. It was a very busy 'oliday both for executives and labourers.

The Officer Dynasty

To my mind the first few months at Kuching can be classified as the 'Officer Period'. Both officers and men occupied the same compound, and it was not until February 1943 that the Japanese segregated the officers in an enclosure two stones' throw away, partly to make room in the enclosure for one hundred extra rankers and partly, without doubt, to weaken camp discipline. When the move was announced, the majority of the rankers thought that it would also be to their own advantage, a view which, in common with a few others, I did not share. The minority proved to be right.

I suppose that the chief suspicion of the ranker was that under officer administration an unfair share of the food would find its way to the officers and their batmen. To some extent, of course, these fears were justified and, as might be expected, preference was given to the officers. As I have stressed before, at no time during the three and a half years as a prisoner of war was a share and share alike policy adopted or, for that matter, anything nearly approaching that idea. The selfishness innate in men precluded them from practising equality, even though the long-term, life-saving effect that this would have had must have been realised by many of the thoughtful. But this much can be said. The officers numbered about sixty or seventy, and the fact that they did wangle just a little extra did not inordinately affect our welfare.

At least, it could be argued that, generally speaking, the rank and file did share and share alike the food provided by the Japanese. This was definitely not the case under the heel of the sergeant major. The old testament words, 'My father also chastised you with whips, but I will chastise you with scorpions', spring to the mind of a ranker. The privileges that the officers allowed themselves never bore any resemblance to the rackets which apparently flourished under the rule of the NCOs. Of course, it cannot be gainsaid that, had the officers remained in charge of the compound, they might not in time have turned a blind eye to the rackets that might have benefited themselves, as food became shorter. The fact remains that organisation was better and fairer under them. In any case, a ranker is less averse to the officer being favoured than a certain section of his own rank and file.

Then again, the officers' influence was greater with the Japanese than that of the senior NCO, and, also, as the officers constituted a comparatively large car-pool of non-workers from which to draw for organisation purposes, a keener scrutiny could be afforded the administrative machinery. Without a doubt, the job of running our lines fairly and efficiently was beyond the powers of the senior NCOs. I feel that the problem of organisation was aggravated because of the diversity of units within the camp and the small remnants of various regiments, i.e. Navy, RAF and Australians, so that there was no regimented honour to uphold.

A word about the organisation of the compound which, as it was arranged under the officers, was to a large extent to remain in being until the end of the war. The British officer in charge of our compound was Lieutenant Colonel Russell. He appointed an adjutant, while various other officers had certain duties assigned to them. For instance, there was one officer, Captain Anderson, appointed to organise entertainment. Captain 'Dipstick' Gardiner, later to be replaced by Captain Spurway, was in charge of the cookhouse. Another officer was in charge of camp hygiene while another, Captain Kettleworth, was placed in command of a squad of engineers. These engineers, formed from just a few men, were made responsible for the maintenance of our lines and for those jobs requiring technical skill. To complete the appearance of normal army conditions, each day there stalked the compound duty officers, from a rota of junior officers, who had no other particular responsibilities.

The officers inhabited a couple of huts near the roadside. Oblong in general shape, the compound was bounded by the road separating it and the Japanese medical officer's offices and sick bay on one of its shorter sides; a track to its other short and southern side, which continued along the west boundary, joined the road at the northwest corner, where the entrance to the compound had been drawn. On the eastern side was the Dutch compound, the track bounding the lines continuing around it, meeting the road once more, opposite the Japanese QM's stores. Just outside the barbed wire, in the southeast corner of our compound, a lookout post had been erected, from which a Japanese guard could also discern exactly what took place in the cookhouse, also that outside our own QM's store, situated nearby. Later, another entrance was made in the northeast corner, and a further guard hut was erected on a made-up green opposite. Each hut within the compound consisted of one long room, plus a small one at one end that was reserved for the sergeant major or other NCO in charge.

Each hut, therefore, became the basic unit of administration, while two or three huts in charge of a sergeant major constituted a company, there being eight companies, A–H, altogether. Working parties were formed, on demand from our commandant, of so many men from each company, it being the responsibility of the sergeant major to determine whether each man was capable of full duty, light duty or no duty and, so, who was delegated to each working party. The men duly paraded, as occasion demanded, in front of their huts before being marched to a small, unpaved square between two huts in the centre of the compound, where the amalgamated working parties were assembled in marching order, and were then handed over to the tender mercy of the Japanese guards.

Messing was also organised on a hut basis. Before each meal the appointed messing orderlies (normally light duty men) had to make their way to the cookhouse to collect the ration of rice and stew in five gallon petrol drums fitted by the engineers with wire handles. The containers were dumped down in front of the company's huts and there, under the supervision of the NCO in charge, the food was equally distributed. After a meal, it was the duty of the orderlies to wash the containers, under one of the three or four taps situated in various parts of the compound, and return them empty to the cookhouse. Food was drawn each day from the Japanese HQ's store, being pushed into our lines on a wagon by light duty men, detailed for the job.

It was fortunate that we numbered among us a bugler, so that reveille, ration parties, working parties, tenkos, lights out and the like, were signalled by the bugle. Also, of course, when orders had to be promulgated, the bugle summoned the duty officer and sergeant major, as the occasion demanded.

Thus, briefly, were the affairs of the compound organised by the officers, and the basis was, apart from the replacement of officers by NCOs, never radically altered. Only the efficiency of the organisation was to change.

On the third day after our arrival, the Japanese demanded that we produce a working party of two hundred and fifty other ranks for labour at the aerodrome. My feet being now more or less healed, so that I could wear the pair of second-hand boots given me in Java, I was among those detailed for the party. After an early breakfast, therefore, while it was still dark, each sergeant major had his men marched to the unpaved square in the middle of the compound. There, under the command of our officers, we were formed up into fifties. For a while, until daylight streaked the sky, we squatted in our ranks, only, just as we were on the point of letting drowsiness take hold of us, to be called smartly to attention as the Korean guards slouched into the compound. After our numbers had been counted and checked – we had not yet learnt to number off in Japanese – we picked up our scanty belongings to be marched out of the compound and down the road to the Japanese guard room. By now, I had bought an army dixie and mug and acquired a pack and a rubberised cape which I carried with me. After being counted and checked once more, we left the camp twenty minutes later to be lined up outside the third milestone on the railway out of Kuching, Batu Tiga. After another wait we were loaded on to the *Borneo Flyer* or *Kuching Express* or whatever it was called.

From the moment that we climbed into the open cattle trucks that were hitched to the train, we felt that there was something phoney about this form of locomotion but, not until we were well on our way and the train had gathered momentum and, as it reached its top speed of about twenty-five to thirty miles per hour, lurching madly to and fro, did the awful truth dawn upon us that she was wood fired. Thus, during the whole journey, we were peppered with hot wood ash. Those sitting with their backs to the engine came off best, but the rest of us spent the journey unsuccessfully dodging flying embers. Experience taught those without army capes to get hold of any old material that could be scrounged, however tattered, to drape on otherwise uncovered legs. We journeyed through about five miles of flat, uninteresting country, the railway being bounded mostly by rubber plantations or rough scrub, or swamp. It was a relief when the train panted to a stop at Batu Lima, and we went on to the aerodrome, where we were quickly formed up, counted (bangoed) and marched on to the runway. There, we were issued with the inevitable changkols and ordered to strip off turfs from the edge of the aerodrome. These we then had to carry to the middle of the runway and stack them into two long lines to a height of about one metre, fifty metres apart, presumably to indicate the best avenue of approach for incoming aircraft.

This work, if work it can be called, was boring to the extreme. In actual fact, very few of us pulled our weight. I remember my own calculations. If I carried six turfs in the morning and six in the afternoon, I had done my share. The guards did not seem unduly concerned or were too scared to force us into reasonable activity. What now surprises me most was that I could have disciplined myself to carry so few. Had I worked a little harder, the day would have slipped by quicker. Yet, I did not have the inclination for consistent toil. Instead, I would first spend about ten minutes hacking out my turf, stroll as slowly as possible to the line pegged out for the earthen wall, probably halt a couple of times on the way to yarn with a mate or drop the turf deliberately as an alternative excuse for a rest. It would demand another five minutes to coax the turf into the right place, a further yarn, lounging unconcernedly against the slowly growing wall which was built in short sections then, a return journey at the same funereal pace and a repeat performance.

The Japanese were, at that time, too confident of victory to trouble over much about the output of POW labour. When, to their mind, the result of the war hung in the balance, they slave drove us, and it was not until the last few weeks of our imprisonment, when ultimate defeat stared them in the face, that working parties became easier again for those few still capable of any work.

Tiffin was brought by lorry. It consisted of bins of rice and green stew (made from kang-kong, a type of spinach) and over-brewed tea (without milk and sugar). Of course, the food was almost stone cold and the liquid contents had been considerably reduced by the jolting of the lorry. Later, the system was changed; tea was brewed on the job but the rice and stew were cooked in the camp the previous night to be carried with us the next day. For the convenience of the Japanese guard, a fairish lunch 'hour' was allowed, so that there was opportunity for relaxation after the meal. Work finally ceased about five o'clock when, once more, we were marched to the railway for another uncomfortable journey back to Batu Tiga. By the time we had drawn our evening meal darkness had fallen. Nevertheless, this meal was the high spot of the day. Usually it was served hot, and the green stew was thicker than at lunchtime.

Once a week, about one hundred and fifty pounds of pork – this for one thousand two hundred men – were issued, diced and cooked with the stew. Occasionally, too, a small quantity of dried fish (ikan) would be provided. These fish, rather similar to whitebait, were baked by the cooks and eaten more or less in their entirety. Once accustomed to them, extremely salty though they were, we welcomed the variety to the diet as they mixed well with the rice. We were also allowed a weekly quantity of coconut oil for frying purposes so that, on most evenings, plain rice was augmented with a small rice rissole fried in the oil. Perhaps, apart from pork, the most nutritious item in our diet was a weekly issue of 'katchang ijau', a type of lentil served boiled which was a comparatively high source of vitamin and protein. Sugar and salt were always short, the former being rationed out each day, a level teaspoonful per man, while salt was added to the stews at the cookhouse. Supplies of salt often ran short so that the stews would be unbelievably tasteless.

Such was our diet. It was not, at that time, particularly deficient in calories, as each man received roughly a pint of rice a day, nor woefully short of vitamins and protein, compared with later times. The canteen organised at that camp could do little to increase these standards, buying mainly out of communal funds the little extra kachang ijau or a supply of chillies, or maybe some fruit. For most extras, as will later be seen, it required individual effort as opposed to communal action to rely on their supply. The establishment taken as a whole did little more than levy a small charge on each working man's pay to finance the so-called canteen. Each man on Japanese working parties received wages varying from ten to twenty cents a day, according to rank, but even this was discontinued later on. A private, therefore, might earn about forty cents a week after deduction of camp levy. This sum, in late 1942, would have bought three eggs, which later rose in price to as much as two dollars each. At that time, therefore, for a week's work a man earned for himself three eggs per week, What could the Japanese expect for such meagre rewards? Yet, they were in a position to demand work even without a payroll, a fact most of us ignored in those early days.

But, gradually, the reins tightened and then there was an incident which took place on the aerodrome. After about two months of this work a Japanese guard, nicknamed 'Doll Face' or 'Moon Face' and, in my opinion, the most detestable of all those actually attached to the camp, called one of the officers to task for not properly supervising the work. Unfortunately, he picked on Captain 'Dipstick' Gardiner, a good-natured officer who was not possessed of much reckless daring, an attribute then perhaps required for the situation which ensued. He was ordered to stand with knees bent, holding a changkol above his head, a performance which is extremely humiliating, to say the least, and, after a short while, quite painful. The rank and file among us thought that he should have refused obedience, but it was not we who were subjected to the ordeal. It is a fact that most probably not more than one in ten officers, and one in fifty of the rank and file, would have disobeyed, but it was doubtful that refusal to acquiesce would, as was feared by some, have resulted in being shot. Probably, at worst, the unfortunate would have been beaten and the matter reported.

None of the young guards would have had the courage to have used his weapon. However, Captain Gardiner obeyed with little demur, although we all wished that Lieutenant Campbell had been put to the test to see if he would have dared. The Japanese, however, knew their man and obedience was exacted. The young guards had proved their authority. The first battle for good treatment and respect had been irretrievably lost. This was really the turning point in our relationship with the Japanese, although sooner, or later, our strength was bound to have been put to severe test, but the rather weak-kneed attitude shown on this occasion precipitated the tightening of discipline. In one brief episode, our weakness had been made only too obvious and our armour had been pierced.

Just prior to this, we had temporarily been given the truly Herculean task of removing the top of a complete knoll, with just the changkol and basket as tools, in order that the aerial approach to the aerodrome might be improved. While on the hill, we were honoured with the presence of two extra guards who were Japanese seasoned soldiers. Although we did work somewhat harder, no real effort was made. Terrorised slavery had yet to be introduced. No one really expected the knoll to be shifted and, after a fortnight's effort, we were sent back to the aerodrome. Doubtless some Japanese engineer had belatedly calculated the number of cubic metres of soil that would have to be shifted, the original conception of the task being based on an amateur's idea of how many man hours would be involved. It was shortly after this, when we were once more in charge of Korean guards on the runway, that the *incident* occurred.

During the period of 'light' duties at the aerodrome, various activities had been inaugurated in the camp. The most important of these were the concerts organised by Captain Anderson, who also acted as MC, and they were, under the circumstances, really first-class. Two or three of the performers were not entirely without experience. However, many of those who appeared on the stage had had no previous training at all. It had taken the comparatively uninhibited atmosphere of a POW camp to discover their latent talents. Some of these entertainers came forward at the outset, while others volunteered only as fresh talent was required during the later stages of servitude. I would especially mention here Andy Hardy and 'Portia' of Priok days, both female impersonators; comedians, Charlie Copper on drums and Lou Levy (RAF), a Jewish comedian of marked ability; Sergeant Ditchburn, another comedian, Tommy Burns a crooner ('Donkey

Serenade!') and Ted Pasquil, a tall Lancashire airman who made his reputation with such songs as 'Steamboat Bill' and impersonations of George Formby. It will be evident, from consideration of this galaxy of stars, that the lighter forms of entertainment were most popular at Kuching. Indeed, this was the case, especially as time wore on, for there was not the scope for serious entertainment, such as theatrical plays, at Kuching. When conditions became tougher, there was neither the time nor energy to put on anything but light entertainment. Thus, songs composed at Kuching, such as 'Sarawakee: Rice and Stew' and 'When we sail down the river to the sea, there'll be happy days for you and me' became minor classics!

All concerts were staged on a platform, with an attap roof, erected on light scaffolding at one end of the unpaved square, where the working parties assembled. Nothing much could be done in the way of curtains and draping, but the stage had been wired for electricity, which was a great advantage as darkness fell at about half past six in the evening and it was impractical to hold a concert during daylight hours on working days. When, halfway through our period of internment, electricity supplies were cut off we had to improvise with small lamps burning coconut oil. There were no extensive dressing rooms, only a sort of screen at each of the wings, behind which the performers grouped before coming on to the stage by means of steps rising from the bare earth to the four feet high platform.

The facilities for the audience were equally primitive. Most of us squatted on the dusty ground or stood uncomfortably at the rear, although many of the officers sat on home-made chairs at the front of the stage. Concerts took place, with Japanese consent, about once a month, although during the last year of captivity, only three or four were staged. We rarely suffered interference from the Japanese, although occasionally two or three young soldiers might be seen standing at the back of the audience, doubtless their motive being curiosity rather than trouble-seeking. In any case, they would have hardly appreciated some of the jokes, although moderation was always exercised, it being policy not to risk annoying the enemy. Only at the conclusion of the last concert, staged before release a day or so after the end of the war, can I remember any lack of this restraint. On that occasion, a deaf Japanese, almost even a dead one, could hardly have failed to have heard the resounding strains of our own national anthem and 'Land of Hope and Glory'. The Proms never could beat this rendering!

Another form of entertainment was debates. Introduced amid great enthusiasm and with competition keen for the platform, yet, rather due to lack of energy than of a failing in standards, they died a natural death long before the concerts ceased to have their monthly performances. Once the period of slavery started, the tired body inclined little towards mental skirmishes. Indeed, the strain of work became so great that few of us wanted to move from our billets after the evening meal. In the last few months of imprisonment, a suggestion of a debate would have been received with derision, yet debates had been as popular as concerts in the early days. For my own part, I had gladly taken part in one of these during early 1943, strongly asserting that professionalism was detrimental to sport. We amateur enthusiasts failed to force home our point of view, but we did not care either way by then.

Lectures were still fashionable, while a new venture was the 'quiz'. It was, however, found too difficult to formulate enough questions that would be less than easy for the few, yet not too difficult for the majority. The result of the contest generally depended on the individual brilliance of one or two members of both teams. These forms of entertainment were, like the debates, to drop into disuse as the general stamina in the camp deteriorated.

One other organisation, formed for our benefit, was the messing committee, consisting of one representative from each company, representatives from the cookhouse, one from the stores, the officers and, of course, the QM himself. This committee must have had as limited a scope as any committee ever formed for such a purpose. I never sat on it myself, yet I believe its sessions were quite protracted and not altogether free from acrimonious controversy. Of course, the committee could not produce food with the wave of a magic wand. Its main function was to determine the method of the division of the allocated food and the manner in which it should be served. Its biggest single problem was how to utilise the coconut oil to the best advantage. As mentioned, the evening meal was usually augmented with rissoles but, occasionally, a so-called 'nasi goreng' was served (this being a mixture of fried rice, diced vegetables and meat) by way of a change, while fried sweet potato was also very popular. I think it is fair to say that the messing committee did their best to provide variety and to augment, as best they could, the rations by judicious purchases, having regard to their meagre resources. The committee was not popular with everyone, as there are, in any crowd of men, the permanently dissatisfied who delight in grumbling and stirring up trouble. Their main complaint at Kuching in the early months was that the officers were receiving extra makan. Doubtless, a few of them were, although not on any appreciable scale, certainly not on the same scale as permitted later under the rule of the proletariat. The messing committee did, however, have its triumphs. Christmas provided the main opportunity. A few weeks before the festival a little of each day's non-perishable rations would be put by and purchases of extra food arranged through the Japanese, so that our stomachs would be full when the great day came. They were always filled. Everyone ate as much as desirable – some a good deal more – and there were no complaints. Variety was achieved as well as bulk. The following menu for Christmas 1943 well indicates this:

Breakfast:	Red rice, porridge, lime and ginger sauce, sugar, two fish rissoles, tea. Tiffin: Kachang ijau, rice, meat stew.
Dinner:	One and a half rations of rice, meat stew, two pork rolls. One cucumber square, fried rice square topped with banana and peanut cream.
Also:	Free issue of half a packet of rice toffee, half a packet of biscuits and bananas.

Many prisoners also roasted jack fruit and concocted blancmange with mashed banana, crumbled biscuits and sugar. They need not have bothered, as at the end of the day the cookhouse had difficulty in disposing of laegi rice.

Christmas 1944 was an even bigger success:

Breakfast: Coconut porridge, sugar, coffee, sweet potato chips, egg on two fried rice squares lump of roasted pork.
Tiffin: curried prawns, rice, pork stew.

Dinner: One and half rations of kedgeree with peanuts, double ration of chicken and duck stew, two chicken and duck rolls, rice square with banana cream.

Supper: Coffee, biscuits and bananas.

There was also an issue of cheroots.

The Japanese allowed us a day off over our first Christmas so, besides Christmas being a day of feasting, it was also a day of sport, treasure hunts and cricket matches, with some very primitive equipment being organised! In those days we were batting on a comparatively easy wicket. The 'sticky dogs' were yet to come.

During the officer dynasty, a radio was put into operation. Constructed of odds and ends, smuggled into the camp from Singapore, and of sundry parts stolen from the Japanese at Kuching, it was secreted in an army dixie and represented the quintessence of the genius of the British prisoner of war within the compound. Mainly responsible for the wiring and assembly was Corporal Beckett, one of the RAF and by trade a radar mechanic. In common with everyone connected with the making and maintenance of the set, he ran the risk of 'kapala katong' (decapitation) by the Japanese if the set was discovered.

The camp security arrangements were excellent. There was always one of our own military police on watch near the gate, often Sergeant Jim Bourne. When not in use, the set was cunningly concealed within the cover of a rice drum and was carried to and from the QM's store and so-called bakehouse, near the showers one hundred and fifty metres away, as occasion demanded. A lookout was posted near to the entrance of the compound. Later, the two entrances were covered whenever the set was in operation. This was usually done by a light duty man like Sergeant Bourne. Should a Japanese enter our lines during this period, signalling devices were immediately set in motion so that the operators had ample time to hide the set. Our captors never guessed about the presence of a radio set within the compound. All they suspected was that we were illegally receiving news from somewhere, attributing the source from over the wire, and that we were contacting certain well-informed natives. Although searches were conducted by the authorities from time to time throughout the various compounds, they presented little difficulty, especially as the most thorough of them took place after the officers had left for a separate compound. No doubt the Japanese calculated that the most likely place for incriminating evidence lurked in the officers' or civilian enclosures, where the brains of the white man resided, whereas in actual fact the one set available to the prisoners never left the compound of the British other ranks. It was that very humble community which boasted the only personnel capable of maintaining it.

Other compounds were kept informed of BBC news to the extent of their needs and abilities and, although instructed not to talk, the news filtered through at fast speed even to the officers after their quarters had been shifted, and they were never in the dark for long. One or two of the younger and more adventurous of them never shirked the risk of crossing from their lines over 'No man's Land', or through the Dutch enclosure, to ours. The Dutch were not wholly in on the secret, because it was thought that there were subversive elements within their compound, so strict instructions were issued to us from time to time not to inform them of what we knew through the wire. There were times, also, when the dissemination of news was stopped because of our suspicion of the Dutch, some of whom were thought to be 'Japanese happy!'

The greatest precautions regarding the operation of a radio were always taken so that, although the penalty of being caught operating the set would probably have meant death, the chances were not great. Thus, no one with the necessary ability jibbed at handling the set, as the advantages were abundant: a highly interesting job, no working parties and extra food. In fact, the radio men had a far better chance of survival than the average prisoner. Not that this detracts from the value of their work, as the morale of the compound was never higher than when BBC news was being received.

The only other source of news, apart from rumours being circulated by the natives, was the Japanese news sheet which appeared periodically during the early part of our internment. Although the European news that it gave was reasonably accurate, the local news was fantastically biased. It was reckoned, on the occasion of a large naval battle, that to arrive at a fairly accurate estimate of the truth the report of the respective losses of the Japanese and American fleets had to be read in reverse.

The set was operated by batteries, a fact which gave rise to difficulties – to be referred to again – for on the continued life of the batteries depended the maintenance of our link with the outside world. During the first eighteen months at Kuching we received no mail, although we were granted the privilege of writing one postcard each soon after our arrival. We knew, of course, that what we said would be severely censored and, as we were also restricted to about two dozen words, the card had little use other than to let our people know that we were still alive at the time of writing. This privilege of writing home was continued for two years, at about four-monthly intervals, but on a more restricted basis. Each man was handed a card with three or four sets of alternative sentences, it being left to individual taste which sentence in a particular group was retained and which crossed out. For instance, the alternatives for one group read something like this:

I am well. I am in good health.
I am wounded but otherwise in good health.
I am fairly fit.

These cards were, therefore, of even less value than the previous type of communication.

Incoming mail was of far more value. Although it was two years before the first batch of letters was sorted, I did eventually receive, at intervals during the next nine months, quite a number of letters, two pages in length, which had been heavily censored. At least I obtained realistic domestic news from home, although my mother received only an occasional card from me, and my fiancée did not receive any. In 1945, throughout the last eight months of internment, unaccountably, we received practically no mail and this fact, at a time when deprivations of the previous three years were taking a heavy toll of life and energies were flagging, constituted a severe blow to morale. It was only after the war was over that stacks of unsorted mail were discovered at Japanese HQ.

Before the end of the officer dynasty, the first death at Kuching was recorded. A burial party was formed and, in the best clothes that could be mustered (whether our own or borrowed), a dozen other ranks, including myself and accompanied by an officer and Japanese guards, marched to the burial ground situated near the swimming pool on the outskirts of Kuching. The actual coffin had preceded us and, at the graveside, a short service was conducted by a padre from the civilians' compound, the coffin lowered, earth scattered and the last post sounded. It is sad to recall that, by the time the relatives heard of the soldier's death probably at the end of the war, he had been completely forgotten, save vaguely by a few of his closest friends at the funeral party itself. By the third part of 1945, funerals were so frequent (more than one a day) that the drama of such occasions became unnoticed.

Not long afterwards, the officers were moved to their own compound so that, for the next two and a half years, though separated only by the Dutch compound and only one hundred and fifty metres away, we rarely contacted them.

Aerial view of part of Lintang barracks, Kuching, Sarawak, where prisoners of war and internees were imprisoned by the Japanese, 1942–5. Other ranks were confined to the central area at the top of the photograph. The author's hut is marked with a cross and the ladies' and children's enclosure is top right. The male internees' and British Officers' compounds were to the left of the photograph. The three symbols on the roof of the building mid-left of the picture were placed there as an answer to questions of the relieving forces at the end of August, 1945.

Top: A portion of Boot Hill, Lintang barracks, with six of the
relieving forces showing respect for the hundreds of prisoners of
war who were buried there under Japanese occupation.
Bottom: Part of the war cemetery at Labuan (an island off the
coast of Sabah, Borneo). Exhumed bodies from Boot Hill,
Lintang barracks are reburied there.
Lady Mountbatten visited recuperating Kuching prisoners of war
in Labuan hospital, October, 1945.

Top: Kuching Docks where prisoners of war unloaded sugar and salt, 1943. The 'White Rajah's' residence stood on the opposite side of the Kuching River, on rising ground.
Bottom: Local inhabitants in Sarawak moving a house. Satan (see chapter entitled 'Satan') forced prisoners to shift a larger one than this with far fewer labourers.

Airmen of 512 AMES (all to become Japanese prisoners of war) relaxing on an island off the coast of Singapore, September, 1941. From left to right of photograph: Ron Lister, the author, Charlie Ward, Charlie Cleal and Joe Fitzgerald. Only Cleal was imprisoned with the author at Kuching, the three other airmen being elsewhere incarcerated.

The Stench of a Thousand Ulcers

Many a ranker muttered, 'Jolly good riddance!' when he watched the officers move out of our compound. I was not so sanguine. Despite the fact that they had enjoyed certain privileges such as a little extra food, services of batmen (some of these shifted with the officers), less crowded quarters and no manual work, I felt that on the whole they had devised a good administrative system. Not only that but, because of their rank, their opinions obviously carried more weight with the Japanese officers and, as at Priok, Lieutenant Colonel Russell was held in great respect by the Japanese, especially by Suga. What would the sergeant major make of the Japanese HQ? Already I sensed the foreboding of evil.

The officers, with Japanese approval, left in charge of the thousand-odd men in our lines and the hundred additional men (including Yanks) who arrived on the day after their removal, were RSM Sunderland, a regular of considerable ability, and Staff Sergeant Southern as his adjutant. In fairness to both these men, I think it must be said that no better choices could have been made and that they did valuable work, especially during the first year or so. Neither of them had had the administrative experience to run the compound with its mixed units on the best of lines. Neither, of course, did they possess the staff to back them up. In the ensuing months, to supply the desired quota of working person-nel, practically every fit man in the camp had to do some work or other. Even the company sergeant majors took it in turn to accompany the outside working parties. Thus the camp staff was very much depleted. While the officers had been in the com-pound, there had never been any shortage of administrative staff.

A trifle under thirty years old, Sunderland was a regular soldier of strong will and of upright, smart appearance, a good regular army warrant officer in every respect, possessing at the outset the confidence and esteem of every man in the enclosure. He appeared unafraid of the Japanese and stood up to them in excellent fashion, but his weakness lay in his unexpected power. In time, harassed by the Japanese, he developed the temperament of a dictator, somewhat out of touch with the rank and file. Like all dictators, he became too isolated and perhaps too fond of his power so that, eventually, a rule of enlightenment became a source of tyranny or so it appeared to many rank and file prisoners. Later, too, a further contingent of fresh troops arrived at the compound, staffed by more sergeant majors. Some of these insinuated themselves into good positions, inaugurating many rackets that Sunderland was incapable of controlling.

Southern was a different sort of a man. Of quiet and sincere disposition, he was at first an excellent foil to Sunderland, but his lack of force was to the disadvantage of the rank and file. When Sunderland became less accessible, gradually donning (as it seemed to me) his tyrant's robes, the second-in-command did not appear strong enough to oppose him to any marked extent. Thus, there came a time when the rankers did not quite know where they stood with Southern. Would he follow the dictates of his own conscience or would he, contrary to his better nature, use the big stick in conformity, so to speak, with the party machine? Under Sunderland and Southern, next in the seniority game were CSMs, such as Scott(Scotty) and sergeants and corporals in charge of huts (such as Eric Oliver and Sergeant Pepler). Below the rank of sergeant, all were more or less equal.

Few, if any, visualised the outcome of the Sunderland/Southern partnership, at the outset. We did not, in any case, anticipate such a lengthy period of imprisonment. I well remember an Australian officer who, a short time before the sequestration of the officers, planted a papaya tree in our compound. We laughed at him saying that the tree would never bear fruit in our time, but it did.

We had no legalised contact with the officers after they left us, other than with the two medical officers, Lieutenant Colonel King and Captain Bailey. These two were quartered on the opposite side of the road about fifty metres from the northwest entrance to our enclosure. There a hut, built on similar lines to those in our compound, contained a sick bay and space for the orderlies. They had a busy time.

Lieutenant Colonel King, the chief of the medical detachment, had been with us at Priok. With bristling moustache and reddish countenance, he was the dream of a music-hall artist or cartoonist, depicting the unbending and narrow vision of the old school of army brass hats. To the rank and file, he appeared an insufferable bully, a man to be feared but not greatly respected. Yet, I would hesitate to characterise him on those lines only. His was a most difficult and exasperating job, treating hundreds of POWs with a few tools of his trade, and with an appalling absence of drugs. Then the Japanese demanded so many working men per day. How was it best to maintain these numbers? How sick must a man be before he dared to take him off duty? I have known King keep a man on working parties, with the most frightful ulcers which were daily increasing in size. Prompt treatment at the outset would, undoubtedly, have prevented a long period of sickness. On the other hand, the rations sent into the camp were based on the numbers on working parties, so the MOs had a very difficult balancing act to perform. Yet in King's defence, it was asserted that he feared pity and the soft treatment of others would lead to a weakening of the will to survive.

Even during the first two years at Kuching a man was as desperate to survive as a hunted fox with a full pack of hounds at its heels. Later, however, daily trips to the cemetery were made and the determination to survive became even more desperate so that doctors did not dare to weaken their resolve. Treat 'em rough and don't let 'em have their own way, appeared to be the approved maxim and psychological way to treat the patient. Alas! their psychology was too often at fault, and how many lives they endangered by the harshness of their methods can only be conjectured, yet soft treatment might have met with no better results in many cases. Besides, how many doctors practising today with an almost unlimited supply of drugs and medical facilities could not look back and dwell on instances where life might have been saved if a different treatment had been offered?

The second doctor, Captain Bailey, was a man of about thirty, a more humane individual but lacking the backbone of his chief. Three and a half years as a POW should have strengthened his character and certainly have added to his medical knowledge, especially with regard to how much the human body can stand when short of nourishment and constantly assailed with disease. There was also a Dutch doctor around at times.

There were all manner of maladies to be treated at Kuching. At the outset, the most common and ludicrous of these was severe soreness and weeping around the genital organs. For similar misfortunes at Changi, in an attempt to make good the vitamin deficiency to which was attributed the root cause of the trouble, a small quantity of Marmite had been daily prescribed. There was practically no Marmite at Kuching and nothing in the way of drying ointments and powder. The treatment, therefore, was of a very simple type: to keep the affected parts dry and to expose them to the sun and air. Sufferers, as they marched past Lieutenant Colonel King, would be greeted with the sight of his hand brushing against his whiskers as the words, 'Keep 'em dry', came from beneath them. It was a common enough spectacle indeed to see half a dozen, practically nude figures, squatting on the steps of their hut with knees upraised and their privates exposed to the sun. They were hanging 'em out to dry!

Vitamin deficiency resulted in many other complaints, the chief ones being pellagra, nephritis and beriberi, all of which claimed their victims. As time (and the years) passed by it became obvious that comrades with light-coloured skin were more prone to skin diseases such as pellagra. Tragically, lads with freckled complexions had slight chances of survival. In an attempt to make good vitamin deficiency, an amazing expedient was later adopted. Large supplies of rice polishings were sent into the camp and each man was allowed a daily ration. Despite the fact that these rice husks were exceedingly dirty, full of weevils and tasted much like dried sawdust, many of us ate them with enthusiasm, if not with gusto, appreciating their food value. Rice polishings, however, offered no resistance to dysentery. One of the biggest scourges of POW camps was undoubtedly dysentery, both amoebic and bacillary. Every effort was made to prevent the spread of this dreaded complaint. Faeces had to be properly covered, all food cooked, water boiled and dixies kept covered and rinsed in hot water before use. Later, more modern sanitary arrangements were installed.

Colourful posters depicting the fly as the arch demon, revelling in murder and human blood, were displayed around the camp. Just as in modern warfare, no impregnable defence can be offered to a determined invader, so, too, could the fly menace be not altogether contained. So thick were these insects that, sooner or later, one infected specimen would manage to fasten its sticky legs to food between the time it was cooked and transferred to hungry mouths, expectorate over an uncovered mess tin, or find its way into a rice bin. Then, of course, man himself, after a strenuous day on working parties, became careless, foregoing the washing of a dixie, chancing some uncooked food or leaving a rissole partly uncovered for later consumption. Moreover, flies had the fiendish audacity to pitch on a man's lip, there to leave the dysentery germ. Stamina was low, and, despite the injection received in Singapore, a serious bout of dysentery followed.

There was only one method of treatment: starvation. With no drugs available and no nourishing foods of the right type, all that could be done for the patient was to put him in the sick bay and feed him on rice water (like a weak starch solution) and nothing else. Sometimes the patient would recover, gradually losing the traces of blood and mucus in his excreta. Sometimes, he never really surmounted the illness, yet managed to survive as it were by sufferance, after concluding a pact with death to the effect that, in later years after release, he would forfeit his lower bowels. Many an ex-Japanese POW, years after the end of the war, had to have his lower bowel sealed off and later removed because of the lingering effects of chronic dysentery. Some sank lower and lower, their only capable movements, it seemed, after days, even weeks, of illness, being those required to evacuate the blood and mucous faeces, fifty or sixty times a day. One remarkable character was said to have had such a will to live that his weight was but little over three stone when at last death accepted capitulation. Sheer heroism had kept body and soul together for days.

Although rarely fatal, yet perhaps more loathsome than other complaints at Kuching, were tropical ulcers. Few men, after six months on working parties, escaped the attention of a microbe that attacked any slight eruption or puncture of the skin, especially on the leg. Once the bug had taken hold, a small hole would develop which, if left, filled with pus. Gangrene was an ever present threat. There was a scanty supply of drugs for treating these ulcers, a little iodoform and a few M&B tablets, the latter to be used only in the most severe cases.

Therefore, to economise on the amount of iodoform, the wound had to be cleaned out very thoroughly with a splint of wood and cotton wool. This cleaning out was a most painful procedure. It was done once a day. Even more agonising was to wake up in the middle of the night with a wound once more tight with pus. The only way to obtain relief was to remove the rags which served as bandages, hobble to the nearest tap and turn it on full bore over the ulcer until it had been washed clean. Indeed, this was efficacious treatment, as the force of the water attacked the infection itself, after the evacuation of the pus. Some ulcers grew to such alarming proportions that a goose's egg would have rested in the hole, with room to spare. When all drugs had been used up, there was only one method to arrest the spread of infection, cut away with a pair of scissors the affected parts. Many a time I heard the screams of patients as, held down by medical orderlies, this operation was performed. We all lived in dread of this, and I for one thank God that my own ulcers never reached such a stage as to require this drastic treatment.

Many a man worked with half a dozen ulcers as big as walnuts holing his legs; another worked with an ulcer on his back (an unusual place) the size of his fist. They received their treatment, if treatment it can be called, at night time. During the worst spells, two hundred ulcerated men turned up on morning sick parade. The stench of rotting flesh, even in the open air, was over-whelmingly nauseating, 'the stench of a thousand ulcers'. One was never free of the smell. On working parties one toiled alongside an ulcer case – mild, average or even chronic – kept on duty by Lieutenant Colonel King and smelt the putrefying flesh, either open to the air or covered by leaves or scraps of rag from worn out underwear, oozing blood and pus. You would sit down to a meal with a suppurating ulcer almost under your nose, or sleep with the stench in your nostrils. You would smell them at the showers even. One loathed them, yet, if not too chronic but chronic enough in the myopic eyes of King to keep one away from the eventual slavery of working parties, one could even bless them.

There were other trials, beriberi, nephritis and pellagra, previously mentioned as well as jaundice and malaria, but none took such a hold as dysentery and tropical ulcers. Nephritis became the worst malady feared in later years, but malaria never reached serious proportions. Kuching and the surrounding districts were fairly free from malarial mosquitoes due to the competent manner in which their breeding grounds had been treated before the war. It was not until 1944 that malaria became fairly common and few fatalities resulted, but, no matter what the complaint there was always Lieutenant Colonel King with his universal cure, 'Do some duty,' modern psychology, of course. If a man was bad and obviously needing rest, then to request it was a certain way to be kept on full duty. If not so bad and preferring to keep going with treatment only, the instruction was to 'Take him off the working parties', or 'Do some duty' and 'Keep 'em dry'.

There was a Japanese doctor called Yamamoto, reputedly a vet in pre-war Japanese civvy street, a man of many moods. Sometimes the devil incarnate, at other times he was as docile as a lamb. From 3 June 1943, the sick bay came directly under his supervision and, when at times in expansive urbane mood he stood on sick parade with King, it might happen that the patient would pass by Yamamoto to hear the words 'Yasumé', only to be confronted by the British colonel a second or two later to hear barked at him 'Do some duty!' or 'Keep 'em dry and carry on'. Perhaps Lieutenant Colonel King never had sores, never sweated on working parties, yet the sardonic Yamamoto, looking benignly on, knew that five hundred men were required for working parties and that the Japanese master intended to get them, come what may. As readers will, before the end of my account, learn with horror, two years hence the urbane Yamamoto would glibly be signing prisoners' death warrants.

In the last instance, Sunderland, since the second day of the New Year, had had to shoulder the responsibility of finding five hundred men fit for back breaking work at the riverside, a task which became more and more difficult. A man of courage, despite his faults, he made repeated efforts to lessen the Japanese demand.

On more than one occasion he was beaten up by the Japanese, but who wasn't? His efforts were mostly unavailing. It was only in the latter months of imprisonment that an alarmingly increasing death roll forced our captors to be content with smaller working parties.

RSM Sunderland must have swallowed the Japanese 'No' more than any man in our compound. In daily contact with the Japanese, he was the intermediary between us and them, a most exacting job although, fortunately, a Japanese civilian with long hair, acted as interpreter. All the enemy's instructions were transmitted to our compound through Sunderland, the penalty for non-compliance being, among other things, a beating for the RSM. His was also the difficult task of voicing our complaints, lack of rations, bad quality of rations, lack of cooking facilities, and the begging of privileges such as the holding of concerts, mailing facilities and extra food for the sick. Perhaps the last request was the least successful. With a typical, Oriental, mixture of topsy-turvy logic and callous common sense, Japanese philosophy included the notion that food was only for those who worked, sickness being but a poor excuse for non-productivity. To them, a sick man meant half rations and, as we could never accept that attitude, selfish though we were, it entailed the fit going even shorter to augment the sick man's diet. Doubtless the attitude of the Japanese towards the sick partly accounted for Lieutenant Colonel King's 'Do some duty' policy towards those afflicted. Perhaps it was a pragmatic doctrine, a short-term policy but likely to pay only small dividends in the long run.

Sunderland could shelve little of the responsibility of personal contact with the Japanese, but he could pass on his instructions. The bugle sounded, sergeant majors hurried to the RSM's room, instructions were conveyed through them to the hut sergeants and so on. Besides his adjutant, Sunderland wangled himself a clerk and batman, privileged men, indeed, as they did little hard physical work, took small risk, yet enjoyed the chance of scrounging extra rations from the RSM's table.

Compared with the rank and file, Sunderland and Southern fared well. Their food, collected separately, was the best obtain-able. Nobody minded this preferential treatment overmuch but, gradually, a snowball began to form. The batmen and the clerk wangled a little extra, then the friends of the RSM and the adjutant and the friends of the batmen (extra food for the radio operator being fully justified). Then the CSMs discovered ways of obtaining more than their share of food – then their friends. The cookhouse staff took advantage of their position, stuffed themselves and cut in their 'muckers' (friends). Then our own MPs, themselves responsible for discipline within the compound, must not be outdone, they and their pals and so on, until the distribution of the food in the compound became a gigantic racket and rocketed out of control.

Sunderland lacked the will or administrative ability to curb this unfair distribution of food. If only there had been fair shares for all! We were never united, probably because the root cause of the shocking distribution of food lay not so much with those in command as in the fact that there were so many different units within our enclosure. There were RASC, Ordnance, Signals, RAs, REs, remnants of various infantry regiments, the RAF and the Navy. There was never any regimental *esprit de corps* because the different units were strangers to each other. Had the thousand or so men in the compound originated all from say, the sunken *Prince of Wales*, from an RAF squadron or from one infantry battalion, then I am sure that the picture would have been very different. Had Lieutenant Colonel Russell remained in charge of the compound, he might have welded the various units into a homogeneous whole, but neither the RSM nor his adjutant, CSM Southern, despite their good qualities, were the men to do it. Yet I doubt whether any two other men in that compound could have done much better.

Poor Lieutenant Colonel Russell! He was one of our first fatalities. Contracting septicaemia, he died rather suddenly on 5 June 1943, tragically, but thirty-two years old. It is often the best apple that is plucked first from the tree! The most loved of all the officers, he was grieved by the whole compound. Even the Japanese were affected, especially Suga who undoubtedly respected and liked him. He was, perhaps, the only European whom the Japanese ever really respected. The death of any other person meant but one less on the ration strength. I only knew of one further death among the officers, a Lieutenant Pool, with whom I had often played chess at Priok.

As at other camps numbers were checked, at first frequently, but after a while, because of the long hours worked outside the camp, tenkos were staged only every two or three weeks. At the sound of the bugle, usually on a Sunday, the Japanese flooded in to count the various companies lined up in front of their huts. We were taught to number off in Japanese and woe betide anyone who missed his cue. I well remember Dr Yamamoto in one of his more expansive moods, teaching a double rank of sick men (the Japanese formed up their prisoners in a double rank for the sake of simplicity) to 'bango' in Japanese. He did not achieve complete success, but we learnt eventually. Before the war ended the men could count in Japanese as quickly as in English. They had to!

We had a lot else to do. As I have stated previously, work at the aerodrome gave way on 2 January 1943 to work at the riverside, about four miles down the river from Kuching. We started with the Korean guards and our own officers in attendance. At first, we had a comparatively easy time, removing an area of compressed attap, a metre deep, from near the water's edge and tipping it into the river. From the surveyors' level pegs, which were well in evidence, it was obvious that we were levelling off part of a large site. Before work at the riverside was concluded, many changes were to take place. One of the most important, the segregation of the officers, coincided with the completion of the attap removal. From that time, they were no longer allowed to accompany us on working parties, NCOs taking their place, a classical example of 'divide and rule'.

The journey to and from the 'docks', as we were wont to call them, (when it became obvious that the Japanese were constructing a shipbuilding depot) was made by native buses. These were small vehicles with two benches facing each other, running from front to rear, and separated by narrow aisles. For our use the seats were crammed to capacity, the aisles packed tight, and even the roofs utilised for carrying still more passengers. In fact these buses were so heavily laden that it was a marvel that they never tipped over. To supplement this native transport, there were also one or two lorries.

At the outset, as I have said, the work was not very arduous.

Provided that we kept pegging away at a fairly steady pace, few complaints were offered. Indeed, when the job of removing the attap was almost complete, the pace was reduced to a dawdle but little notice was taken. I remember squatting the whole of one day around the stump of a rubber tree, slowly chipping away at it, with the guards apparently unconcerned whether or not I hacked it off that day, or the next. It was that unnatural quietness that sometimes precedes a heavy storm. However, after the removal of all the attap and the chopping down to ground level of a few trees, we were given the task of making a roadway leading from the main road, obliquely to the docks and skirted on the right side by a saw mill. The roadway presented no great engineering problem, consisting of nothing more than the removal of the top vegetable soil for about six metres wide, forming a camber and the digging of two wide dykes longitudinally to take away storm water. There was no pitching, blinding or surface dressing to be done.

The job started slowly enough but, suddenly, as though at a pre-arranged signal, when nearing the end of the job, heat was applied. We found that we had to changkol away as fast as we could and that any attempt to take a breather only afforded the Japanese a good excuse for practising the gentle art of 'bashing up'. This change in tempo was quite a shock to us, though the pace set was moderate enough, compared with later requirements.

Prior to the beginning of what can only be termed as absolute slavery, we had learned a lot. Throughout imprisonment, a man on Japanese working parties (termed 'the working man', a phrase more appropriately used then than in modern days) could only enjoy the benefit of a little extra food (without which his chance of survival, over the days ahead, was slim) unless he risked participation in some racket outside the wire. Unlike his fortunate 'stay-at-home' comrades i.e. cookhouse wallahs, administrative staff and the like, the extra food he procured was at the risk of a 'bashing' or worse.

Generally speaking, the system worked this way. The natives at that time were not particularly short of money or certain foods, but they were short of clothing. In the rankers' compound, and even more so in the civvies' enclosures, there was some surplus clothing, for which we could clandestinely barter through the dividing wires. Unfortunates like myself, in contrast to those who had worked in the POW camps in Java with their kit intact, had no spare clobber. I cannot avoid stressing that little official attempt to make good this discrepancy was ever made. This neglect left the enterprising poor relation with the chance of personal gain. If he could contact some well-clothed man who was willing to part with, say, a shirt, he could agree to sell the article to the natives for a commission of ten per cent. Once on working parties, it would be up to his own initiative to contact one of the natives, also working on the site, to strike his bargain in either cash or commodities like sugar, salt or eggs, and make an undetected exchange. Not many articles of clothing changed hands at the riverside because, at that time, clothing was generally considered more important than money. Later, however, under different conditions, the opposite theory was more popular, but it was at this time that the barter procedure was first learnt. To be caught exchanging goods meant a beating for certain but the far greater danger, if discovered in contact with the natives, was to be judged guilty of espionage or fifth column activity. For this, the only penalty, as will later be seen, was death.

At that time we received payment for our work during the shaping of the roadway, so there existed also a legitimate buying power with facilities for purchasing, a life-saving boon. Besides the luncheon interval, a ten-minute break was allowed in the middle of the morning. During those times, native vendors offered for sale a limited supply of fried banana slices, fried sweet potatoes, fried rissoles and other titbits. There flourished another, more underhand, method of obtaining food. Eggs, for instance, were not usually among the wares offered officially for sale. Just off the new roadway crouched an attap house behind which the audacious might hope to contact the resident or some other native to purchase duck eggs which, in those days, were eight coins for a dozen. The main risk of detection was the discovery of the eggs during personal searches, which were usually conducted before boarding the buses for camp. Although investigations were not pursued with the vindictiveness later shown, to hide some eggs otherwise than in an ordinary army pack, being the main object of searches, was still chancy. The alternatives were false bottoms to water bottles and false crowns to hats, sometimes adopted to prevent detection. We had learnt something else in order to survive!

We learnt even more, namely, to rely increasingly on ourselves and less on the pooling of resources. As mentioned previously, at Priok four of us had decided to share and share alike, the ideal policy it seemed to us. At the docks, however, we quickly discovered that this same principle was not going to work very well. Whereas three of us were prepared, in varying degrees, to risk punishment in order to obtain extra food, a fourth member of the gang would not take the slightest risk and, therefore, not without some justification, it was agreed to share current assets, disband the combine and work independently. It was a decadent step, although I for one never suffered materially from the dissolution. This step, together with the refusal to pool resources, so criticised by us as the fault of those in command, further hardened our natures and grew the seeds of selfishness. I still assert, however, that the sin of selfishness spread from the top downwards rather than vice-versa. Among the rank and file, individual effort to share met with no encouragement from above. The strong, the senior NCOs, perpetrated the law of 'survival of the fittest', with themselves being the fittest and determined to remain so. Can one then blame the individual if, in his fight to survive, he gradually gave up the effort to share, the primary instinct being self-preservation?

Before moving from the roadway there are two memories of that time, one amusing, the other gratifying. One man tumbled, without hurt, into a cesspool and those sleeping next to him swore that he stank for days afterwards. Then, later, a native, sitting outside his abode near a rubber factory, pressed us to accept a gift of some local rice wine; nobody claimed a teetotal tendency!

Yasumé – Lucky for Some, Brutal Life-sapping Working Parties for Others!

The enslavement soon became complete but, upon its inception and because of a worsening of my tropical ulcers, I was invalided off working parties for which I was not sorry. Throughout my imprisonment, I freely admit that I preferred loafing inside the compound doing little, to working outside the wire, whether exacting or not. Life in camp, though, was thought by the majority to be detested more than the working parties, save for those times when outside parties were exceptionally arduous. Many men who survived endless back-breaking working parties would have found it difficult to live through the boredom of camp life, yet I preferred it. If there was a dearth of reading matter, I never lacked a pencil and scraps of paper with which to agreeably while away the time. Yasumé inferred rest from working parties as well as the usual Japanese order to 'down tools'.

During the second quarter of 1943, no one could have failed to benefit from a period inside the bounds of the barbed wire. One could not but hear, with heartfelt sympathy, the reports of those on working parties of worsening conditions. Work on a new section of the 'docks' had begun, which entailed filling in a depression near the waterfront with earth obtained from two or three hundred metres away. The traditional changkol and basket were used, the earth being heaped into the baskets which were then stacked beside the rails, on which ran a number of skips. When these vehicles returned empty, having deposited their contents near the waterfront, the earth from the refilled baskets was heaved over the edge of the skips and was heaped up as high as possible. The skips were then pushed back to the waterfront as quickly as possible and unloaded again.

At first, about ten trips a day were organised, but gradually the pace was quickened by the Japanese to twelve a day, after which prisoners could return to camp, but twelve were accomplished before the buses made their scheduled return so they were told, 'Well, you can therefore do more than twelve a day! Do fifteen, then go back to camp.'

Again, these were done before the arrival of the buses so, 'Do twenty and then return to camp.'

Before the buses rattled by, the target had been again reached and twenty five became the standard. Too late, the men perceived wisdom in making twenty-five last the whole day and they whispered this among themselves. There were, however, the means to step up production by brutality, a speciality of the Japanese. So, thirty trips a day were obtained. The chaps on the docks thought the limit had been reached, but they were wrong. By heaping brutality upon brutality – for would not Suga keep his promise to lighten our load all he could – forty trips a day were made.

Thus had the ancient Egyptians forced more and more production out of the Israelites. The maximum output had been achieved despite the greatest of efforts on the part of the Japanese, frequent bashings and the daily visit of three Japanese soldiers, headed by a particularly brutal guard commander nicknamed the 'Stamper'. He it was who made certain that the earth in the baskets was not placed loosely but 'stamped down' without loss of speed. No wonder the working site was immortalised by the name of Lekas (Quick) Corner! Later working parties at the docks had to contend with an even worse guard, the 'Gorilla', who outdid the Stamper in brutality and was the most feared man in Sarawak. Men worked at fever pitch. Those with changkols slashed and cut like mad, those carrying baskets stooped, picked up and stacked all in one movement, straining their guts out; those managing skips not only helped to load, but pushed with all their might at the heavy vehicles, feverishly emptying them at the waterfront, running back with the empty trucks as though in a race for life itself. In a way they were, too. For every bashing received for alleged slackness, a man's expectation of life was cut short by days. Many a man died, albeit a brawny ex-miner, dock or brewery worker, not altogether because of the sapping of their physical capabilities, but because of nervous exhaustion. All lived in mortal fear of Japanese blows, some coped better than others where nerves were concerned. You had to be cool enough and re-sourceful enough to take a breather when the backs of the Japanese were turned; to use less force with the changkol than action suggested. One man was scared into such a frenzy of exertion that he worked like a demon all the time, no matter where the eyes of the Japanese guards hovered. His fires were soon burnt out and, after a short period of illness in the camp, his life just ebbed away.

It was sad and frightening to hear of what had befallen the working party at Lekas Corner but, meanwhile, after a short period of 'yasumé', I was placed on light duty and appointed as one of the ration party. Each morning, at the sound of reveille, out of bed and down to the cookhouse I went. First come, first served was the custom and it became a point of honour to collect the rations quickly so that the working parties were not kept waiting. After the meal we washed the bins – at lunchtime and after the evening meal, also.

Precious few chances of extra food were offered to the ration party. The most that we selfish beasts, who yet mourned the treatment meted out to our comrades on the docks, could hope for were the scrapings of rice left at the bottom of the bin after the rations had been split. Food was becoming more and more important. It meant energy, but it meant even more than that psychologically. Some enjoyed eating after the others had finished. Thus two or three would endeavour to make the eating of a meal, a lengthy procedure, picking and nibbling, even interrupting their mastication to search a loincloth for lice or pay a visit to the urinal, all for the sake of eventually having the pleasure of eating after the others had finished. Still others fiddled and faddled, putting a little in one dish, a little into another, like Chinese connoisseurs. Others ate all but a quarter of their rice which they would put by for a meal later on, so that others then could watch with greedy eyes, although delayed mastication increased the likelihood of dysentery! Who would dare criticise these poor creatures now!

I was not blameless. Besides being on ration party, a squad of light duty men had each day to present themselves in front of the Japanese QM stores with an empty wagon. This was, under the surveillance of the Japanese QM, loaded with rice and vegetables. Then the cart had to be pulled and pushed into our compound under the supervision of our own QM. It was a tiresome job. Those manhandling the cart did not so much hope that the wagon would contain more than average supplies, but that a vegetable (such as kang-kong, a type of kale) might fall off, which could be secreted about their person or, perhaps, a rice bag might be holed to give the opportunity of gathering up a few grains for personal cooking pots. When detailed to the party, I shared these base sentiments, and the wagon rarely reached the cookhouse before thoughts of lifting a vegetable from the cart or holing a sack of rice, not merely scrounged spillages, had entered my head. The penalty for being caught was severe, while conscience, weak though its voice, yet still articulated 'No'. It was wisest to hope for loose grains of rice and stray pieces of vegetable left in the cart after it had been unloaded at our own QM's stores, as sole reward for our labours.

During my period of light duty, another venture was launched, camp gardens. Under the personal supervision of ex-vet camp doctor Yamamoto, a portion of a rubber plantation was developed, westwards from our compound and between us and what was to become the ladies' camp. All the rubber trees had been felled by the wood party and, initially, it was the duty of the light duty contingent to grub out the stumps, not an easy task. Besides excavating around the trunk, the roots, sometimes bunched and knotted together, had to be cut through with small axes which were never very sharp. Yet, we worked with a will. There was a certain incentive. Yamamoto promised that when a party of men (working in fours) had removed the stump allotted to it, its members could down their tools. Unlike the Japanese at the docks, he kept his promise so that often we were back in our huts well before lunch. Simultaneously, with the clearing free of stumps, other light duty men were changkoling the ground in preparation for the sowing of sweet potato plants and greens.

While we 'ulcerated legs' worked in the gardens, those on working party drove relentlessly on at Lekas Corner. There were few deaths but, during this period, many so weakened themselves that ultimate death was the only sequel. Unpleasant though my ulcers were, the rest they afforded me probably saved my life.

A further advantage of light duty was an opportunity to appreciate something of what had transpired and what was going on in the compound. One of the most important developments was undoubtedly the improvement of sanitary arrangements. The primitive slit trenches had been superseded by small wooden structures erected throughout the compound by our engineer's staff. Each convenience contained two or three closets provided with cased-in lavatory 'buckets' (in reality these were empty petrol drums) which could be covered after use. These arrangements, after the makeshift trenches, were extremely popular. There was, too, a little privacy, although in one corner of our enclosure, near the engineer's depot, there still remained a batch of lavatories which were not divided into cubicles. Each day, the buckets were emptied by a 'benjo' party. Four in number and heftily built, they needed to be strong. They trudged through our lines with a large bin, its weight taken by two poles passed through on opposite sides, each man supporting the end of one pole. Into the bin, the contents of the lavatories were poured, ultimately to be tipped into cesspits some distance from the compound.

While on light duty, I helped to excavate one of these large pits under the supervision of a most detestable guard. We had our laughs also, though. We were informed one day that a Japanese general would be visiting the aerodrome before lunch, for which we were instructed to appreciate the supreme moment and honour the spotting of his incoming plane. Later, as we worked, a plane was indeed heard approaching, although whether it contained the general we never knew, but the Japanese guard called us to attention anyway. The plane was sighted three or four miles away, but our guard forced us to salute it. Our grinning faces contrasted sharply with the ecstatic look of adoration imprinted on the face of the Japanese, as he saw nothing ridiculous in the incident.

A not so funny incident occurred one day, with regard to the benjo party. One of the bearers – I think it was Lou Levy – slipped under the weight of a full tub of ordure and the contents drenched him, although, after a good wash, his ardour of the job was maintained. The job of emptying and cleaning out the latrines was not as unattractive as it might appear. Similar work was also carried out in other compounds, including the Japanese billets and the women's compound. Besides being a regular job, it resulted in satisfying a personal want of the Japanese, so that the benjo wallahs were not persecuted by them, and there were also opportunities of procuring a little laegi (extra) food. Above all, the carriers were exempt from normal working parties.

The engineers, another small bunch of fellows jealously regarded by the outside working fraternity, were fortunately not restricted to constructing latrines. They also fitted covers to the rice and stew bins, fashioned wooden rice boxes to ease the carrying of cooked rice especially on working parties, improved cookhouse and washing facilities, constructed containers for the QM's store, and, of course, assisted in shaping parts for the radio and the installation of warning devices.

Food during this period was still reasonably good, albeit basically of rice and stew while the canteen continued to augment supplies, to a limited extent. One of the most intriguing purchases was a substance called blachang, a type of strong fish paste. Purple in colour, it was a by-product of native cured fish, very strong in flavour and saved only from complete rancidness by its high salt content. Its strong flavour added an exciting flavour to plain rice.

Occasionally, a little curry was obtained or, maybe, a few chillies or some extra salt. Once or twice, an issue of prawns was obtained which, curried by the cooks, offered perhaps the most delicious dish during our stay at Kuching. The meat supplies fell off a little, later to cease altogether. Even at that period of relative plenty, it was our custom to count the number of lumps of fat pork received with our weekly ration of pork stew. Our rivalry started as soon as the stew bins, one for each hut, were brought from the cookhouse. Floating on top of them were the larger cubes of pork, succulent and mouth-watering. Some contended that it was better to be first in the queue, others that more meat could be expected when the level of the stew had dropped nearly to the bottom of the bin. Others contended that it made no difference, being entirely a matter of luck. All I know is that when it came to my turn for rations, whatever position I stood in the queue, the lumps of floating pork rarely failed to wriggle tantalisingly away from the scoop which had been fixed by the engineers to a dipstick. It may be difficult to believe that grown men could gloat over the fact of receiving three lumps of meat to others' one but, in retrospect, the idea seems quite natural to me. Even now, I can imagine the pangs of jealousy that I felt as I perceived my comrades, like Corporal Sheldrick, counting three or four lumps of pork while I could boast only one and, conversely, the satisfaction of knowing, and this was a rare feeling, that I had gathered more than my neighbour!

During my period of light duty several important events took place. Until now, the women, numbering about two hundred and forty and including a party of nuns, had been quartered behind the Japanese office, but on 10 June 1943, soon after the death of Lieutenant Colonel Russell – surely a far more important event – they were shifted to an enclosure prepared for them the other side of us, just a hundred metres down the lane from the sick bay. Here, they were to remain until liberation. Part of their previous quarters was taken by a small party of Dutch Fathers, while the Dutch officers were shifted to quarters behind the Japanese HQ, formerly inhabited by Dutch native troops who, in their turn, were re-billeted overlooking the open space by the Japanese offices and QM's stores. This left only the English male internees directly in contact with our compound, somewhat enlarged, through the wire. The security of our compound was unintentionally tightened up by the Japanese sponsored moves.

June 1943 was quite an eventful month. Besides the rearrangement of the various compounds, there was the visit of the Japanese general (already referred to) and also the staging of a cinema show on the open space by the Japanese offices. For this purpose, a large square of canvas had been strained taut to a wooden framework erected in the middle of the clearing. On 13 June 1943, to this open space, all walking prisoners of war and internees of both sexes and all nationalities were marched and marshalled, on both sides of the screen. The POWs were allotted space on the side of the screen opposite the projector and, on being confronted with a Chinese view of the screen, yowled at in Japanese and with no intelligible subtitles, it is easy to imagine the difficulty that we had in following the action. This entertainment obviously divided itself into three parts, firstly, a martial piece of propaganda, secondly a short Japanese romantic musical and thirdly, some type of comedy. The only one of the three from which we derived any enjoyment was the musical which purported to be a delightfully sweet Japanese love song, which sounded as sad as one from *Madam Butterfly*.

The only other comparable entertainment staged throughout the whole of our internment by the Japanese consisted of a Japanese band concert. We were never sure whether we were allowed to attend these concerts out of Japanese kindness or our captors' hope of impressing us with Japanese culture. Meanwhile, our own concerts were being held regularly about once a month. These never waned in popularity throughout our imprisonment. We might have tired to some extent of one performer, but there were always others to step forward. On the other hand, the debates ceased altogether as there was no energy for such features. The only other organised form of popular entertainment was listening to men talking of their pre-war jobs or discoursing on subjects which interested them. As time went on, the one subject of conversation was food, food and more food!

The Japanese found plenty of energy for activity, both individual and communal. During the English summer months of 1943, a hate week was organised. Whether this sprang from the instructions of the Japanese High Command or Major Suga was never quite clear. What was clear, and abundantly so, was the determined effort on the part of the Japanese to make us realise that a hate week meant exactly what it implied. Japanese guards would stroll around the enclosure during both hours of daylight and darkness and, at the slightest pretext, hand out a bashing. For example, one man smoked without a bowl of water to hand; this man's demeanour as he bowed suggested pride; this man did not spring quickly enough to attention and one man's face bore traces of disrespect. Members of working parties, too, were yanked out of line and beaten unmercifully on leaving and entering camp. It was indeed a reign of terror though, fortunately, never repeated on the same scale notwithstanding the fact that, throughout our internment, 'hate days' were from time to time organised. Sometimes the camp thugs were reinforced by the odious Kempei

Tai (Japanese Gestapo). We were never given a reason for these bouts of special brutality, but I suspect they coincided with Japanese defeats.

One of the most distasteful of all attacks (not during 'hate week') occurred just outside our enclosure. Returning from a visit to the Japanese offices, one of the ladies was suddenly and without apparent cause accosted by 'Doll Face' and brutally slapped across the face. A year previously, such an attack might well have produced a violent retaliation within our compound, but we had been softened and the will to resist had been stifled. By now, the one thought uppermost in our minds was to be submissive at all costs, hoping only that we could hang on to life until the close of hostilities.

In July 1943, the piped water supply petered out. This was due partly to an unusually dry period and partly, we suspected, to misuse and waste elsewhere. Thus had failed our greatest amenity. Arrangements were made for the cookhouse staff to draw enough water for cooking but, for drinking purposes, we had to fetch it from a large pond at the edge of the compound and a short step from the ladies' lines. As for washing, at first we simply went without, a denial not unbearable had it not been for the lost opportunity of bathing ulcerated legs and sluicing filthy rags. As it was, the stench from rotten flesh became even more objectionable, if that were possible. Fortunately, however, towards the end of a three-week period of drought, the Japanese allowed both the light duty men and the men returning from working parties a daily dip in the pond. I enjoyed this and found that I could still swim without undue fatigue despite ulcerated legs and general weakness. The piped water supply never again entirely failed, although near the end of captivity we did, for a few days, have to eke out our supplies by drawing from the pond.

Meanwhile, memorable events were taking place at the boat building depot. So successful had the expansion there been that on 30 July the first boat made of wood was launched from the so-called 'docks'. Importantly, it was named *Borneo Maru*. Celebrations were ordered in Kuching while, at the docks, an imposing ceremony was performed. How many of the pompous little Japanese attending that ceremony, I wonder, then imagined that before the expiry of two years the industry was to be blasted to bits and that in two years' time anyhow, the war for them would be lost! In camp, the momentous event was celebrated by the organisation of a concert on the open space in front of the Japanese offices. After such a long lapse of time, I am uncertain whether or no this was the occasion when the Japanese band visited us. I think that they must have been there, as the only other general concert staged that I can recall was one presented by the prisoners themselves, other than a film, that is. Excellent performances were given by most enclosures, including the ladies', but I must in all fairness state that half of the concert's duration was given over to our own artists, whose costumes had been tailored by the female internees.

This concert was staged on 15 August 1943, it being the first anniversary of the initial setting up of the POW and internees camp at Kuching. It also afforded an opportunity for another speech by Suga. He 'shimpashised wid us' and still hoped that we would return safe and sound to our loved ones, as indeed we should if we obeyed his instructions. Alas, speeches were the only indications that he showed of wanting to further our welfare. No doubt this 'shimpashy' for us quickly faded away as the Japanese had scant cause for further self-congratulation.

August was, indeed, quite an eventful month. There arrived on the 26th of the month from San Dakan thirty-three officers, and from Kuching came nurses and one or two civilian doctors who had, until then, been employed at the civilian hospital just outside Kuching. Apparently, security arrangements were being tightened. Prior to this, too, several hundred prisoners, mostly Australians, had stayed in our compound a night or so on the way to British North Borneo. Poor devils! No one was to survive. It would have been better if they had all met the same fate as one of their party while still at Kuching, who accidentally stepped on a live electric wire and was electrocuted!

Visitors of a different kind were Japanese senior officers. Apart from the fact that our huts were given an extra clean and the gardens and paths tidied, I can remember little result. We were supposed to have received a double supply of meat that week, but I cannot say that the stews showed much evidence of this benevolence.

While I was still doing light duties in camp, the Japanese Kempei Tai carried out a thorough search of all the compounds. We, in our compound, were lined up and 'bangoed' on the road.

An event of some personal importance occurred on 23 September. My tropical ulcers had made no headway and eventually became so bad as to qualify me for a period of sick bay treatment. By now, owing to such a large number of 'stingahmatis' (or 'half deads', those very sick personnel, many of whom would not survive), the sick bay across the road was used only for the more serious cases. As there were no beds, I was given lying space on the boards of a hut within our compound, about seventy metres from my usual quarters. At about this time, most of the patients were suffering from either dysentery or tropical sores, with little treatment for either although a limited amount of iodoform was still being used. Complete rest was the main advantage and, to my surprise, my ulcers improved rapidly. While in the sick bay, I developed a fever and diarrhoea. It was thought that I might be troubled with dysentery.

Fortunately, there were now, under the supervision of a Dutch doctor who had been attached to the sick quarters across the road, limited facilities for bacteriological examination. A sample of my excrement was taken away for scrutiny and it was soon discovered that I had contracted hookworm, a parasite picked up through walking barefooted. This was understandable as most of us had worn out our irreplaceable boots and padded around in bare feet. I understand from medical authorities that this Oriental and thriving parasite enters through the feet into the bloodstream, eventually to reach the intestines, there to hook itself a permanent abode where it may cause chronic anaemia. Fortunately, as the first case diagnosed, I was lucky enough to be given treatment, although there were in the camps only a few capsules of the liquid poisonous to these parasites. On release, I had to have further treatment as, indeed most prisoners had to have after release, in order to free them from these troublesome parasites, not to mention the more resistant strongyloides, the successful treatment for which was only developed when the US Army were in Vietnam.

Towards the end of October, I was eventually discharged from the sick bay and, after another week or so on light duty, I resumed working parties. So, back with the changkol and, when the guards' backs were turned, to fascinating discussions on food with such mates as Bill Dunkerley, Brian Curran, Corporal Burnham, Corporal Sheldrick, Les Ward and Corporal 'Jimmy' (Tom) James.

Rissole Hill

I tumbled out of the buses and, with the others, walked towards the 'docks'. Halfway to the waterfront, I spotted a small attap constructed shed. Its appearance seemed to act on my comrades as a red rag flaunted in front of a savage bull. In a mad rush, they careered towards it. I was flabbergasted as to what was the object of this but, to my disadvantage, I soon gathered why. In front of the shack, the ground was littered with the leftovers of half a dozen large changkols and a similar number of very large rattan baskets. Always preferring a changkol to a basket, I picked one up and discovered that it was as heavy as lead. Hence the rush, as all the light tools had disappeared with the earlier arrivals picking the lighter tools and baskets. It was a wild and undignified scramble with rough words and near blows used in the tussle. It felt all wrong, and although I could, under the prevailing conditions of our slavery, well sympathise with the overwhelming desire to grab a light tool, I knew immediately and beyond all shadow of doubt that the practice should be stamped out. Possession of a light changkol, or small basket, meant an easier day's work and the burning up of less precious energy, a greatly added facility in the use of the tools and the less likely therefore the possessor had of a bashing and, in the final issue, a greater chance of survival. Thus to men who for months on end had worked and quailed under the most terrible conditions, any sense of indignity might have well been immaterial.

The NCOs in charge did not work. They had nothing to lose by any unfair allocation of tools. I cannot understand, to this day, why it was that they did not enforce orderly distribution as part of their duty and see that the men approached the implements, laid out in orderly fashion on the ground, in single file and that they were picked up in sequence. Every man, then, would have had an equal chance of procuring a favourable tool and the weak, the slow and the diffident would not have been put at a disadvantage to the strong and bold. POW life was, of course, the survival of the fittest, but men should never have been allowed to degrade themselves when watched by the Japanese. Such baseness lessened the enemy's respect for us, so that we could, with less justification, blame them for treating us increasingly as dogs. Not for the first time, I thought of the officers leaving our compound. Such exhibitions would never, under their supervision, have been allowed.

However, I soon had other matters to concentrate upon. On my first morning, the changkol men were set to hack away at a high piece of ground, filling the baskets of those who carried them. The 'basketeers', with their loads above their heads, jog-trotted fifty metres to tip their earth into a depression. By now, I was given to understand that the tempo of the work had slackened somewhat, but we were, nevertheless, kept hard at it all day long. The camp guards demanded full baskets, so that some of the 'basketeers' had the greatest difficulty in lifting their loads above their heads. Although each day, a Japanese officer or senior NCO, accompanied by two privates, made their rounds, insisting on full baskets and utmost speed, the famed 'Gorilla' had ceased to supervise. Not a man, however, dared to be seen slacking, although in truth I was amazed at the fear still shown by many, a fear that goaded men to work and expend unnecessary calories much faster than they needed. For myself, I soon learned when to work and when to ease up, which guards to fear and which to take liberties with. I discovered that all these gentlemen sported nicknames, for instance, Joe Louis, Big Pig, Little Pig, Maggots, Makan Basher, Big Annie, 'The Bear', Doll Face, all brutes. Others were sometimes severe, at other times 'cushy', such as Kempy's Mate, and the Stutterer, while one or two were always as humanitarian as they dared, never beating a man without some provocation. Of this latter category I especially remember Moray and a stout character we called Tubby.

This latter man was the senior non-Japanese guard attached to the camp and was later put in disgrace and demoted because of his leniency to the prisoners. Yet few, with Tubby in charge, slacked. They yet maintained a good steady rate. With other supervisors they worked with unceasing furiousness, not caring to ease up even when the 'slant eyes' were averted! For this they paid with their lives. Who could reproach them? Not I who had missed months of absolute slavery. You had but to cast your eyes towards that line of basket men, with their loads above their heads walking towards the tipping point, only to see bodies, naked save for a brief loincloth, with matchstick arms supporting the piled up baskets on their heads! This method of transportation pulled so taut against the ribs with their dreadfully thin cover of flesh that one might think a tap on the diaphragm with a drumstick would evoke a sonorous boom from the hollowness of the emaciated torso.

Onlookers saw less a man in his prime than a walking skeleton, pitiful to behold. The majority of the Japanese saw no pity, only a fast running-down machine, still capable of doing work. Thus, perhaps, did our forebears see their slaves as they sweated in the sugar and cotton plantations and shouted, 'Move quicker', 'Pack those baskets denser', 'Strain those muscles', 'Get those loads above your heads!' If any man could not, it was not weakness but laziness. What one man could do, another could! I saw a figure unable to raise his load, fearful of the consequence of shaking out some of the earth to lighten the load. He had beseeched his mate to help him hoist his burden. No wonder that small baskets were at such a premium and no wonder that those who fashioned the baskets, incapable of routine work and under Japanese eyes, made them as small as they dared!

After less than a week of this task, however, we were moved back to the waterside. Here the main job was to drive in some wooden piles, under the supervision of Japanese civilian engineers. Any prisoner who had thought that the Japanese civilians were likely to be less brutal than their military counterparts had soon been disillusioned. The two in charge of the operation were like pressurised steam in a closed cylinder, in that they harboured fearful tempers. Provided that the operations proceeded smoothly, they were pleasant enough but, at the slightest hitch, their 'valves' jerked and they broke into towering rages, lashing out with sticks at anyone within arm's length.

In the main, prisoners of war were divided into two parties, those manhandling the pile-driving monkeys and those working up to their armpits in mud, as they initially adjusted the piles and breakwater timbers. Strangely enough, the latter task was thought by many to be preferable as the mud served as sanctuary. The Japanese, not out of humanity, but because of the unpleasant smell of the muck, rarely struck at a man mud-caked. The greatest danger spot was to stand overlooking the mud bank. Nothing delighted the sadistic Japanese more than finding an excuse to knock a man into the filthy morass. To my mind, because of the spells of inactivity and thus my reason for tagging on to this party, the men strung out along the ropes operating the monkeys had the easier time. Yet, every now and then, and for no apparent reason, the Japanese would lash out left and right with anything to hand.

Apart from the violence of the Japanese civilians, my most vivid impression of this phase of activities was the ceaseless industry from the nearby carpenters' shops. Woefully short of tools and machinery, save for the nearby sawmill, the natives axed to the correct shape and curves all the timbers for the boats that they were building. To watch the accurate chipping of a dozen axes was a fascinating occupation. Never once, it seemed, was the finest shaving ever taken off in error; never did I spy a wasted stroke. Always the axe, with amazing speed, carved with precision, so that the timbers seemed of their own accord to bend and curve to the exact shapes and curve willed by the carpenters.

After a fortnight near the carpenters' shops, we were shifted to another part of the 'dock' area at the back of some nearby stables. Again the changkol and basket, the same dreary routine, taking soil away from here and dumping it there. Gradually, however, the tempo of the work was eased although no slacking of any kind was tolerated. The Japanese could be tolerant during break periods. Lunch was eaten on a hillock nicknamed 'Rissole Hill' near the excavations. Within easy reach of the road, it attracted native vendors whom the Japanese allowed to display their wares. On platters, they brought fried pisannes, goola balls (sugary balls covered with grated coconut), fried rissoles, slices of papaya and pineapple, pomelos and coconuts. Money, officially or unofficially come by, therefore, could be expended on extra food. The drawback was the shortage of popular lines, above all rissoles, so that an insensate rush developed to buy first. None of the NCOs in charge appeared capable of controlling the rush and the tussle for food was almost as undignified as the scramble for changkol and basket, a practice which still continued.

During that period, a profitable egg racket had also developed. Unlike rissoles, eggs were not openly offered for sale, but there were other ways and means. I soon discovered that the easiest method was to buy through the native workmen. Making contact unbeknown to the Japanese presented the major difficulty, but the natives in the tool shed, partly out of a desire to make a little on the side and partly, too, I think, out of compassion for us, were very co-operative. One of the first lessons that I learnt, while working, was to knock the blade off my changkol and thus gain permission from the Japanese to change it at the stores. During the exchange, there was often an opportunity to slip a native a dollar while he put my eggs in an army water bottle especially adapted for the purpose. We had strict orders not to take anything back to camp and we were usually searched before boarding the return buses. So far, however, the Japanese had never discovered the water bottle ruse, so I became bolder. Why not buy two or three dozen eggs? I could then, after retaining three a day to mix with my rice ration, sell them in camp at double the cost price and use the profits partly to increase my capital resources, and partly to spend at 'Rissole Hill'. So, I learnt each morning, after grabbing a changkol, to leave a purchased army pack holding two or three bucks, near the stores. At eventide, the eggs would be within the pack left near the shed and somehow or other I would get the plunder back to camp, a few in the water bottle, some secreted about my person e.g. under my hat, and a few at the bottom of the pack hidden beneath an upturned mug. Of course, in time, I was inevitably caught and received a thorough bashing, while the eggs were distributed amongst the rest of the squad, half of which were returned.

I cannot remember that the incident quelled my ardour over much, though, of course, I had to practise more caution in the future, as the risks taken in getting extra food were well worth the while. Few Kuching prisoners who, day after day, week after week and month after month, appeared on working parties, lasted the three years unless they risked unauthorised trading. Those who took risks suffered many a bashing, but the extra nourishment obtained preserved their lives. What should have been planned, of course, was a co-operative and highly organised system of bringing in extra food for the general good of the community, but the launching of such an enterprise was beyond the capabilities and imagination of those in charge. When later an organised method was introduced in other localities, it benefited only a few.

At the riverside we finished working as we began, changkoling away at attap, now on the Kuching extremity of the shipbuilding yard and emptying baskets into the sea. The pace, too, became more in keeping with our earlier exertions, with a good deal of 'slapping' being still quite popular! During this phase, we spent two or three bad days shouldering long heavy poles from the extremity of the riverside enterprise to the tool shed. This operation would not have been so bad had we been allowed to carry it through in our own way, but the Japanese insisted on two men to a timber balk, when four were reasonably required. Many men gave way under the strain, especially when struggling over plank bridges spanning shallow declivities. The ducking and muck did not matter, but the subsequent bashing did, and a few more men were accelerated towards their graves. Yet, even this operation had its advantages, as extra contact could be made at the tool shed with the excellent native storekeepers.

In mid-December the working party consisted of only one hundred and fifty men, because of sickness. We had been worked out and the Japanese knew this, as well as we did. Their shipyard almost complete, why should they worry? On 31 December, therefore, the last working party returned from the 'docks' and not a prisoner was sorry to leave the river 'resort'.

Long periods of slavery were yet to come, as we were beaten time and time again and made to work on even less rations on a seven-day week working schedule as opposed to the previous six-day one. Further, we were to re-encounter the 'Gorilla'. In retrospect, however, the period at the shipbuilding yard would, by and large, be voted the worst phase of the lot. Although the percentage of those who died during 1943 was small, scores of men wore themselves out slaving on Japanese working parties, especially at Lekas Corner, and death claimed them before the cessation of hostilities. Tropical ulcers, to those who suffered from them, were often a blessing in disguise.

Satan

Simultaneous with our exertions at Lekas Corner and Rissole Hill, another form of work was being performed some little distance from the main road which ran from the aerodrome to the camp. To reach it, we turned down a road opposite the main approach drive to the golf course, which we also later worked at. There, a remarkable Japanese sergeant, nicknamed quite aptly, Satan, wielded absolute authority over the fifty POWs sent to him each day. A blacksmith by trade, he actually employed two or three of our men about his workshop, but the majority performed rougher jobs, digging air raid shelters, improving roads, levelling off ground and other such lowly tasks. The work was not quite so hard as at the boat building site: it certainly could not have been harder, but few men would have elected permanently to have thrown in their lot with Satan. At the best, it could be said that a day on Satan's party constituted a change and not a change that was as good as a rest!

Satan's main quality was the most uncertain and violent temper. At Lekas Corner, the threat of a severe bashing was never absent but, generally speaking, a man could squeeze through a day unscathed if he worked hard enough, never, for one moment, letting up. When a beating was received, though frequently, the reason was generally evident, however slight the provocation. With Satan, it was the unexpected that made life so unbearable. You could not guard against punishment because so often it was administered without the slightest warning and without, so far as could be seen, the slightest cause. When upset, his rage knew no bounds. At times, quite content to watch men pressing on steadily, though not breathlessly, at other times he was not even placated by the greatest exertions. Prisoners might be diligently working, concentrating on the job, when suddenly, like a tornado, he descended upon them and, lashing out left and right, did not cease his exertions until every man lay flat on his back. The wallop he packed was proverbial, among us POWs. It was rumoured that he had, in his time, been a boxer. I cannot vouch for the veracity of this, yet it is well known that boxers of old would often train for fights by working at a blacksmith's forge; certainly Satan had a mighty strong arm. Violent and savage as he was, however, his methods never compared in animal ferocity and cruelty with the exploits of the 'Gorilla' whom we shall, ere long, encounter once more.

As I recall Satan, one particular incident sticks out in my mind. It was once required of us to shift a shack built of bamboo poles and covered with attap. Satan suggested that we might lift it bodily and so carry it to the new site – 'Lekasio' (Hurry Up). Twenty men, therefore, arranged themselves about the structure, found firm grip where best possible and at a word from Satan took the strain. Not an inch did the building budge. Again, came the order to lift. Again, we failed in our efforts. We knew the task to be beyond our capabilities. In this knowledge there was an exception, Satan. Herod (which might well have been a more appropriate name!) in all his rage could not have been more terrible. Cursing at the top of his voice, he rampaged around bashing out with a heavy stick unmercifully. We wilted beneath the blows, but heretofore undiscovered reserves of strength flew to our aid. Up from the ground rose the hut and we found that we could actually shuffle along with it. More miraculously still, we struggled with it to the proposed site a hundred metres away. Satan had won, as he did so often.

Before leaving His Satanic Majesty, I would like to add that adjoining the shelter, less than fifty metres from Satan's black-smith's shop, where we ate our lunch, it was said a brothel reposed. It was, indeed, further asserted that one of the prisoners who worked at the blacksmith's shop had found solace there. Be that as it may, is it surprising that Satan ensured such an amenity for his domain?

Confined to Barracks

Work with Satan lingered on a short while after work ceased at the 'docks' but, with the cessation of the major operation, the emphasis was laid on gardening.

It transpired that few in 'civvy street' enjoyed gardening, even fewer expressed a partiality for it under the Japanese. Besides the development of Dr Yamamoto's gardens, opposite the sick bay, a new project was the laying out of gardens behind the quarters of the Korean guards. Each day, therefore, a party of gardeners was detailed. These men came under the control of a regular Japanese NCO, a rather surly individual who was quickly nicknamed 'Mr Middleton'. As usual, the tools provided were changkol and basket, and we did little else than make paths and hack level the plots. We were really nothing more than labourers, although one or two privileged prisoners did actually assist in the planting of sweet potatoes, brinjals and greenstuff.

Meanwhile, now that every third day each man stayed at the camp, various enterprising prisoners began to stake out a claim to pieces of untilled ground about their huts, despite their dislike of horticulture. With a mate, I cultivated a small, though useful, sweet potato patch at the bottom of our own hut, and from it we reaped benefit both from the potatoes and from their tops. There became popular the daily boiling of green tops to eke out our meagre rations. Three or four prisoners would pool their supplies of greens, whether from their own small gardens or stolen from the Japanese gardens and, in tins scrounged from the Japanese or found on working parties, boil the greens over home-made fires. It was indeed, at this time a very common sight to see, dotted about the compound, little groups of prisoners bending over fires preparing their 'stodges' as these concoctions were commonly called. The greatest problem was the provision of fuel, and the detailing for a Japanese working party outside our enclosure was welcomed for the chance it offered to forage wood, if nothing else. However, enough could never be obtained in this way, so our buildings suffered. Pieces of wood serving no apparent usefulness in the construction of the huts would surreptitiously be taken, unessential parts of lavatories mysteriously disappeared overnight, the sides and divisions between the showers rapidly vanished, with the result that ultimately all showers were taken in public. Despite the scrounging and pilfering, wood supplies were still insufficient and a good deal of jockeying for position over the fires would take place. Jones, for instance, might start a fire when along would come Smith asking if, for the contribution of a piece of wood, he could share the flame. Yes, would say Jones, then along would come Brown and Williams, until about six cooks, all attempting to attract the greatest amount of heat, were clustered around the fire bending over their stodge pots. Sometimes, there were quarrels and perhaps blows were struck.

Simultaneously, with the development of individual gardens, each company was, on a communal basis, cultivating a portion of the environs of their huts, so that the company stodge was eventually enjoyed once a fortnight. Two men from each company were appointed company gardeners and, eventually, a valuable contribution to the diet was evolved. A shock, however, awaited the individualists. When every foot of available land had been dug up and planted, an edict was issued to the effect that all individual gardens were to be confiscated and embodied within the company gardens. This was most unfair as those who had made no effort of their own, and I am not including the sick, were to receive the same benefit as those men who had worked hard in their spare time. As in most instances when authorities attempted to pool resources, they mistimed their effort, so that not unjustifiably it was whispered that the pooling was done for the benefit of the few. Of course, all gardens should have been pooled and even those who had laboured at their own plots had said from the outset that such enterprise should not have been left to individual effort. Gardens, they said, should have been developed jointly under authority. It was only when development was complete that the authorities stepped in, stifling individual effort. The high-handed, ill-timed attitude, left a bitter taste in many a mouth. Despite it all, though, the 'stodge' craze never quite died out, although the wherewithal was not so readily available, as to fill the stodge pot there remained the problem of purchase, scrounging or theft, particularly on a working party.

The temporary cessation of outside working parties coincided with the failure of medical supplies. Such a woeful shortage we had never known, as always for the treatment of ulcers there had been something or other in the way of drugs. Now, there was nothing. My own ulcers had broken out again and the outlook was bleak. There were only two methods of treatment, one being the application of salt appropriated from the rations, rendering stews even more tasteless, but the salt was of more use to ulcers than watering tongues and, until further limited drugs were available, filled the gap tolerably well.

Drugs would not have been quite as short had it not been for a remarkable theft that had taken place some time previously. In the sick bay, the MOs had jealously treasured a small supply of M&B tablets, invaluable under the conditions. Suddenly, without trace, they disappeared. Despite a thorough investigation, they were not officially discovered, although suspicion was directed to one person, a medical orderly, who subsequently lost his position. Thereafter, tablets could only be obtained on payment of fantastic sums of money and I think it can be hazarded that the reason for the culprit's inviolability was because the favoured few could still buy what was not now generally available to the rank and file. If so, this was a most shocking and disgraceful state of affairs but, then, as I have mentioned often, the encampment was never run fairly with regard to the common good, only largely for the welfare of the few. When once a large sum of canteen funds had been stolen, the culprits were energetically hounded down and punished. There was, on that occasion, nothing to be gained by sheltering the malefactors.

By now, we had been allowed the privilege of maintaining discipline within our own compound and, to this end, MPs were appointed. This innovation should have been to our advantage. In practice, however, and because of the most flagrant abuse of power, it had in the main, the opposite effect. One or two of the MPs were okay but some abused their position, were allowed to abuse it and became mixed up in the very money rackets that they were supposed to be suppressing.

Four or five men were chosen as MPs and their task was one of the most envied. To begin with, it entailed neither working parties nor manual work of any kind, the main job being to ensure that men, already made wretched slogging their guts out for the Japanese, should toe the line within the confines of the barbed wire. This task should have been carried out with tact and humanity, but because of lack of management control and the appointment of the wrong type of man, in several instances injustice resulted.

Regular MPs were chosen, men used to imposing the rigid discipline demanded of the army under normal conditions on fit men, trained for concerted action under enemy fire who, undisciplined, would only constitute a rabble. In this case, we were not being trained to fight human adversaries. We would never be able to fight again, but only have the energy to combat death, the arch enemy. For the most part, neither the MPs nor Sunderland or Southern seemed to realise this. In not appreciating the fact that men could no longer be reckoned as cogs in an unfeeling army machine, but rather as brothers in misfortune, they made a gigantic error. The truth was that we were missing the humanity of Lieutenant Colonel Russell. If we had to have disciplinary executives, then to my mind and in the first place, the term MP should have been replaced by such nomenclature as 'security guards' or such, and secondly, regular MPs should not have been chosen for this task, that is to say, men not usually renowned for welfare gifts, and certainly two of these decidedly were not such as this. Furthermore, those chosen should have had it impressed upon them that discipline must be tempered with understanding and humanity. As it was, from the rankers' conception, the opposite seemed to have been advocated. Little humanity was displayed, though a lot of brutality was practised. 'Better to reign in Heaven than serve in Hell,' was the popular dictum. Without doubt MPs let power run to their heads. They were curbed very little.

A small hut which was to serve as a detention barracks was constructed by the engineers. Its interior was more dreaded than the sick bay. Men knew that, at all costs, they must evade the clutches of the MPs, but it was too easy to slide into trouble and set in motion the machinery that steered the way to the detention barracks. Initially, a delinquent would, in true army style, and escorted by an NCO and two other men, be marched in front of Sergeant Major Sunderland. He might prove his innocence and be let off scot-free; he might be adjudged guilty of a minor offence and, under the surveillance of the MPs, be allotted only extra fatigues or, for major offences, be sentenced to a period of imprisonment within the detention barracks, ranging from two or three days to two weeks.

Some of our own MPs mentally destroyed fellow prisoners. Hard as the Japanese worked POWs, the yellow man's yoke was never so harsh as that of the MPs. Perhaps these tormentors, determined to prove their own white 'racial' superiority, took pride in working men as hard or harder than our captors. The hard work imposed by the Japanese was, on the limited rations available and under the pitiless rays of the tropical sun, so sapping a man's energy that many would eventually die. Few of those confined for long in the detention barracks survived the ordeal unscathed. These doubly imprisoned wretches were kept hard at it from six o'clock in the morning until nine or ten o'clock at night during hours of daylight, working furiously with a changkol about the compound, doubling to and fro and, at night times, polishing buckets with sand. They could not stand it and they did not.

It must be recorded, however, in all fairness, that one or two of the more humane MPs did at times ease up, even allowing their charges to stop altogether if out of sight, while others abated their efforts to kill not a jot.

It was sadism at its worse. These petty tyrants, having all day hounded men nearly out of their lives, graciously allowing their victims to slurp at some maggoty rice like starving dogs, had the temerity to draw extra rations with callous indifference. No wonder that they were amongst the fittest and most detested men in the compound, strapping fellows, not appreciating, in their own self-centredness, the poor stamina of the men entrusted to their care, or so it seemed to the ordinary hoi-polloi like myself.

I am not asserting that men were, without provocation, punished with a lengthy spell of confinement. They were not. Indeed, two or three of such culprits were among the worst antisocial types, real bad hats, capable of the greatest meanness, but they did not murder and they did not deserve the death sentence which, in effect, they received.

The worst case concerned the three men who stole from the ladies' compound. Clothed in nothing but loincloths, they broke camp by crawling under a culvert, crossed the patrol track bounding our compound and went over the wasteland at the bottom of Yamamoto's garden. It was then a comparatively easy task to break into the ladies' enclosure. There, they stole what they could lay their hands on and frightened the nuns by, allegedly, appearing before them in the nude. I doubt whether they actually did this. More likely the nuns, being inadvertently disturbed in their rest, were so frightened as not to notice the loincloths. What we understood as nude might be differently interpreted by these staid ladies. Anyhow, having stolen all there was to lay their hands on, the thieves crawled back to our compound with their booty, or that part of it that was left after they had eaten all they could manage.

They were caught and, it was rumoured, as a first step, severely beaten in the Japanese manner – so very uncivilised were we becoming. This was carried out by the strongest fellow in our compound and, incidentally, the biggest racketeer of the lot. Thereafter they were confined to the floor of the detention barracks. Even at the commencement of this double imprisonment they were sadly emaciated, below the average in physique and mentality, more objects of pity than animosity and spite. Never did men work harder under the heel of the MPs than they. One of them actually died before completing his sentence. Neither of the other two 'sailed down the river' again. They had sealed their own doom as surely as ever any convicted murderer in a totalitarian state. The nuns must have had no idea of the punishment meted out to these poor men.

We POWs did have less despicable contact with the ladies' compound. Some were detailed to grub out rubber tree stumps at the bottom of their garden, the wood party supplied their cookhouse; the benjo party cleared their latrines while parties of us were occasionally detailed to weed the track round their enclosure. Of all our contacts with the ladies' compound, however, the most pleasing occurred to a party of men under the gentle guard, Moray. To the wire he summoned a Mrs Swan whom he asked to sing for us. She possessed a beautiful soprano voice and this unexpected civilised entertainment left a lasting impression on the men.

A less praiseworthy contact with the ladies was made by an English sick orderly. His clandestine midnight rendezvous with a Dutch Eurasian resulted in the only confinement at Lintang Barracks. What befell the lady I do not know, but the culprit was severely punished by the Japanese, being shut up for two weeks in the their guard room where he was frequently beaten. Even officially, however, we contacted the ladies' compound far more often than any others, probably because the Japanese could see little danger in it.

The Japanese were always afraid of contact between the various enclosures, although they occasionally allowed, under guard, the civilian internees to meet their wives in the ladies' compound. Although we could risk conversation and even exchange of goods with the civilians through the wire which separated us, we rarely had an opportunity to exchange words with the small contingent of Indian troops quartered in a small hut opposite the sick bay. They were a most stalwart body of men, who, despite severe pressure from the Japanese, never wavered in their loyalty to the Crown. In the early days, it was said, they had been cruelly treated, but latterly they were given more consideration than we Britishers and never subjected to rigorous working parties, being mainly employed on various tasks near the camp. Always most patient in their demeanour, they were well disciplined, having their own officer quartered with them. Perhaps their greatest problem was to reconcile their different religions and customs, as Muslims and Hindus were placed together. I never really knew whether or not they refused the pork sent them by their captors.

The Japanese showed a certain religious toleration. Each Sunday they allowed us to hold religious services and, had the request been made, would perhaps have sanctioned other days too, provided there was no interference with work. Furthermore, they allowed a Church of England bishop (formerly resident in Kuching) entry to the compound to conduct the Sunday services. An altar was improvised between two of the huts and services were held there, although sparsely attended. Occasionally, Holy Communion would be celebrated. Camp-made wafers and wine, made from rice, were used. Later the bishop's visits were suspended, not I suspect without justice, on the grounds that he acted as a channel of information between the various compounds but we could, if we chose, still hold a service. The Roman Catholics within the compound were also allowed facilities for worship. The right of Christian burial was another Japanese concession. Services at the cemetery far outnumbered others.

It is said that cleanliness is next to godliness and, during this respite, we became more body conscious. Showers were taken perhaps twice a day, teeth were cleaned more often, faces shaved more frequently and haircuts studied. The easiest ablutional act was washing. Besides showers we had, within the compound a row of taps emptying over a washing bench. One of the few commodities other than food issued to us by the Japanese was soap and, coarse though it was, it was of inestimable benefit. With it, we not only kept our bodies clean, albeit a sparing usage as, apart from its limited supply, it was not too good for the skin, but rinsed our clothes out on the washing bench. Despite the great exertions, however, we could not prevent the spread of lice. Washing was not enough. Lice and nits, skulking in the seams of clothes, were untouched by the most thorough washing. The only way to keep reasonably clear of them was to work in nothing but a loincloth and to sleep without a stitch of clothing on, relying only on a blanket for warmth. At one time there was a typhus scare and Lieutenant Colonel King, quite rightly, ordered that any person whose clothes became infected with lice should have both them and his blanket disinfected in a rather primitive steam disinfestor which had been made by the engineers. The biggest drawback was the extra wear that this placed on the clothes and it was for this reason that the disinfestor was not very popular. For a while, however, sterling work was done and typhus never became an epidemic despite one or two suspected cases.

The lice, however, won in the end. With the resumption of

working parties, there was not the time to disinfest the clothes and less attention to cleanliness was paid. We could wear very little and regularly ran through our scanty wardrobe, killing all the visible lice and nits. It became a common sight to see a man picking at his shorts, ape-like, in search of lice. I cannot ever remember seeing the results of successful searches being eaten but, had I seen such a performance, I would scarcely have been surprised. Another good way of keeping lice infestation in check was to leave a garment untouched, hanging on a line out of doors for a couple of weeks, if a spare rag was available to wear in the meantime.

The cleaning of teeth, however, presented a major problem, so much so that many neglected the task. For my part, I tried to do what I could with an old toothbrush plastered with salt or charcoal. Others did the same. My friend Williams was the most meticulous of men with his appearance, spending at least an hour on Sundays, cleaning his teeth, trimming his moustache and shaving, this being our rest day. Shaving constituted an even greater problem than teeth cleaning, as razors were scarce and blades never issued. All that could be done was to retain old blades, sharpen them against the sides of a tumbler, of which in our compound there were few, and borrow a razor if without one. It was always a laborious, painful business. As a rule, I shaved once or twice a fortnight. Some managed to shave more frequently, others less. Many grew beards. The strangest sight of all though was to see a man with a long beard, yet in Japanese fashion, with a shaven head. I always thought of these men as 'moon' men. I don't know why!

When it came to haircuts, one could always sit for one, provided that the time was available. The Japanese allowed a couple of light duty men to act as barbers so that the difficulty was not so much finding a barber as finding the time to locate him, especially when Sundays also were decreed working days, during the second half of imprisonment. Of course, shaven heads entirely eliminated the danger of head lice. Perhaps, that is why the Japanese popularised the fashion. On the other hand perhaps their heads became so swollen that they were shorn as an alternative to the issue of bigger hats. I do not know!

It was a pity, however, that all parts of the body could not have been treated in such a manner as to have immunised us from skin infestations. Two of the greatest scourges of the camp were skin irritation and scabies. Largely due to malnutrition, the first of these afflictions sometimes affected practically the whole body, causing unbearable itching. It was not unknown for sleepless men in the middle of the night to stumble outside to seek relief by rolling, animal-like, on the rough surface of the ground, but more common for the sufferers to squat on the steps of their huts, picking away at themselves, oblivious of ought else. Once all the water pimples, which closely dotted the affected parts, had been burst, the irritation ceased. Apart from the active discomfort caused, such an affliction sapped the energy, contributing to the cause of many deaths.

Scabies was, under the circumstances, a particularly dirty disease. All parts of the body, but mostly hands and rump, were attacked. Lacking in medical supplies as we were, we often discovered that the eruption had turned septic. With only rags for covering, the awful mess can be well imagined. Eventually, the Japanese were persuaded to send a supply of sulphur into the compound. Thereupon, the engineers constructed a large concrete bath near the sick bay. Water, heated first at the cook-house and later over a fire nearer the bath, was passed by chain in buckets by the fittest patients from fire to bath until it was half full, the sulphur added and stirred well in. With this concoction ready, six patients at a time were able to enter the healing waters, there to soak at leisure and scrub their scabs. In May 1944, I underwent a course of four days' treatment, receiving surprising benefit from it, although I cannot describe the experience as being enjoyable, sitting up to my armpits in water floating with scabs, and an unpleasant odour never absent. When not undergoing a course of baths, sufferers scrubbed off their scabies' scabs under the various taps about the enclosure. I never really sustained a really bad attack myself although, early in 1945, I can remember once a day scrubbing the scabies scabs from the buttocks of Freddie Pafford, a task I found quite as unpleasant as scrubbing my own few pus-holding sores.

In the early months of 1944 dysentery rode again, causing great anxiety and claiming its fatal victims. Precautionary measures were redoubled and a general epidemic arrested.

Enough of disease: it is again necessary to revert to the subject of food yet, and if I mentioned victuals on every page, I could hardly be reproached on the score of exaggerating their importance. Food was the one subject of conversation interesting to all of us. It formed common ground for the bank clerk and the labourer, for the business executive and he who heaved coal. On working parties and Japanese fatigues, it was customary to help stifle the boredom and, where possible, discussing among ourselves various subjects of mutual interest. The range was extensive but always the subject eventually palled, unless it was that of food. Grub constituted the one enthralling subject: discussion on present rations, on what we had eaten in the past, on what we should eat in the future, on recipes and the like. Every man became a potential chef. When free, we were going to cook this and that and the other. Cooking would be a fascinating pastime. Even though we freely recognised that we were biased, nevertheless, we were certain that we should all become ardent cooks, even allowing for every contingency. I wonder how many of us did become so! Certainly, I have become a defaulter but then, equally with the rest, I would be guilty, no matter how interesting was some other subject of conversation, of returning to the food topic. No man who has been a POW would, I am sure, prescribe to the theory, as advanced by certain psychologists, that sex is the primary instinct. No! Self-preservation is, without a doubt. No one had time or energy for sex yet, soon after release, smutty jokes were the vogue.

Again, back to food. On 28 March 1944, a great event took place. A supply of Red Cross parcels, containing mostly food, arrived. On distribution, one parcel was shared between six men, a proportion being withheld for use at the cookhouse. It is impossible to describe the pleasure, let alone the benefit, that we received from these supplies. Each mouthful, were it corned beef, spam or tinned fruit, would be turned over on the tongue with greater relish than the world's greatest gourmet ever knew. As chances of receiving further parcels seemed very slim, most groups rationed themselves so that their extras lasted as long as possible. They were wise, for we received no further Red Cross comforts until the war was over. Besides the food, the supplies included a few pairs of American boots, but the only pairs which saw the inside of our enclosure were given to the three Americans among us. These men, on the strength of the goods having been supplied by the USA, also received a parcel of food each. In addition to the Red Cross supplies in May 1944, our first letters from home arrived. The pleasure we derived from them cannot be accurately assessed although, of course, they brought also spasms of pain. On the whole, however, the effect on morale was good.

Upon release, I dug up a tin which I had buried in which I had meticulously recorded (not without risk of 'kepala katong') scores of dates from the time of my capture. From the notes it was clear that in the spring of 1944, two or three hundred further prisoners of war, many of them ex-Singapore volunteers, arrived at Kuching. One hundred of them, with a like number of our original party, later left for Labuan. The others stayed with us permanently. How lucky they were, as the Labuan men fared no better than the previous contingent that had passed through the camp on the way to British North Borneo. The Japanese organised death marches towards the end of the war in northeast Borneo ensured that there were no survivors from two and a half thousand prisoners, save for six who miraculously escaped.

Another contemporaneous event was the increase in our pay. Was it to offset the rising cost of living? Certainly, the struggle to live at all was to be made more difficult for, on 16 July, we were placed on half rations. A wave of consternation swept the compound. To survive on the new rations would be impossible! We should all starve. Hardly had we began to readjust ourselves, however, that the inevitable outside working parties recommenced. It was an exciting day, especially as the Japanese agreed to increase the food again, somewhat, although the level of rations was never again to rise to what it had been.

Working with the 'Gorilla' at the Aerodrome

Not being detailed for the first day of resumed working parties, nevertheless I was, during the day, often in spirit with the workers. How had they fared? When at nightfall eventually they returned the reports were good. Apparently work had recommenced at the aerodrome, but it had not been at all onerous and the guards, exchanged for our camp guards at Batu Tiga, had been mostly of non-Japanese origin and pretty 'cushy' by comparison. I was, therefore, quite pleased to find myself among the party of about two hundred and fifty men who were, the following day, detailed for duty.

On arrival at Batu Tiga we had to wait quite a while before the train pulled in from Kuching. Our camp guards, being in a fairly easy frame of mind, perhaps because they would not set eyes on us again until the return to the station in the evening, allowed us to squat at the roadside despite the fact that we were still formed up in parties of fifty.

I was one of the last party farthest from the station entrance and I noticed that, after the stagnation of routine camp duties, a rather good-natured, lackadaisical atmosphere prevailed. Not even the chug-chug of the approaching train aroused much excitement although, when its smoke plumed into sight, a few men stirred lazily, struggling to their feet, as though there was all the time in the world. Indeed it seemed there was, as before we boarded the panting train, it lurched another hundred metres before allowing the Japanese guards to alight so that they could conveniently station themselves in order to see all parties bangoed by the Korean guards. Hardly had the train stuttered to a standstill, however, than I heard the POW sergeant in charge of the first party sharply call his men to attention. I peered down the ranks and an amazing spectacle met my eyes. Every man of the first two parties was frantically gripping his mess tin (or whatever odds and ends were carried) to scramble to attention in an obvious endeavour to form one of an orderly, well-disciplined double rank. Why this, I thought? Surely such commotion was unnecessary for easygoing non-Japanese guards! Such soldierly alacrity had never been displayed before.

Have you ever been present in the lazy good-natured atmosphere of a county cricket field when a popular batsman has, unbeknown to the majority, just completed, say, his thousandth run? A small section of the crowd, at some distance from you, appreciating the significance of the last scoring shot, commences to clap. The clapping is taken up quickly by the adjoining section of the crowd and so on, like a Mexican wave, so that racing towards you comes the beating of hands. Thus appeared the activity of men down the rank. It spread from number one party to number two party, from number two party to number three party and so eventually to our party, until I, too, at the tail end of it wonderingly (but knowing it to be wise) pulled myself off my haunches. Behind the movement came the hush and then the four syllables passed in bated breath from one man to another, the 'Gor-ill-a', the 'Gor-ill-a', ' the 'Gor-ill-a'. Dread lurked in the faces of my companions, while the knees of one of my friends were actually quaking. Can he be as terrible as all that, I thought? Even the Korean guards were obviously ill at ease.

Having never seen the gentleman before, I was itching with expectancy, later to wish I had never set eyes on him. In a moment, I was to see a man scarcely more than thirty years old, of medium height, sturdily built with a bluff handsomeness, less Oriental than normal. He looked brusquely efficient. He was. Never were two hundred and fifty men more quickly bangoed and despatched to the trucks. Never did men more quickly haul themselves up the sides of the trucks, each fearing to be last. The 'Gorilla' and his three or four Japanese (not native) henchmen strode towards the first of the carriages, the only closed one at the front of the train, taking little notice of us. Few men spoke during the five-mile journey. Those who did made only low utterances as to what to expect on arrival. I still remained expectant.

Nobody fussed on arrival at the aerodrome. A quick, efficient bango and we were hurried off towards the flying field, eventually being halted at its extremity, opposite where we had first spent our so-called working hours. Obviously, an attempt was being made to lengthen the runway, using the inevitable method of changko-ling away earth from a high point, basketing it to skips, pushing them to where the ground fell away, emptying, levelling the soil and ramming it to the right level. To assist in our efforts, those of us working at the high level (of which I was one) were also supplied with pickaxes, the ground there being very hard.

There was no need to be told to work hard, without rest, when the 'Gorilla' was around. Everybody took such a requirement for granted. Hardly a word was spoken, as men worked as though their lives depended upon their exertions. Frankly, I did not see the exigency of this, but kept up with the rest though without panic. Indeed, there seemed to be no particular need to worry. True, the Japanese guards stationed at strategic points were obviously vigilant but of the 'Gorilla' save for occasional brief visits, I saw little as he was mainly supervising the tipping of the trucks. Not once did he start trouble, there was no shouting, no PT, no bashings. Punctually, we stopped worked for lunch. Nearly two hours were allowed. Rations were brought in a lorry and dished out in orderly fashion. We ate under three or four nearby shelters, one of which was reserved for the Japanese. The 'Gorilla' never once interfered in our shelters and not a man could grumble.

The afternoon dragged by in much the same way as the morning, and we re-boarded the train, cheerfully. Conversation on the return journey was breezy and hopeful. Perhaps HE had changed? Perhaps HE had been ordered by Suga to be more humane? Perhaps the urgency of the aerodrome work was not such as to merit Lekas Corner treatment? With the reasons still undecided, we were marched away from Batu Tiga by Korean guards in as good a humour as twelve hours earlier. We enjoyed the meal that night. We enjoyed gossiping about the change in the 'Gorilla' and we enjoyed ourselves. Moreover, I was pleased to find myself detailed for the aerodrome the next day. At the recommencement of working parties we were to be required only two days out of three.

We were soon to be disillusioned. The 'Gorilla' had been feeling his way. We were at the beginning of another Lekas

Corner, which mercifully, however, did not last many weeks. After two or three days, this monster began to bare his fangs. The tempo of the work increased. Once more, fear reigned supreme. The 'Gorilla' was to exact from us the last ounce of strength. Bashings became as frequent as cups of tea passed around at ladies' meetings on thirsty days. We learnt that we dare not pause long enough to wipe the sweat from our brows. If the 'Gorilla' spotted this indulgence, it was a bashing for certain. He argued that such a movement of the arm was wasteful, as it entailed one less blow of the pickaxe or changkol. He boasted the quickest eyes in the whole of Borneo. With his back to a squad of men, he would suddenly whip around to spot a malingerer, even though the culprit had been peering at the 'Gorilla' intently from the corner of his eye in readiness to increase his efforts the moment the guard commander turned. There seemed to be no interval between the moment the hated head began to move and the detection of any slacking.

We learnt that it was unwise to wear any untoward garment that caught the eye. A hat with a red band, a white neckerchief or a colourful loincloth would attract his gaze as a bull is furiously attracted to a red duster. In fact, he might have been more aptly called a bull than a gorilla, as he was neither simian in feature nor action, but fearless, fierce and at times as rageful as a maddened ox. He was also devilishly cunning. On more than one occasion, he strode past a line of working men to pick out two or three whose backs were greased with less sweat than those of their fellows. These, too, could not be expending the maximum energy. There was no trial, no inquiry, just a rapid punishment. It is a fact that we could work at times furiously under the tropical sky without visibly sweating. The blood had thinned, the moisture had already departed from our tired bodies; the humidity and sun were less exacting than usual. I learnt to ensure perspiration by drinking more liquid, but it was not easy to outwit the 'Gorilla'.

He packed a very hefty wallop, sometimes insisting on a man holding his arms raised in a knees bend position, a changkol or pickaxe above his head for unbearably long periods, yet he obviously believed in more violent forms of punishment. The chosen victim would be yanked out of line, growled at and then swung at with both hands until felled by the force of the blows. To pretend unconsciousness was inviting near-annihilation. If at all possible, the unfortunate must spring to his feet immediately, only to be knocked down again. The 'Gorilla' had a demoniac gift for knowing just how much a man could take, so that usually the victim was left dazed but not quite senseless.

At times, a whole party of fifty was made to suffer. Lined up facing each other in pairs, each pair had to swap blows until ordered to desist. Blows to the face were administered in turn, first with one hand and then the other. We attempted to hold back our punches and ride the blows. It was no good. The 'Gorilla' always knew if the punishment was not being meted out with true Nippon ferocity. To suspect leniency was the signal for him or his guards to step in to deputise, and as hard as we might hit they would always strike much harder. Many a man, however, fell senseless under his partner's despairing blows. Personally, what I disliked as much as the physical pain was the awful indignity and humiliation of this mass punishment.

One particular incident I shall always remember. Another prisoner and myself were accused of slackness by the 'Gorilla'. I admit that I had been attempting to 'swing the lead' not for the first time (nor for the last) and could, under the circumstances hardly grumble when the 'Gorilla', after initiating the punishment, forced us to face each other, rhythmically to commence the usual slugging contest. We both knew that it was but a minute or so to 'tiffin', as the rice bins were already being unloaded and, as the 'Gorilla' had wandered off a little, we started to hold back our punches. Therefore, before either of us was hurt, yasumé was called. Tacitly, we congratulated ourselves on our good fortune. Alas! The 'Gorilla' approached, eyed us with suspicious derision, bashed both of us unmercifully and ordered us to continue our exercises, while the others lunched. He retired to his shelter one hundred metres away, yet neither I nor my companion dared to ease up for we were certain that his eyes were riveted upon us. After a short period, I realised that, although I myself was still quite strong, my comrade was becoming weaker and dazed. His blows now had little force, albeit delivered with effort and at last, gradually, I found the courage to let up my exertions. Yet, for both our sakes, I knew that to ease up too much would court disaster. My comrade began to sway. I knew that I was knocking him out. It was a strange sensation. Putting a man out in a fight is one thing, but knocking out a companion in cold blood is another. Yet what could I do? At last I realised that, come what may, I must hold back no more punches, but rather strengthen my blows in an attempt to administer the *coup de grace* as soon as possible, thus shortening the agony. I struck hard again, and down went my human punchbag. He was out. I looked at him sympathetically, yet felt even more sorry for myself as the 'Gorilla' came bounding up, yelling 'Bagairo' (Japanese swear word). Now it was my turn to be bashed into unconsciousness! However, he stepped first to the fallen man, peered at him intently, satisfied himself it was no sham, then gruffly, but not without pleasure, I thought, ordered me to my lunch. I am glad to say that, after a medical orderly was called, the unconscious man soon came round.

After a few weeks spent lengthening the runway, we were moved near the control tower. However, two incidents merit reporting before sweating once more with changkol and basket: the first, especially in the light of future happenings, was interesting, the second was of remarkable brutality.

Towards the close of one day's work, aeroplane after aeroplane – fighters and bombers – touched down on the aerodrome until almost a hundred littered the field. An ominous sign, I thought. If the Japanese could muster such numbers on an unimportant aerodrome, what must their total strength be? In our position, such a display of air power filled us with anything but cheerfulness. Even the inveterate optimists held their tongues. The planes were gone by the next day, however, and never again did such large numbers appear, although for a time a few used the runway. Within six months, allied planes were to cross the Kuching skies. Then the enemy could only make airborne two or three 'self-respecting' planes to offer a token resistance. In retrospect, it seems obvious that the hundred Japanese planes used the aerodrome merely as an emergency rendezvous, having probably just been forced to evacuate stations further south.

Billeted at one side of the aerodrome were fifty prisoners of war who had been at Kuching before our arrival and who did not join the main contingent until two or three months later. Until then, they never worked with us, but acted as a general fatigue party attached to the air station. Their washing facilities consisted of a pond alongside the railway about one hundred metres from where we caught the train to Batu Tiga. It had been a comparatively quiet day, and we were, under the surveillance of the 'Gorilla' and his guards, squatting near the track which led between the prisoners' billets and the gap in the fence alongside the line from where we gained access to the rails and through which the aerodrome party passed on their way to and from their bath. About ten men were at the bath and, when cleansed in ones and twos, they turned towards their billets. We saw the 'Gorilla' motion and grin wickedly at his henchmen. There was devilry afoot and, as the first cleansed man appeared through the gap, we held our breath. Just as the man came alongside our party, the 'Gorilla' stepped forward and without warning knocked him to the ground, kicked him and then forced him to bow respectfully.

We had by now become accustomed to bowing to all Japanese, whether they were officers or not, but apparently discipline was slack on the aerodrome. The 'Gorilla' would change all that. He would teach them. He hustled off the badly shaken man before the next victim arrived upon the scene. Again, there was no bow and the 'Gorilla' repeated his brutality. It was obvious that our guard commander was enjoying himself immensely. He was in high good humour, springing upon each helpless man, knocking him down and bustling him off again before the next returning bather realised what had befallen his mate! Only the last two or three of the bathing party had, from the pond, seen enough to realise that to bow would probably mean the escape of punishment. Altogether, it was one of the most cool, brutal attacks of all that I saw or heard of at Kuching. Doubtless the 'Gorilla' staged the exhibition as much to bolster up his own ego as to impress his fellow guards and prisoners with his power. Smike could not have been more in terror of Squeers than as we were of the 'Gorilla'.

We were not to see much more of the 'Gorilla', although his successor, nicknamed Rastus, during his short spell of command, was thought by some to be as dangerous. Personally, I do not think that he could compare in brutality with his better known compatriot. Before we meet that gentleman, let me recount one more incident concerning personal contact with the famous 'Gorilla'.

After being transferred from the far extremity of the runway we were set to work once more with the familiar tools – pickaxe, changkol and rattan basket – at one side of the main entrance to the aerodrome, hacking away at a high embankment, the spoil being whisked away as usual in skips. Despite the efforts of a couple of Japanese in loosening the rock encountered with dynamite, the work was as arduous and boring as before. One day, however, the worst of the 'Gorilla's's stooges was standing just behind me and decided to make life a little more exciting by insisting that I should work closer to my neighbour, a sergeant friend to the left of me. We both wielded pickaxes and the danger of working too close to each other was obvious. For a while, I endeavoured to disobey the guard's instructions but a blow in the legs with a rifle butt advised me in which direction lay the greatest danger. It was not long before the accident that I had anticipated happened.

As I started to lift my pickaxe, I administered a glancing blow to the head of my sergeant friend who was simultaneously directing his tool downwards. He fell, momentarily stunned. As he began to come to his senses, a sick orderly was called who assisted the victim to a tent nearby where the 'Gorilla' was relaxing. Meanwhile, I continued my labours in an attempt to put the incident out of my mind, only to be summoned to the 'Gorilla' five minutes later.

'*Bagairo*! What happened?' he asked me.

I tried to explain the circumstances, but no excuse ever satisfied the 'Gorilla'. He gave three successive blows to my head and down I went. On scrambling to my feet, I expected further blows but the 'Gorilla' was otherwise engaged. He was attending to the recumbent form of the wounded sergeant, who bravely endured the blows without a murmur, not administering medical treatment (that had been done by the medical orderly), but kicking him in the groin. Poor though my mastery of the mixture of Japanese, Malay and English was, I knew it to be obvious that he was telling the unfortunate sergeant that if I had been punished for my clumsiness, he was being punished for getting in the way. What can you make of such a brute?

Rastus worked us no less hard. Violent at times though he was, he lacked the emotionless brutality of the incomparable 'Gorilla'. I never found that he was to be feared. He was less cunning. With Rastus in charge, I discovered that I could quite easily pretend to be exerting every ounce of strength while, in fact, I was merely waving my changkol or pickaxe at the basket. Regardless of any effective result, I was conserving calories. Neither did Rastus possess the 'Gorilla's' uncanny ability to glance quickly over his shoulder to spot a man who had been 'going slow'. I appreciated Rastus, in fact, and could never understand the fellow who still worked unceasingly at top speed whether eyes were or were not turned upon him. Such men were signing their own death warrants, but then I had never been subjected to the torture of Lekas Corner.

Opposite the embankment grew some ubi-kayu and, with Rastus in charge, I dared to wander over to this on the pretext of changing a changkol or pickaxe from a supply laid out on the ground nearby. On several occasions I managed to pull up, undetected, some of the half-grown roots, to park them nearby my pack in which I could secrete them at the end of the day. The roots contained calories. I was never caught, although more by luck than judgement. Others managed similar feats, but I wonder how many of us would have dared to do so with the 'Gorilla'.

Nearby was a Japanese cookhouse. Every day, two men under the general supervision of the sick orderly, Sergeant Connolly, were detailed to help with the chores. On one or two occasions, I managed to scrounge myself on to this party and never failed to reap reward, the theft of sweet potatoes, fruit or coconut oil. No wonder Sergeant Connolly was becoming quite fat! Once I remember watching a Japanese cook turning out the thinnest and lightest omelette that I ever saw from a large built-in cooking pan, in which he had wiped a thin smear of fat. Egon Ronay would have been proud of him.

There were other ways of obtaining extra food, but under what can only be termed as deplorable circumstances. The train now took us right to the entrance road of the aerodrome about which was a native kampong. Near the terminus fermented a garbage pit to which each morning, immediately after the train had stopped, half a dozen POWs would wildly stampede in the hope of scavenging something edible, like starving dogs. In the main it was partly rotted fruit discarded by the natives. It was a disgusting and degrading sight, never stopped by the Japanese, as why should they mind if we so-called superior whites demeaned ourselves to such an extent in the eyes of the natives! Yet, this was another example of the lack of control exercised by our senior NCOs. Such acts of humiliation and shame should, under pain of reduced rations or something of the sort, have been forbidden, but they were not. No! Day after day, self-respecting prisoners must watch this pitiful sight, note the surprise of the natives and the mixed satisfaction and disgust of the Japanese. It was, I am glad to record, always the same few who sank to the level of the native dogs and, strangely enough, not always those to be expected. True, there were, among the garbage fiends, the usual two or three gormless and somewhat naïve prisoners, but there were also an equal number of well-educated men who had been the revered rubber and coconut plantation bosses, the Malaysian equivalent of the Colonial Indian pukka sahibs. How easily, under such circumstances, can men sink to the level of beasts.

Equally degrading was the practice of squatting, dog-like, around the Japanese while they ate their midday meal. Often our guards did not want all their rations and were seemingly generous enough to pass their leftovers to nearby POWs. Actually, they must have derived a terrific kick from watching the envious appealing eyes of those few who sat around waiting for the scraps from their masters' tables. Members of this small, shameless band were rarely disappointed, although often the guards, having eaten their fill, kept their human whelps, with mouths slobbering, in agonies of suspense. They placed their Japanese dixies lidless on the floor nearby them, almost under the noses of their watchers, teasing and enticing but seeming to disregard the hungry mouths until, near the end of the tiffin hour, they beckoned their dogs to approach, at last to empty the contents of their own dixies into the empty British ones proffered them.

Most disgusting of all was the rush for the durian nuts. Of all the fruit in the world, the durian is surely one of the most delicious. Growing on high trees, about the size of a melon, it contains within its tough prickly exterior, kernels the size of chestnuts, surrounded by a soft, sticky, whitish substance. It is this latter substance that possesses the truly wonderful but indescribable taste, approaching nearest to a concoction of banana and sweetened condensed milk with a haunting flavour that might be onions but which is not. The drawback of durian is its smell, not only existing in the fruit but residual – stronger by far than pickled onions – so that Europeans never eat them normally, except when out of contact with their countrymen or at special durian parties. The natives believe them to harbour aphrodisiac properties. Perhaps that is why the Japanese ate them, though women, apart from regular prostitutes, must have been difficult to come by despite the occasional visit to Kuching of Geisha girls. However, they enjoyed the fruit. Having sucked away the sticky flesh, they spat out the nuts. Thereupon a few men, mainly the garbage fiends, would scramble for them. Sometimes they even transferred the nuts straight to their own mouths so that those who still appreciated self-respect were made well-nigh sick; always the nuts were, for ultimate consumption, later baked over a fire. It is painful to record such un-English acts, but I desire not merely to portray the heroism of camp life which, as can be seen from the text taken as a whole, always glimmered through the miasma of meanness, but the sordid side of POW life, omitted from so many POW books. Hardship of the type we sometimes endured brings out not so much the best, but the worst, in man. In retrospect, however, I realise that surface dross often hid the inner sterling.

Although such acts of indignity were indicative of the great suffering that the prisoners endured, nevertheless, they were beyond the pale. Nothing but dire starvation should have justified them. Many of us were not over-squeamish or scrupulous, rarely drawing the line at petty theft, bargaining with our captors for articles that we had to sell or even soft-soaping a Japanese for ulterior motives, but sinking to the level of dogs? Well, it was not an option for the great majority.

The Japanese were usually keen to conclude a business deal.

They would buy watches, rings, fountain pens and similar valuables, and many who had until then hung on to these articles, for want of nourishment, at last threw their sentimental prejudices to the winds and sold. Those on working parties wanting to sell did their own bargaining; those in camp appointed an agent on the understanding that the latter should receive a percentage on sales or, say anything over and above a reasonable sum asked for by his client. Prices, however, were fairly stable, so many dollars, say eighty for a fourteen carat gold ring and so on. The Japanese did not like paying cash and hit on the expedient of paying out in books or as part payment. Printed on rice paper, these were, in the absence of anything else, ideal for rolling the coarse native tobacco. As a cigarette paper cost a cent and, say, twenty of them could be cut from a single page of print, a book of two hundred pages (a hundred leaves) would be worth twenty dollars, a fantastic sum. Small keepsake flimsy-sheeted Bibles were almost priceless.

To be fair, the Japanese were, as a rule, pretty honest in their dealings, more honest than some of their captives. For instance, it was not unknown for an agent to swear that a Japanese had requisitioned an article during the bargaining process, without payment, when in actual fact a fair price had been reached and the money paid over. Others would assert that they had received less than they had. Matters came to such a pass, indeed, that a man could not unquestionably trust his best friend, yea, not even himself! The eighth commandment had long been out of fashion, in so far as the Japanese or even the natives were the victims and it was but a short step to steal from friends. A lot of this was done.

Because of the prolonged, brutal, inhuman treatment imposed by our captors, to some extent or other, ninety per cent of the compound (including myself) practised deceit or petty theft, not always excepting one's comrades as victims. The relatively decent man, if I may use this term, only deceived and stole to a conventional degree, only practising selfishness to a point. To steal or to deceive or to indulge in selfishness is a sin, no matter what the degree, and as we became deliberately and knowingly more selfish, it did sometimes occur to me that, under the circumstances, complete selfishness was not a fault. The man who went so far usually drew an imaginary and arbitrary line between what was fair cheating and what was not although we are told that we cannot serve two masters. Either you are on God's side of the fence or the devil's. Nevertheless, if thievery was, therefore, under the prevailing conditions admissible in moderation, albeit contrary to the eighth commandment, then were not those of us, given all the extenuating circumstances, who did not let conscience or hypocritical pride hinder some infringement of the eighth commandment, more virtuous than those who wandered further into the devil's territory, but no so far as altogether to lose sight of the glimmer of heaven? Such it might be argued.

On the other hand, it might be held that man's primary duty under those conditions was self-preservation, not only just for one's personal gain, but also for the sake of loved ones at home. If a man stole and cheated for his own ends, then the chances of being in the flesh reunited with his loved ones were greater. Maybe the end justified the means. Perhaps the truth, as often it did, lay along the middle road. Provided that the prisoner stole and cheated only to an extent that benefited himself and his loved ones more than it harmed his comrades and their loved ones, then his breaking of the strict code or morals did not damn him. However, the genuine saints, like many valiant colleagues, did not barter, steal or scheme for personal advantage but allowed fate to take them willy-nilly along, like surf on an incoming tide. They died unmourned, but unstigmatised by selfishness.

One of the greatest blows dealt to my own preservation took the form of a terrific downpour of rain. It was the end of the afternoon's work and was first noticed as a black cloud that had gathered above the hills whose summits etched the sky a few miles from the aerodrome. Suddenly, the whole cloud mass commenced to race at a tremendous speed towards us, as though to obliterate not only us but every inanimate object also. With such force and malevolence did this huge, hell-born monster bear down upon us that its very appearance was frightening. When still two miles away, the rain could be heard as though there approached all the devils of hell. I dreaded the impact. Once overhead, however, the terror dissipated in the heaviest downpour of rain that I have ever experienced. Within a few minutes the landing ground was rendered unusable, literally covered with a sheet of water. I had experienced many thunderstorms, most of which sprang up late in the afternoon and, because of their frequency, I had invested in an army groundsheet. This, in its worn condition, was absolutely as incapable of keeping out the pelting rain as a house made of matchboxes could have withstood the charge of a bull. Before we reached the train, I was soaked to the skin. The full force of the storm was fortunately soon over but, as we cowered against the sides of the open trucks, it rained heavily all the way to Batu Tiga. However, by the time we had reached the camp the rain had ceased. When we had managed to drag ourselves to our billets and commenced to towel ourselves down with odd pieces of material, I for one found that my teeth were chattering. I had heard of this phenomenon, but hardly credited the fact that such an involuntary action could not be halted by exercising self-control. Yet, despite the greatest effort on my part, it was quite some time before I could stop my teeth from chattering. It was a nasty experience and weakened my resistance.

Fortunately, we rarely got really wet and cold. As a rule, the Japanese would allow us to knock off work and seek what shelter was available when the rain fell heavily. I suspect this practice was less for reasons of humanity than a realisation that a heavy downpour made working conditions almost impossible. In any case, they doubtless disliked standing guard in the rain.

Occasionally, too, our departure from camp was delayed because of a heavy downpour during the early morning. Once we were confined to our billets for a whole day, for it rained incessantly. In twenty-four hours, it was said that ten inches of rain fell, a terrific downpour for Sarawak, despite the fact that yearly rainfall averaged something over one hundred and fifty inches. The absorbent nature of the soil and the deep ditches prevented serious flooding. Moreover, the attap roofs of the huts stood up surprisingly well and, the huts being raised on piers, no appreciable amount of water penetrated our quarters.

Soon after the downpour that flooded the aerodrome, and because the task of removing part of the embankment opposite the Japanese cookhouse was nearing completion, men were being detached from the main party for work elsewhere about the aerodrome. As the increasing toil had once more taken its toll of health, all fit men, without regular camp duties to perform, were called upon every day for work at the aerodrome. A change of work, therefore, was the only rest, but there was little attraction about working at the nearby quarry. Each day, several men were now detailed to manhandle large stones dynamited from the quarry face at the back of the aerodrome. To lift these stones into the waiting skips was a hard and boring task. Sometimes at least, we worked faster than the Japanese dynamiters and could rest between explosions. Truck pushing, too, was a diversion. We took it in turns to push these vehicles to the stone-crushing plant. To urge them up the slope leading to the platform from where they were offloaded into the machine was hard work, but it was fun to stand on the back of the skips as they careered at speed, swaying down the ramp on the return journey, thus nostalgically remind-ing us of fairground dodgems.

Small parties were also formed to extend and improve aircraft dispersal points. Away from the main party, discipline was usually slacker and occasions to buy arose once more, although the opportunity was paltry compared with what was to come. This was to be the most exciting and rewarding period for the enter-prising. Other parties were engaged in excavating gun sites and air-raid shelters, a very healthy sign. A fellow from one of these parties was knocked out with a hammer by a near maniac of a guard. This incident constituted one of the few cases at Kuching when really dangerous brutality was practised, although at the time we wondered whether a new wave of terror was about to begin under the auspices of Kempei Tai but, before the isolated nature of this incident became apparent, I was transferred to a special party during the first two or three months of 1945. Thus, for me, began my best spell of imprisonment at Kuching.

To maintain some sort of chronological order, I first ought to make mention of other special parties that were formed, not only during the period between duty at the boat building yards and the second aerodrome parties, but simultaneously with our second dose of slavery there.

Here and There

Of all the miscellaneous Japanese working parties, perhaps the most exciting were the half dozen organised to unload ships at the godowns in Kuching itself. In the first place, it was stimulating to be driven through civilisation, although Oriental. The journey from Lintang Barracks entailed travelling along part of the main road from the aerodrome, past the golf course, past the turning off to Satan's HQ, past the swimming baths and the museum, past Kuching Cathedral, past the native shops and so to the river. Opposite the godowns, across the river, reposed, white against a background of peaceful green, the ex-white Rajah's palace, peering at us with benign indifference as if, boastful of its own seemingly timeless surroundings, it wished nothing more than to remain aloof from our sad predicament and impermanence.

Once at the godowns, there was little time for fantasy. We were there to work and the Japanese were present to ensure it. Nobody, in fact, except for the Japanese, stood idle. Besides POW labour, native labour was available. We were the less valuable asset, as the native stevedores were tremendously active, performing almost unbelievable feats of strength. Used to carrying heavy loads from adolescence, their shoulder and leg muscles were extraordinarily developed. I once saw one native shoulder three large sacks of rice; yet another native was remarkable for his height, at least seven feet; a third man was an albino. I wonder what stories this oddity could have told of Japanese questioning!

The natives usually unloaded one end of a ship and we the other, so that there was at times little chance of contact, although those POWs shifting goods from the quay to the warehouse as distinct from those in one of the ship's holds, continually passed the Kuching stevedores, but there was no cover. Cargoes varied, but most frequently consisted of rice, with sugar and salt being the chief alternatives. All three commodities were packed in bags so that the job of those in the hold was to load the bags into the sling attached to a crane. When the crane had dropped its load, other prisoners on the quayside dragged forth the bags to carry or push them in trucks to the warehouse and so on, until the ship was unloaded.

It was hard work but not, except when it came to the salt, unduly unpleasant. Many of the bags, whether they contained rice, sugar or salt, were broken, so that their contents were spilled throughout the hold. In the case of the rice and the sugar, we were not in the least worried, but the third commodity struck terror in our hearts. Troubled with uncovered or but poorly covered sores as we were, we discovered that the salt, creeping into the wounds, caused agonisingly sharp pains. Although doubtless it exercised on the sores a cleaning and healing effect, those who suffered failed to appreciate that fact.

Of course, salt, like rice and sugar had its advantages, one being that it could be consumed but it was the least favoured of the three commodities. Sugar took pride of place. While actually at work, we were allowed to eat sugar to an almost unlimited degree. Huge quantities were consumed with gusto. Doubtless a little was both stimulating and valuable, but few could exercise self-control so that severe sickness and diarrhoea often resulted. Rice and salt could also, if required, be eaten with freedom but the prospect was without attraction.

The big snag was not being allowed to take either commodity away although few were the prisoners who, at one time or another, did not disobey this injunction despite the risks. Almost invariably, there was a search when leaving the docks and often another less thorough search when returning to camp. Many ruses were adopted to escape the vigilance of the guards; stolen liquid in a water bottle, small packages secreted under the armpit, under a cap or under one's loin cloth, to mention but a few of the ruses practised. Again, one of the disadvantages of salt, was its irritation to sweat rash and other skin diseases. Of course, the Japanese eventually discovered these somewhat personal hiding places; even the water bottle ruse was rumbled in time. To escape detection, therefore, prisoners had to be content with hiding only a little in those ways. Booty piled under an upturned mug in a pack was (as mentioned before) another ruse often successfully adopted, although all packs had to be opened up.

A few men ingeniously provided false bottoms to their packs: a kati of food might be carried in this way. To be really ambitious, however, a man must get back to camp a whole pack of rice. I managed to do this on a few occasions, as did others. The best method was to fill a pack with rice and secrete it, before we had finished work, near the exit from the docks. To be searched, we were lined up and bangoed, prior to leaving the quayside. The Japanese passed down the ranks, investigating each man individually. Not everyone boasted a pack, so its absence, provided that eating utensils were on view, would not excite suspicion. The search over, the pack had to be surreptitiously snatched up on the way out. Other men, on the approach of the searcher, passed their pack to an accomplice in another rank, a risky operation as the guards often separated the files by a couple of metres. By whatever method the full pack was smuggled from the docks, the next prayer was that no search would be carried out at the entrance to the camp. If we were examined, then we would once more hope to pass a pack to a man already searched, or to entice the guard's suspicion to the armpits, for instance, while the pack lay hidden behind a pair of apprehensive legs.

Despite our ingenuity, we were often caught with the 'blag' and severely beaten but, although less risks were taken, the practice never ceased altogether and, doubtless, those who obtained extra food illegally increased their chances of survival. Besides rice, salt and sugar, we managed, at various times, to steal tapioca powder, soap and even dried fish. Much else was out of the question, for imports appeared to be restricted to bare necessities.

The natives were also short of food. I once witnessed quite a rush to sweep up some grains of rice that had fallen on to the highway running parallel to the godowns from a split bag as it was jolted at the back of a lorry. We were able to turn this shortage on the part of the natives to our own advantage. As I have already mentioned, we could hardly eat large quantities of rice in its raw state during the working day, but if we could get it to the natives we might receive in return items of food that could be eaten there and then. We soon discovered the way to do this for at the back of the warehouses, into which we stacked the bags or rice, were one or two small openings. Through these we managed to pass small quantities of rice, receiving in return fried bananas, fried sweet potatoes, goola balls and the like. I cannot remember anyone being caught red-handed at this.

One of the biggest disadvantages with dock parties was that it entailed Sunday working. This I resented so much that I decided to rest on the job. Tiffin was taken near the main entrance to the godowns where there was a shed, half of which was taken up as a timber store. Planks of wood were packed right up to the roof couples and I discovered that I could, undetected by the Japanese, lie on top of them. The idea of doing this while the Japanese thought that I was working attracted me immensely. Why not, therefore, take my Sunday rest as usual? Thus I ate my lunch in the wood shed and lay down afterwards on top of the wood pile so that, when work resumed, I stayed hidden. I think that some of my happiest moments as a POW were spent thus, dreaming of the past, of one day sailing down the river to the sea, and of the future, not to mentioned the satisfaction of outwitting the Japanese. It was fun, too, after an hour or two of rest, to creep out like a schoolboy who had played truant. I was never caught emerging and had little fear of it. The biggest risk seemed that I would fall asleep on the wood pile to be still there while being 'bangoed' at the end of the day. Perhaps it was these escapades of mine which led to my nickname, 'Dodger'. Perhaps I was wrong in all this; perhaps I should not have slacked while my comrades slaved. Yet why not? Of all the working parties, the docks were the most envied and, once work was finished there, back it was to the aerodrome or to whatever other work was in hand. Anyhow, were we not concerned solely with our own welfare? No one would worry if I received a bashing for stealing while others' packs remained undetected, so why should I worry about others? Thus, many of us, when we could, generally chose the easier tasks while vindicating our somewhat ruthless selfishness.

At the dockside the hardest job was, immediately prior to a ship's departure, shovelling coal into the hold. The Japanese seemed to abhor slacking on this task more than thus offending on the ship. As the coal could not be eaten, shovelling it provided few charms. Besides, this exercise usually heralded the cessation of another spell at the godowns and back to dreary routine.

Not only one of the first forms of alternative drudgery, but also one of the hardest, was the wood party, which was, for some weeks, sent to the jungle a couple of miles on the other side of the fourth station, Batu Ampat, out of Kuching. About fifty men, in addition to the usual aerodrome party, were required each day for this work. Despite the fact that volunteers came forward for permanent duty on this party, the majority had to be detailed especially for it, and it was with dread that most prisoners listened each morning to the duty list being read out by the CSM or his deputy. The one thing in the party's favour was that it was less boring than the aerodrome party, but to detail men haphazardly for this work was another example of the lack of thought and humanity exercised by the staff. Though the pace set at these parties was nowhere near as fast as on the aerodrome, yet the nature of the work required more than average strength. On being detailed for this party, I quickly realised that all the volunteers were comparatively strong men.

Besides there being a shortage of firewood in the camp at this time, the Japanese wished to erect some additional fences. So, immediately on arrival at the site, we were hurried into the jungle to fell saplings and small trees suitable for posts. An axe was perhaps shared between six men, and when the selected tree had been felled we had to lop off all the branches and carry the trunk to the side of the track some distance away, a task which was by no means simple, as we had to negotiate the rough scrubland in bare feet or thin Japanese-issue rubber galoshes made from crude rubber. For the volunteers, I noticed that this task compared pretty favourably with the work at the aerodrome, for they knew where to find the best trees and had accustomed themselves to their tools. Above all else, they were strong and well-shod. For the ill-shod, the task of struggling with the trunk over the rough ground for marshalling the cut timber on to the track was a most painful one. The worst part of the day had yet to come, the four miles of carrying the logs back to camp. Economy was the rule: if a smallish tree trunk, then only one man must carry it; if determined medium in size, then two men; if large, then perhaps four men. The Japanese, and who could blame them in view of our own officers' neglect, failed to appreciate the difference in the strength and staying powers of men of varying sorts and sizes. Two strong men, they calculated, ought to be able to carry such and such a tree for four miles. Well then, what two poor devils could carry, two more could. Thus, therefore, to the fit volunteers, the journey home meant only a hard pull after a moderate day's work. To the weak, it meant an hour and a half of mental and physical agony.

I was stronger than some, though by no means as muscular as the volunteers and some others, and never did one of these trips without feeling at one time or another that I could not go another step. Between halts, we rested on the road or trackside about every mile, but I always managed to keep going. Others were less fortunate. Now and then a man would collapse, quite unable, without an extra rest, to go any further. Sometimes he was allowed a breather, either by sufferance of the Japanese or because the lines of struggling men had become so strung out that the dropping of his load went unnoticed; at other times he was allowed no respite, but brutally punished and forced to resume his march until again he collapsed, sometimes becoming so utterly incapable of further work that at last the Japanese were forced to realise that, even under pain of death, no more work could be exacted from him. The worst episode that I saw was when six men decided to shoulder a particularly large trunk. Such a large gang to one tree enraged the Japanese and, although even at the first instance the men had with the greatest difficulty raised the tree to their shoulders, two of them were made to drop out to find another trunk, while the four struggled on alone. Their shoulders sagged, they buckled at the knees, yet, they had to carry on. It was too much, for the four could not manage their burden, despite the brutal blows, and the Japanese were forced to add another man to the task. Had our own administrative staff exercised discrimination in their detailing, untold agonies would have been spared. If they did not know of what was happening, then more shame to the uncaring sergeant major in charge of the party.

There was a lighter side to the party. Alongside the jungle track trickled a peaty stream in which fish were reported. I never saw any myself, but some of the regulars had fashioned themselves fishing lines, hoping to augment their meagre rations.

A mile or so further down the track was a quarry. Here, too, a party of approximately a dozen men were sent under the guard, Doll Face. This most detestable of all the camp guards was a little quieter when on his own, although he never shed his very treacherous nature. Yet I dared, while on this party, to take one of the biggest personal risks that I had so far taken. Our job was to hew out a pile of stones, which we had to carry a distance of about one hundred metres along a winding tree-lined path to be heaped up ready for haulage by lorry. The work was boring but not very hard; best of all, it was ill-organised. Doll Face, when at the quarry, could not watch the men who were carrying the stones to and from the road. Neither did he seem to know who was doing what. The nearness of a pineapple plantation, therefore, tempted the more enterprising to sneak away for a few minutes to eat the fruit. Although one man was actually caught and subsequently brutally punished after emerging from the bushes with his booty, Doll Face seemed so dull-witted as never to notice any shortage in numbers.

So one day, I thought that it would be pleasant to munch my stolen pineapple near a tiny stream that sparkled between the pineapple plantation and the semi-jungle surrounding the quarry. For perhaps half an hour I relaxed completely, the only time in three and a half years that, in the isolation of natural surroundings, I ever did so. The experience was extremely exhilarating. One of the worst features of a POW's life was the lack of privacy and quiet: a man could not get away from the crowd. Always, in the air, there hung incessantly the intangible, yet tangible, feeling of other people's broodings, their resentments, their jealousies, their hopes and fears and their hates. On the physical plane a man was lucky if, save in the middle of the night, he could enjoy a shower in privacy. He was still more lucky if he could, in solitude, allow his thoughts to stray. Yet, here I found that I could for once free the spirit from its earthly trappings and let it soar unhampered, unenvied. For a while then, I was able to fling wide the shutters of my subconscious self so that my soul, as it were, entered into rapturous communion with the flaming fertility of the tropical vegetation. For once I knew a peace and contentment of mind not experienced for two years. It was half an hour before I once again caged my restless spirit and took my body off towards servitude to emerge undetected near the quarry, a much refreshed man from pantheistic experience.

A more refreshing type of job should have been the golf course assignment but it was not, for changkol and basket appeared equally to be the tools of the groundsman as of the excavator. Already mentioned as being spread over land, just off the main road from the aerodrome to Kuching, the golf course was crossed at one end by the road that bypassed the town and led to the riverside boat building industry. The clubhouse was at the opposite extremity. From there, we collected the tools, and so on to the hallowed turf. I never really knew exactly to what end our efforts were directed there. Who cared anyhow? Whether we worked at the aerodrome, in the shipbuilding industry or on a sports ground, it seemed that we could not escape the changkol and basket and the old dreary routine of shifting soil from one spot and dumping it in another. The only advantage of working on the golf course was being responsible to only one Japanese guard. I never saw a professional Japanese groundsman, although the course was put to its normal use, proved one day when a few Japanese suddenly appeared complete with clubs, balls and caddies. Playing in pairs, the Japanese sportsmen appeared to take the game very seriously. I could only hope, however, that their aim with a rifle was no better than their aim with a golf club.

I also worked, not far from Lintang Barracks, with changkol and basket at some sort of Japanese shrine, probably a burial ground. Here we improved the driveway. The pleasure of digging graves for the Japanese, however, was denied us, but at least stolen fruit from some carefully spaced out lime trees was some recompense.

As rubber trees surrounding the camp were felled, so were gardens started. Besides the development of gardens within the actual bounds of the camp, much of the land just outside the wire was changkoled over and planted with tapioca plants. These grew with remarkable rapidity, soon reaching a height of over two metres. Periodically labour was required to weed between the rows. This was supplied partly by POWs and partly by internees, both male and female. It was sad to see not only English wives but also nuns toiling in the heat of the sun under 'benevolent' Japanese supervision. But we had, of course, our own troubles and had little pity to spare. Tiresome and joyless as must have been the life of these women, it should not be forgotten that the hardships they endured, great as they were, in no way compared with those of us POW other ranks: our death rate was about forty per cent, theirs but one per cent. I do not think either that the ladies were forced to work, although they probably had, of necessity, to do so under threat of reduced rations if they did not. More touching than the sight of women working under such conditions was to see each day a woman call at the Japanese guard room for their milk ration, about a quart between two or three hundred women and children. In actual fact, of course, the milk was for the very young children whose numbers I never learnt.

We also weeded and generally maintained the unmetalled road surface of the camp approach road. No task was more boring. Worse still, it was near the Japanese guard room so that we could always expect a very tough time of it indeed. The only attraction was to hope for an opportunity to steal from the hands of green bananas, so temptingly clustered against the huge, ragged leaves of the banana trees which had been cultivated at the side of the road. Only once was I able to grab any fruit, but a remarkable piece of good fortune did one day come my way.

In the heat of the afternoon, we were startled by a noise from the sago tree plantation where, apparently, two or three oxen had sought shade. It was very funny, although the humourless Japanese did not think so. Funnier still, however, they ordered the POWs to drive them from the plantation. We jumped to obey, dashing into the plantation as though for very freedom itself. Completely hidden from the Japanese, once well within the wood, it was a heaven-sent opportunity to pull up young roots and, especially by those who were clothed in something more than a loincloth as I happened to be, to secrete them about our bodies. We did far more damage than the oxen, who eventually emerged into the road of their own accord and, there being no search, boasted full stomachs before seeking the hardness of bare boards for the night's repose.

Another garden was started on quite a large scale, a mile from the camp, off a track that served as a back entrance to the boat building industry. Here, under the supervision of Big Pig, Little Pig, Doll Face and Joe Louis – the very worst of the guards, it seemed – we worked feverishly. The initial objective was to rough-changkol the whole area, already cleared of trees and brushwood. An ingenious method was adopted. Perhaps a dozen or twenty men would be lined up in close formation and ordered to advance, changkoling. However, they must keep in line. Some men were inclined to changkol with greater energy than others, some less thoroughly. They progressed rapidly, but with those men every other prisoner would have to keep pace. Keep up with the leader was the order, or...! To men who were less strong or inclined to be more thorough than their fellows, the pace was killing.

I also worked in a lime plantation near the Japanese shrine, weeding between the growing bushes. The stolen limes were luscious!

I spent two further days at a small factory alongside the main road to Kuching, shovelling rice polishings into sacks. These polishings were, as previously explained, to be eaten neat in an attempt to augment the vitamin in our food. While I loaded the sacks with an Australian soldier, I had an argument which led to an indecisive scrap back in camp. After going at each other hammer and tongs for a couple of minutes, the pair of us became so exhausted that we did not continue the encounter, but we never forgave each other.

I also assisted another prisoner cleaning out a midden at the back of Dr Yamamoto's office. We were provided, for this delightful task, with a long ladle and a large drum drawn on a pair of trucks. When the drum was full, we pushed it to a cesspool, emptied the contents and went back for more. As a reward for work well done, however, we were each given a bowl of katchang ijau, a leguminous vegetable. I worked also for the Japanese in their pigsties. These were at the back of the their HQ, built at the head of a pond on which thickly grew a type of green vegetable used as pigs' food. Besides being required to clean out the pigsties, we were also ordered to wade in the pond to cut the green stuff. I was also for a short while appointed to a small party working immediately behind Suga's HQ. There we assisted in mixing concrete for the piers of a new hut. We also widened and weeded paths.

A rough track was constructed around the perimeter of the collection of compounds which formed the entire camp. With this work, too, I assisted. During the construction, I had a remarkable experience which threw some light on the Japanese character. Four of us were hauled up in front of the Japanese guard nick-named Big Annie, for infringing some unwritten law, and he commenced to bash us. As I was standing farthest from him, I was therefore accorded the dubious privilege of watching my com-rades beaten first. Each of them, as the blow was about to fall upon their cheeks, involuntarily flinched. By the glint in the eyes of the guard, I could see that it was because of this understandably involuntary reaction that subsequent blows were meted out with added vigour. I was determined, on grounds more of plain common sense than courage, to discipline myself not to shrink at the first blow. My turn came, the arm strained backwards, a tremendous blow was aimed and I stood unmoved. The guard's hand stopped only two inches from my cheek. Candidly, Big Annie surveyed me, back with the arm once more and again the blow was directed. Once more the hand stopped short of my face. A third time, he tried but I was not to be shaken. An approving Japanese grin, the gift of a fag but without a word, and he let me go. As a sequel, I must mention that before freedom, despite my greatest efforts not to flinch and despite my knowledge of the consequences, I found myself quite incapable of refraining from doing so again. By then, my nerve had broken and I had lost my 'bottle'.

I also had a hand in constructing a grass-covered roundabout as a site for a guard box off the main square, in the apex of the triangle formed between the entrance road to the camp and the road running past our compound. From thence, a watch could be kept over the extra entrance made nearby into our enclosure.

I also worked at one end of the women's compound, digging out the stumps of rubber trees. I wish I could honestly say that I found satisfaction in doing this. I did not. Rather did I harbour a feeling shared, I have little doubt, by most of the others who worked with me, that, as the women were not fit and strong enough to do the work, the male internees could have been roped in. Such a task, I felt, could have been justifiably excused the POWs of no rank though we were: the far fitter internees would, I am sure, not have begrudged this service to their wives.

Not once during the work did I have an opportunity to converse with the women. They must have had strong injunctions not to contact us, although perhaps the nuns and the prudes would not have appreciated speech with our ill-kempt, practically naked, skeleton-like frames. Anyhow, in her book, Mrs Keith did not feel that many of our efforts were worthy of mention, not of our occasional weeding of the paths, not the carrying of wood into the ladies' enclosure nor the fact, as will later been seen, that daily, for week after week, as we passed by their compound to and from the site of another stupendous task which was yet in store for us, we were searched before continuing. Many a man, perhaps even myself, must have been seen being beaten up for attempting to smuggle food into the camp and would surely have been seen by Mrs Keith, as later mentioned.

During one task allotted to me, I had no opportunity of obtaining extra food. This was at a small Indian cattle farm. A mate and myself were allotted a task by the Japanese to emphasise our ignominious dishonour as prisoners of war. Standing unshod in cow manure almost up to the knees we had to muck out a byre while the Tamil peasant incredulously stood idly by.

Special Assignment

For the second time, work at the aerodrome was petering out, but one evening, before it was to cease altogether, I learnt that I had been detailed for the morrow as a member of a special party of about fifteen men which daily had to be formed. Reports of the advantages of this party had already filtered our lines, so that I counted my appointment as a slice of good fortune. As far as I could ascertain, most of its members were regulars and I determined that, if the work was to my liking, I would also endeavour to stake a permanent claim. I was fed up with the aerodrome and even more fed up with the Japanese guards with whom we had to contend. Of course, the ideal party never existed – one without a guard – for the Japanese never failed to give us unrelenting attention.

The following morning the fifteen of us, under a Sergeant Fleming, a particular friend of mine, were paraded in the usual manner and marched to the guard room. There we were met by the Japanese guard in charge of the party. A relatively good-natured and harmless individual was the first impression I had of him, and his smile of greeting seemed to suggest appreciation of my appraisal. When clear of the guardroom, his smile became even broader. At last, perhaps, apart from the odd one or two attached to the camp, I had encountered our first easygoing and responsible Japanese guard. Such a phenomenon savoured of incredulity. It was no wonder that I still harboured doubts. Before tiffin, however, my mind was made up. I would, if possible, stick tight to the special party. This guard was to be respected rather than feared and, before the end of the day, I had ingratiated myself with a Japanese, a performance never to be repeated. Working with a will, I did all that I could to convince him that I was a very glutton for a hard day's work and, during the afternoon, I thought it opportune, through Sergeant Fleming, to beg him to issue instruction that I should be regularly required for his party.

Unenthusiastically, but without the slightest demur, he agreed. Thereafter, I was never missing from the special party and served on it until its dissolution about two months later. It was not only the happiest but the most beneficial period that I spent at Kuching.

This paragraph is unique for it is in praise of a Nip. Our special party guard – I have forgotten his name – was a kindly junior NCO and, if not pro-British, at least not anti-British. Perhaps he was a Christian – I do not know – but at least he displayed humanitarian principles. If there was no work of urgency to be done, we idled under cover of the rubber plantation. Of all the regular Japanese he was the only one who would not work us solely for the sake of adding to our burdens. Other Japanese, if no other task suggested itself, would have set us aimlessly clearing jungle. This gentleman preferred that he and we should hide away from roads and tracks in the thick of the jungle, where we would doze and talk as inclination dictated. During some of these periods he spoke of Japan, not disguising the fact that the tide of war was turning in favour of his country's adversaries and that Japanese defeat was not far distant. Most of all, he showed kindliness in his attitude towards our buying. Appreciating the paucity of our rations, he often encouraged us to trade with the natives. Indeed, on occasions, he, himself, went so far as to barter with them for easy terms, not seeking, as some Japanese did, the private rake-off. Then his face would beam with pleasure as he watched us eating our tiffin, augmented by purchases that he had arranged or shut his eyes to. Furthermore, at nightfall, on reaching the guardroom, he made a point of informing the Korean guards that we carried no contraband, thus ensuring that we marched into our lines without the customary search.

In return for such consideration, however, he expected us not only to work, but to work hard when occasion demanded, so that his kindliness, though unpremeditated, was not without common sense. Of all the tasks we carried out, the most common was the shifting of petrol drums. These were transported to within a mile or so of the aerodrome and offloaded at the roadside. There we took over, manhandling them over a ditch and into the semi-jungle beyond, to hide them under the thick undergrowth. The reason for this was obvious, the safety of the petrol supplied in the case of an attack of the aerodrome from the air.

A short while previously, we had indeed, for the first time for about three years, been brought into direct contact with the war. It was Palm Sunday 1945 and, although by now we were working a seven-day week outside the camp, for some reason or other I was labouring in the camp gardens on that memorable day. Suddenly, late in the morning, the stillness was broken by the noise of an approaching aeroplane, not the familiar burr of a single-engined 'kite', but the concerted roar of the engines of a large plane, a sound that we had not heard for a long time. Our eyes searched the skies, and an excited shout went up, 'There it is!' Low down towards the aerodrome a large bomber was spotted. It seemed only a few seconds later, certainly not long for we were still idly wondering what plane it could be, when we heard the harsh clatter of machine guns. We jumped for joy, hardly daring to breathe the words that formed on the lips – 'A Yank plane!' Then, as more gunfire was heard, we broke into an excited chatter. It must be the Yanks. It was the biggest thrill ever at Kuching, even more exciting than the arrival of the food parcels. Our part of the world was not altogether forgotten, the war would soon be won. We would be free again. It was too good to be true. We laughed. We nearly cried for joy. At that time, indeed, with a mounting death roll and with no news – the radio's batteries had several months earlier given out – morale had sunk pretty low. This was the fillip that we needed, as hopes were revived. Blast the Japanese! We would beat them yet.

The plane, a Liberator or Flying Fortress – I forget which – hovered around for about half an hour, and then slowly and deliberately flew off, carrying all our best wishes with it. Obviously, we reasoned, the Allies must be not more distant than the Philippines. That they were a good deal nearer, however, operating from the other end of Borneo itself, was proved five days later on Good Friday when several Wellsian-looking planes – twin fuselage Lockheed Lightnings – machine-gunned the aerodrome. They met with little opposition and zoomed and wove their patterns low against the sky over the distant aerodrome for almost half an hour. We did not witness the whole performance for the Japanese insisted that those in camp stay put in their huts, although this injunction did not prevent us from darting out now and then to report progress. I was, on this occasion, working within our lines. This futuristic display was far too good and thrilling to miss.

On each occasion, those working on the aerodrome had had a much better view. No one was hurt, for the guards had hustled the working party off the flying field before the fun started. But, there were one or two narrow squeaks and empty shell-cases were later proudly displayed in our lines.

Thereafter, the appearance of Allied planes became common-place. Slit trenches were dug about our compound and to these the prisoners were herded when Allied planes were about. Mercifully, they rarely, if ever, came over at night time and never attacked the camp or its vicinity. The opposition to be encountered at Kuching was not enough to justify night flying. Only on one or two occasions did we ever see Japanese planes show fight, for reasons, I imagine, not of cowardice but of shortage of aircraft.

While working on the special party, our airborne friends appeared to put on a first-class performance for my benefit alone! During luncheon hour, usually taken under cover at some spot a mile or so from the aerodrome, it was usual to sneak off on foraging expeditions, after having eaten our regulation rations. I had discovered a garden which cultivated brinjals (a fruit I had never sampled in England, now called aubergines) about half a mile from one of the trips that we made to have tiffin, this being about one hundred metres off the road. To this haven I would, when in the vicinity, wander about twice a week. On this occasion, I had barely reached my 'patch' when I detected the noise of approaching aircraft. Looking up, I eventually picked out about twenty planes flying towards the airfield in fairly close formation. So purposeful were they, and unconcerned in their approach, that they looked for all the world like a flight of large birds leisurely betaking themselves to a distant tree top. As I waited, however, I saw plummeting to the earth, as though from the bellies of the birds, huge eggs that I knew were bombs. Terrific explosions followed half a minute later. But the planes, if planes they were, continued undeviatingly on their course, unmolested. I also continued on my way, quite unperturbed, plucking my brinjals and rejoining the rest of the party. We had by now become used to planes: brinjals were more important than bombs.

While shifting oil and petrol drums, I lost a hard earned ten dollars. This caused me undue grievance as, though making money fairly rapidly, I was becoming 'cash' conscious. I decided, therefore, that I must recompense myself by some means which normally I could not adopt. But how? Theft from a fellow prisoner suggested itself and such an enterprise would not present many difficulties but, despite my acquired hardness and cynicism, I could not bring myself to do it and nosed around for other possibilities. Believe it or not, a profitable line at the time was the trading in Castrol oil. Its frying properties were excellent. Rissoles browned in this oil were delicious, although the cook had to be careful to drain off all superfluous fat before eating or other well-known properties of such rich and sickly oils would have had drastic effect. One or two fellows who had been brought into contact with the oil drums had managed to fill a water bottle. At five dollars a pint, I could, with one bottleful, pretty well clear the deficit on my account. I was not working with these drums, but I ascertained that about two hundred metres from where we took our tiffin, there were some drums secreted in the jungle at the roadside. I decided to attempt a 'big steal', but the risks were great.

To steal from the drums necessitated a journey up and down the road from the only access through the thick undergrowth. Short though the distance was, I risked being halted and questioned by the Japanese. To be caught actually stealing from the drums would almost certainly result in a charge of sabotage, but the loss of the ten dollars rankled me so much that I determined to take the risk. One tiffin time, therefore, I strode briskly down the road with a water bottle strapped to my side. Halfway there, but going in the opposite direction, a Japanese lorry passed me. I endeavoured to assume complete nonchalance. I do not know whether I achieved this object, but at least the Japanese on the lorry showed no interest in me. A minute later I was, with the feverishness of an Arabian Bedouin, undoing the bung of one of the barrels. Into the bottle I tipped the oil, stoppered it and thankfully reached the road undetected. My luck held. Neither pedestrian nor vehicle passed me on the way back to our party. I would recoup my ten dollars. Wisely, however, I never again tempted Providence in this way. I did not replace the bung.

Another, though smaller, 'luncheon' risk that I took nearly resulted in disaster. Opposite where we had our lunch was a track which wandered off through the semi-jungle more or less at right angles to the main road. Two or three of us could not resist the temptation to see what lay at the end of it. A native house it transpired, and there we transacted some rather good business.

The following day I decided once again to 'chance my arm'. Just on the point of rounding a bend in the track, however, I spotted a Japanese only fifty metres away. Mercifully his eyes were on the ground, and, doing a snappier about-turn than ever was done for the strictest of sergeant majors, I darted, undetected, back down the track. Another adventure never to be repeated!

We did not spend all our time trundling petrol drums. There were days spent transporting bombs from the aerodrome a distance of over a mile to unload them at the roadside. Once there, we had to manhandle them to a stone-built hut seventy metres into the semi-jungle. This was very heavy work and four men had to strain themselves to their utmost to get the crated bomb up the sloping track to the hut in one lift. Unfortunately, too, while put to this task we suffered the attentions of a second Japanese of less easygoing habits. It appeared to be of supreme importance that the greatest haste was made, so we trembled lest we had to rest en route. My greatest fear was that I should collapse under the tremendous weight. I never did, but seldom covered the last few metres without the greatest difficulty.

We became acquainted with a kampong a couple of miles on the other side of the aerodrome. Excursions thereto corresponded with air raid warnings received when working near the aerodrome. The Japanese with whom we worked, and who can blame them, were for once of the same mind as us, to shoot out of danger as quickly as possible. So the handiest lorry hurried us to the first kampong where, until the all-clear was given, the Japanese could chat with and bully the natives.

On one or two occasions, we drove further inland by about

two miles. Ammunition again! It had been thought necessary to store bombs all within a mile of the aerodrome, yet small arms ammunition, for some reason or another, had to be gathered four miles from the aerodrome. So we journeyed by lorry from the aerodrome with boxes of ammunition and unloaded them at a native house. The rounds were found to be in such a rusty condition that we were given the task of rubbing them smooth with glass paper. That this task was thought probably to be contrary to the Geneva Convention, as also was the shifting of bombs, did not unduly worry us. Why should it? If we did not glass paper bullets someone else would, and was it not easier work to do this than wield a changkol? Sabotage of machinery at Kuching had never been possible, but on this occasion, at least, we made certain of shoddy workmanship.

There was another advantage to this chore. Discipline was slack, so that one of the party could keep watch on the roadside for possible vendors. Moreover, behind the house smiled a well-cultivated garden, from which we stole vegetables, a crime which, ashamedly, left us in stitches of laughter.

Under Sergeant Fleming, we had organised on a communal basis illicit purchases and theft when legitimate buying was not possible. The booty was pooled with an extra rake-off for the organisers. When cleaning the small arms ammunition, a second Japanese was in attendance, so consequently we had to purchase illicitly. In turn, therefore, a man kept watch on the road while two of us, being the boldest, decided at an opportune moment to raid the gardens at the back of the house. The moment arrived when we were actually carrying the arms from the roadside to the house. The guards would not miss a short absence of two from our party. So, with empty packs and with Ian Farquharson, I dashed into the back garden and in next to no time, not only packs but pockets and dixies were full of brinjals, cucumbers and large chillies. About to sneak back to the house, we were startled by the appearance of a Chinese woman. Saying nothing, however, we made for the house, reaching it unseen by the Japanese. By now, it was my turn to keep watch for possible vendors at the roadside and, not unwillingly, I took up my position.

A few seconds later, I was listening with apprehension to the excited cackle of the Chinese woman, then the more restrained voices of the Japanese guards. Obviously, the theft had been discovered. Somewhat shamefully I remained put, wondering what would befall Ian. Without doubt, the matter would have to be cleared up, for the cackle of the Chinese woman was growing louder, faster and more passionate. I admit, that I had little care for her plight but a lot for whether or not I should receive a bashing. Ruefully, my conscience got the better of me and, as I could not let my pal 'carry the can' for both of us being caught at the scene, I was goaded into action and, like a dog, reluctantly returned to an irate master. I limped towards the house where the Chinese woman was still jabbering nineteen to the dozen, while the two Japanese faced her and my guilty-looking comrade but, with relief, I noticed that the Japanese were more amused than enraged, and, thus encouraged, boldly admitted my part in the affair. The upshot was that we had to empty our packs. At the sight of what tumbled to the ground, the cackle of the woman rose to a new crescendo. Now, to pay for our sins but no, the guards, obviously relishing the joke, ordered us to hand back the booty. Reluctantly we did so while the Japanese muttered 'bagus' (good). The woman still seemed loath to go, so the Japanese hustled her off, cursing and laden with vegetables. We departed unpunished, followed not only by the laughter of our mates but by that of the Japanese, also. For once, their sense of humour coincided with ours, as we all had a good laugh. What is more, we thieves had got away with only light admonishment, but with profit, for our dixies and pockets were still full!

We not only shifted small arms ammunition to this house, but also to another house the other side of the aerodrome about four miles from Kuching and opposite a pineapple plantation which, of course, received our attention. We also carried out many other miscellaneous tasks such as digging dugouts and clearing jungle for gun emplacements, but of more interest than these were the jobs that took us through Kuching.

On one occasion, we drove through the town with heavy boxes of ammunition which had to be carried up the steep slope of a rubber plantation. In doing this we, as did our own guard, took orders from a large Japanese with a huge handlebar moustache. His looks lent force to the rumour that he was a man of remarkable ferocity, and so we strained our utmost to lug the boxes up the hill as quickly as possible. I suspect that he was far less fierce than he looked, for he gave not the slightest trouble. He was no 'Gorilla' or 'Satan'!

Returning from one of these urban assignments we were, due to the local activity of American planes, forced to spend a couple of hours sitting at the roadside on the outskirts of the town. Although we saw little of the planes, we could hear them bombing and machine-gunning down the river in the locality of Lekas Corner. Later, we heard that the boat building project had been completely wrecked. No one, it should be recorded, who suffered there at the hands of the 'Gorilla' and the Stamper, died of a broken heart at this news. They died of broken bodies! As we sat by the roadside on this occasion, however, I know that our attention was far more directed towards a lime tree whose branches curved invitingly within our reach. As was usual, under such circumstances, we failed to observe the eighth commandment.

A later expedition – one of the last of the special party – was even more rewarding. We had been detailed to shift some ammunition to a suburban house, some sort of Japanese Battalion HQ, I imagine, in Kuching. No sooner had we started the journey from road to house than a lone four-engined bomber appeared, an almost daily occasion now. As far as we could make out, in leisurely fashion it began to shoot up the buildings overlooking the river, unmolested. The Japanese officer who had temporarily replaced our regular guard ordered us to take cover under some trees that shaded the highway while the Japanese themselves retired to the house. Nothing could have pleased us more, as some of the trees were pendulous with limes. I do not for one moment suppose that we rivalled the bomber in the devastation inflicted, but I'll wager that we reaped a greater satisfaction from our depredations.

Before I had served long on the special party, all work at the aerodrome ceased and the party of fifty prisoners who had been stationed there were sent to join us at Lintang Barracks. In the meantime another task had commenced, the making of an airstrip a mile or two from camp, at what was termed 'San Mile' (third mile). This enterprise too, it was said, presented plenty of opportunity for the ambitious businessman. So, despite the fact that we never again saw our kindly Nip, I did not suffer over-whelming disappointment when the special party was disbanded.

Before moving on once again to join the main working party, let us for a short time return to the affairs within our lines.

Boot Hill

Before dealing with matters of the gravest significance, I shall now discuss the affairs of our compound covering most of the time that I served on the special party and 'San Mile'.

First and foremost, food. In 1945, the standard and amount of food officially allocated to us were abysmally low, fatally so, in fact. In previous years, bad as the food had been, we had not been seriously rationed for rice and, although our rations had sadly lacked quality, a fair amount of energy could be derived from them, so much so that at one time, in an effort to reduce the risk of beriberi, I had foregone part of my rice allowance. But now, the Japanese had the greatest difficulty in maintaining their supply lines and, as comparatively little rice was grown in Sarawak, we were put on very short rations. Instead of three dishes of rice per day, the allocation of dry rice was so reduced that three such dishes a day became one a day, the evening meal. We were to be expected to start the day's work on nothing but a small flat cake made of tapioca or sago, or a small ration of 'gloo-boo', a gelatinous substance concocted of sago flour and tapioca. For tiffin, we had a pint of mixed rice and green stew, on return from work, a pint of green stew, three-quarters of a pint of steamed rice and a small rice rissole fried in coconut oil.

How many calories a day's fare contained, I do not know, but obviously they were pitifully low for slaves who toiled long hours under the remorseless rays of a tropical sun. Supplies of meat and fish were luxuries of the past; fruit, save for a few persimmons, was practically nil. Short of energy foods, drastically deficient in proteins and vitamin, it was no wonder that, after the strain of Lekas Corner and the aerodrome, we saw our ranks rapidly thinning as death took its inevitable toll. No wonder too, that men, even the most restrained, began to jostle for position on the laegi queues (if any). An extra spoonful of rice was jealously regarded as an extra leash of life. No ordinary worker now dared to refuse rice; no ordinary duty man dared now to worry about the beriberi risk of too much rice. Energy to work, energy to retain enough strength daily to hobble out on the working parties with the chance of scrounging extra food was man's supreme ambition.

At the end of 1944, my weight had dropped to nine stone. Before imprisonment I had scaled about twelve stone. By remaining on working parties I managed, I should imagine, never to lose more than another six pounds but it was only by hogging all I could that, I stuck to what must, comparatively speaking, have constituted the middle-weight division. Thankful I can be that at no time did I look a human skeleton as the majority did, but I had my frights. On two occasions, after a successful theft or racket, I consumed a surfeit of badly cooked ubi-kayu, with the results nearly fatal. Even now, vividly imprinted on my mind, is the first of these episodes. Waking up in the very early hours of one morning I felt an urgent desire to go to the lavatory. More asleep than awake, I stumbled outside to be unable to go more than ten metres before being forced to an abrupt stop. My heart beat within me like a steam hammer. I thought that it was the end of me. Not long previously, a man had collapsed on the square to die before treatment could be administered. Doubtless he had been stricken as I was. However, sinking to my haunches, I summoned up all my will power and physical resources, remaining motionless until the pounding had ceased, chronic palpitations, I suppose, caused by severe indigestion and general debility, and slowly, and with infinite care, picked my way to the lavatory and back. The second attack, equally severe, but not quite so terrifying, convinced me that to eat too much ubi-kayu might prove disastrous, but restraint was difficult.

Rice, rice and more rice! Although I always endeavoured to maintain a sense of proportion, I once, in the middle of one sleepless night, sneaked out of my hut becoming obsessed with the need to consume as much of it as possible. I crept to the so-called bakery and eased myself under a piece of loose boarding. I crawled to a rice bin inside and liberally helped myself to some boiled rice. Mercifully, I regained my hut's protection without detection.

On only one other occasion did I steal in our lines, and that was after I had been the victim of a dirty trick perpetrated by an Australian. Again, like a crook, I waited until after midnight to slink to a small patch of ubi-kayu owned by the Australian in question to pull up several stalks by the root. Most were too young for harvesting, although I did scrounge a couple of meals. More importantly, however, I had earned my revenge, although careful to cook thoroughly the stolen garden produce and eating it a little at a time.

I am glad to say that I never again gave way to such temptation. The truth of the matter was that, desperate though I had become, the chances of being caught were rather too heavily weighted against me and punishment would have been severe. Moreover, I still nurtured some principles. To steal from the Japanese and from native gardens was all right but I resisted the temptation to steal from my mates, although some variation of domestic theft was not uncommon. This was true not only in the letter of the law but far more so in the spirit. I mean that those in responsible positions, although not actually engaged in the physical act of stealing, were mixed up daily in sharp practice.

Lack of food sapped our energies for entertainment as well as for work. It had become not only too much trouble to make our own entertainment, but to walk to the square to see concerts, few though they had become. Worse, the effort of stirring from our quarters after an evening meal to visit, say, a pal in the sick bay less than one hundred metres away, was usually beyond us. The majority of those on working parties now desired to do only one thing once the evening meal was over, and that was to lie on the bare boards or home-made wooden beds and engage in desultory talk of the day's happenings, the past and of what we would do in the future, with less zest than hitherto. Speaking for myself, at that time, I preferred lying on the boards and listening to a 'mate' (Private Brown), nostalgically sing the 'Lost Chord' – the only song that he knew – than travelling to the square, there to stand uncomfortably watching the same faces on the same stage.

Lassitude was not the sole reason for this mood. By 1945, when most it was required, there was no electric light. The only light available in our huts was from burning crude rubber or coconut oil. A candle would have been a luxury. To attempt to read, write, or maybe make something in these dim lights, framed with grotesque shadows, was most unattractive.

Nature's own lighting system remained unaffected by the war, and the stars, though not as brilliant as in Java, shone with greater intensity than in England. I had discarded my Javanese habit of tracking down the constellations, yet one night, after lights out, feeling particularly depressed, I stumbled outside to squat on the stump of a rubber tree there to cast my eyes heavenwards. As usual, after a little quiet meditation, my troubles slipped away from me. I am convinced that, if intending suicides would first consider their infinitesimal importance compared with the vastness of the universe, few would then proceed as planned. Certainly, on that particular night, before creeping back to the hut, I once again experienced a blissful peace of mind.

For some, there was no peace. Although there were, surprisingly enough, no suicides at Kuching, one or two prisoners lost their reason, so that a small hut – a 'geela' ward – was constructed near the sick quarters by our engineers to shelter three or four men reputed to be in various stages of insanity. None of them, I believe, was raving mad, so their supervision was not difficult. Actually, as regards one of the inmates of the geela ward, an airman, I was never really certain whether he was mad or merely wiser than I, whether indeed his insanity was not feigned to evade working parties.

As regard the happenings in the camp, there was for me, a ranker, a lot to be uncertain about and much that was too difficult to understand. All I could be sure of was that many of the activities of those in responsible staff positions would not bear close scrutiny, as was proved one day when one of the medical orderlies ran amok among our lines. Chased by two other well-fed orderlies (ex-MPs), he must have raced three times around the compound before, like a runaway horse, he was captured and bridled. What had caused this remarkable episode? Tongues waggled, and soon very strong rumours were afoot that this man had broken down after having, for a long period, been subjected to the illicit and unnatural passions of some of the fitter men amongst the medical staff, even the name of a doctor was freely quoted. Such an idea might seem inconceivable, yet I never heard cogent claims for an alternative explanation. The man in question did not survive.

All things considered, I think the homosexual theory was correct: the lad in question was almost pretty, highly strung and just the type that one would expect to attract unnatural affections. Moreover, homosexuality was beyond all doubt proved in another instance, when a member of the RAF contingent was involved. Apparently, encouraged by the offer of extra food, he had agreed to submit to the will of one of the MPs. The airman freely admitted to me and others of his comrades that he had accepted the food but denied that he had actually made the final submission. While doubt lingered in our minds, however, we did not condemn our RAF colleague, but the MP lost his status.

It is sad to think that sodomy was practised, yet I cannot deny the fact that it was by certain camp workers who, doubtless, because of extra food and better conditions, were at least not unnaturally feeling sex-starved. For myself, I never knew the sex urge, but then I do not wish to appear self-righteous as I rarely experienced the surplus energy required! After the Japanese, in an endeavour to increase their war effort, had exacted all the energy they could from me, any spare energy I boasted – and I am by no means certain that I should be proud of this – was directed towards the augmentation of my food by engaging in one racket or the other. As a result of one of these I found myself hauled up in front of RSM Sunderland.

It happened like this. Large profits were being made by working party members on goods bought, stolen or otherwise acquired outside camp and sold inside it. To many this activity, summed up, spelt unwarranted profiteering. It could, indeed, be argued that it was fundamentally wrong for those fit enough to venture forth on working parties to sell at double or treble the purchase price goods acquired there to those, including the sick, inside but, these high prices were common to all, not only to the sick, but also to some of the fittest men in the camp, the cooks, the MPs, administrative staff, the burial ground and benjo parties, the men who blessed their stars that they had found a nice safe niche in the camp or had sheltered occupations. Their companions, on the other hand, their poor relations, literally worked themselves to death in the roughest of all worlds.

To discriminate between the fit and the sick, when fixing prices, was of course unrealistic, for what, in fact, the man who did business was doing was simply procuring the best price he could for his article, having regard to the general economic law of supply and demand. When, therefore, RSM Sunderland decreed that working party members selling in camp should charge only a ten per cent profit, he was acting unreasonably. Men were certainly not going to risk a bashing as punishment for being caught with illicit goods for small rewards. Besides, the very act of barter meant the expenditure of extra energy, and a man first had to ensure that profits were large enough to provide enough food to compensate for valuable calories expended in its acquisition. Naturally, therefore, it was asserted by the so-called profiteers that Sunderland was unfair to them and that he was acting not in the interests of the sick, but of those of himself and his camp friends. Why wait so long before he thought of the welfare of the sick? Why had not a share and share alike policy been adopted ages ago?

I liked his 'one-tenth' decree no better than the others and certainly did not intend to restrict myself to such a low profit. So I sold some native tobacco at twice its cost price. The purchaser, a man himself who had in the past made his profits, reported to the MPs that he had been exorbitantly charged. Naturally, I refused to admit this, was charged and, in due course, marched in front of Sunderland. I had few worries. When shown the tobacco that I had supposedly sold for two dollars, I knew immediately that some had already been taken. By discreet enquiry I ascertained that the plaintiff had already rolled one or two cigarettes and, perhaps, a mate had had one also. Of course, such an indeterminate statement was just what I needed and I had no trouble in convincing the RSM that, despite the fact that he had acquired a pretty good idea of the price of the commodity, no one could tell exactly how much tobacco had been used.

To my mind, men who chanced a beating, or even a charge of espionage, for sneaking food into the camp on a profit-making basis were not the blackguards that some people made them out to be. The working party businessman priced not so much the article as the risks taken, and the risks were great. To be caught with 'blag' carried a minimum punishment of a bashing. As a maximum, a few days would be spent in the Japanese guardroom, where a bashing could be expected on every change of guard, apart from the incidental discomfort, lack of food, space and sleep. To be caught red-handed dealing with a native might evoke a charge of subversive activities.

There was the case of Sergeant Bent, one of the most fearless of all men and one who could handle the Japanese, but he went too far. One day, he was whipped away never to be seen again and later we learnt that he was charged with spying and, after prolonged interrogation, doubtless third degree stuff, was moved elsewhere. I never, for certain, knew the ultimate outcome, but I believe that he may have been executed. Previously to this, a strong rumour circulated that an Australian officer had been to Kuching from up-country, where he had acted contrary to the interests of Dai Nippon Gun. It was said that, following his decapitation, he was transported to a remote spot and buried there. Sergeant Bent was not the last victim. Some time afterwards, a private from our lines and one or two civilians were arrested. They, too, it was whispered, lost their heads.

While some men suffered, others prospered. Our MPs continued to use the big stick. Originally appointed to enforce internal military discipline, their duties were later expanded to ensure that the cookhouse staff took no more than their fair share of makan. What happened before long was that the cooks bribed the MPs to keep their mouths shut. The rapid increase in the weight of the police was alone sufficient to prove this but, apart from such physical evidence, it became common knowledge that dixies of food were passed over to the MPs from the cookhouse staff, especially at night time. Wheels within wheels! It was inevitable, of course, that, having regard to his autocratic selfishness, Sunderland appeared to turn a Nelsonian eye to such irregularities. In fact, practically everyone holding a regular camp job was, in one way or another, obtaining an unfair share of food. No wonder, then, that working party personnel took it hard when under the guise of not exploiting the sick in camp, we were ordered to make only a ten per cent profit on sales. We were certainly not going to sell goods to their fat, regularly employed camp staff brethren for such small returns.

The price control law, however, though never officially abrogated, soon became a dead letter. Sunderland obviously came to realise that its enforcement was impracticable, and I hope my own successful defence of the tobacco sale assisted him in this realisation. In Sunderland's own defence, of course, he was never cut out for authority under POW circumstances. An excellent disciplinarian, I would not deny and, as a first-class man in the field of battle, there were few better I am sure, but the task assigned him at Kuching called for a mixture of military authority, great diplomacy and social welfare. That is why Lieutenant Colonel Russell had been so popular for, surely, there had been a man cut out for welfare work, besides the exercise of more material forms of authority.

The poor members of outside working parties had other trials besides restriction of profits. By now, wood was so scarce that each day a party of about thirty men had to penetrate the semi-jungle over half a mile from our compound to fetch it. A regular wood party of about ten men had been formed, but twenty had still to be detailed. As was usual, the regular members of the party – and who can blame them – had quite naturally cornered the best work, that is the felling of the trees. The casuals were left with the difficult job of dragging the trees from the jungle to open land. This was not only arduous work but painful work as, being at this late stage mostly without shoes, we found the scrub played havoc with our feet. Such an obvious fact was never appreciated by the sergeant major in charge, who had developed into as ignorant, ruthless and as callous a man as ever I had set eyes on. He was far more to be feared than the Japanese who escorted us. I regret that to say that he was unrivalled would be to leave out of the reckoning a sergeant major who sometimes accompanied us on a working party. Less of a tyrant perhaps, he was nevertheless more cowardly so that when I once, under great provocation and in Australian manner, called him a bastard, he could but stutter and bluster, only summoning up the courage to charge me when I refused to retract my statement. I got away with it because of his poor handling of the case. What misguided military command had promoted these men, Heaven only knows! All I can say is that they were far more fitted to reign in hell than to serve in Heaven.

I was less fortunate with the wood party sergeant major. Near the end of the war, I was discovered absent from active duties stealing ubi-kayu from a small clearing, one hundred metres from where we worked. On return to our lines, I was directed to the detention barracks. In a fit of temper, upon being shuffled into the hut, I struggled with an MP. It was an inadvisable step, for I was immediately set upon by two or three of them and severely cuffed. My blood welled up and I fought like a tiger. After three years as a POW, I had lost control for the first time. I would have taken on fifty men, yea, fifty Japanese! The result was that I received as big a hiding as ever I had had. Moreover, I discovered that MPs had become so callous as to be able to vie with the Japanese in literally kicking a man when he was lying down. I learnt something else during my two days' stay in the detention block. It was in the middle of the night and, despite the fact that I had slaved throughout the day weeding paths, trimming edges, cleaning out ditches, I slept fitfully and, turning over, smelt food, delectable food. What was going on? Opening one eye I saw, with amazement, that the sergeant major was tucking into an enormous meal of rice and mixed vegetables. I knew that the MPs were neck-deep in rackets, but never had I imagined that certain senior officers were hand in glove with them. No wonder that the ordinary soldier was getting less food than he thought he should. I complained, but found that you cannot beat the system, as I learnt again during my last days at Kuching.

However, to revert to the wood party. At the end of the day, when the wood had all been dragged to the side of some cultivated ground at the edge of the jungle, it was loaded on to an ancient wagon and slowly pushed back to our lines. We had to pass the lookout platform that had been constructed above the level of some nearby rubber trees across the unpaved square in the front of the Japanese billets, where the Korean guards practised bayonet drill, past the Japanese HQ and the nearby workshop, where a party of nuns laundered their captors' clothes, then down the hill to the Japanese offices. We bought wood for the Japanese, for the ladies' compound and for our compound, wood for the daily pint of rice, a cup of green stew and a tapioca rissole!

Yet, despite it all when, once or twice weekly, Suga (now Lieutenant Colonel Suga, Commandant of all Sarawak POW camps) royally motored among our lines, when in residence at Kuching, one would have thought that he was inviting applause from the gallery for benefits that we had received. He passed between the six huts harbouring the sick, and turned not a hair, 'shimpashizing wid us', no doubt! I do not think that he ever made a tour of the sick bays. At least he was not hypocrite enough to walk smilingly between the double row of sick men who were rotting away in the six huts. We, who had formerly inhabited Hut Number 17 had, in order to accommodate the growing number of casualties, been forced to shift to another part of the lines. Some of these men were already dead. They still breathed, their hearts still beat, they still, meaninglessly, ate three times a day, woke up in the morning and went to sleep at night. Yet, to all intents and purposes, they would never again awake. Devoid of hope, of pain, of the will to live and brought low through starvation and sickness, they were in a comatose state. One felt that the resources of the best hospital anywhere would now be too late for them.

It is a fact that, on more than one occasion visiting a friend in the sick bay, I felt the presence of death in the room. Palpably, in omnipresent manifestation, he brooded over the recumbent forms of perhaps two or three who lay on the floor. It was as though the body lived on, without the spirit. Losing the will to fight, to live, these men had died prematurely, their spirits shaken loose from their flesh before their bodies were ready to let them go. Thus, perhaps they perched on top of the body, patiently awaiting the ceasing of its seemingly automatic functions, until they could take final leave to the open arms of hovering death. Is this mere fantasy? Perhaps! Yet, I still believe that certain men of living tissue were in fact dead, that is, the finest medical treatment in the world would not, at that late stage, have saved them. However, had treatment suddenly been made available to other men of more spirit but of equal physical disability, the result would have been different.

Although my closest friend, Charlie Cleal, was still pretty fit, many of my other friends died during 1945. Norman Williams was amongst the first. Kidney trouble and dysentery were the physical causes, though a man of sterner stuff would, I think, have lasted longer. Freddie Pafford, my fellow escapee, had also died. Never in the best of health, yet, he too, I believe, should have done better with a more valiant will, for he had been fairly well looked after by the compound 'administration'. Two more RAF personnel died, with whom I had been brought into close contact. One, AC1 Stiven, the a European dance champion, another, McGowan, the ex-film extra. The latter was another example of one who, not of poor physique, should have gone the distance, but, a stooge of Stiven's, he rarely showed strength of character. Lieutenant Pool, one of the officers, died in the camp sick quarters and, to his credit, he did not forget his friends before he died for, through a medical orderly, he sent me a dollar. Many other of my nearer acquaintances died, one of the three Yanks also. In 1945 the death roll in our compound mounted rapidly – sixty-eight in May, eighty in June, one hundred and thirty-six in July. By such progression, few would still be breathing by the end of the year. The percentage increase in deaths was even more alarming. The roll was, I believe, between six hundred and fifty and seven hundred and fifty when the war ended. Yet, there was no such mounting death roll among the other communities. Lekas Corner and the aerodrome had done their ghastly work. The Stamper, Big Pig, Little Pig, Joe Louis, Doll Face and, above all, the 'Gorilla', were reaping a rich harvest, not to mention the obvious callous smirk of Lieutenant Nekata (Suga's number one and camp commandant) as he watched us returning to the camp after a day's slavery.

Yet, little concrete sympathy was displayed by the management. Sunderland, most of the sergeant majors, the MPs and the cookhouse staff still retained their flesh and still made no effort to ensure the proper division of the food sent into the enclosure, save that some of the cookhouse staff were belatedly sent on a working party, while their places were taken by those who had worked outside fairly regularly. Only a few were affected, while those ex-cooks who went out to work were still in cahoots with the retained original staff, so that another racket sprang up.

Meanwhile, Lieutenant Colonel King had little medicine to

dispense and, seemingly, very little more in the way of sympathy. On sick parade, one evening towards the end of our time at Kuching, I well remember watching the MPs march a Corporal Collis, who had been despatched to detention barracks for disobedience, in front of our friend King.

'What's your trouble?' rasped King.

Collis pointed to bruises on his face. 'The MP struck me here, sir,' he blurted.

A fierce brush of King's moustache and, 'H'm! Can't see anything,' barked King. 'Is that all?'

Collis then displayed the long welts that angered his legs, other evidence of DB cruelty. 'Can't see anything, Corporal Collis!' again barked King. 'Take him away, sergeant!'

Off the corporal was marched, doubtless for another walloping. Had I read of such an incident with regard to normal army life, I would have attributed it to a writer's zest for the extravagances of the typical army martinet, whom music-hall artists love to parody. Yet, it was in the misery of a POW camp that I witnessed this sort of thing.

No wonder that some men thought that their deceased mates were better off on Boot Hill. For some time now, the practice of taking corpses to Kuching for burial had ceased. In lieu, a portion of a rubber plantation had been cleared some distance behind the officers' enclosure and in 1945, each day, a small cortege would wend its way in that direction, from the sick quarters opposite our lines. Light duty men were used as bearers, although the actual grave-digging party had, since the beginning of that year, consisted of regulars. Theirs was a good steady job. It had a certain security about it, as the grave diggers knew that this job would be open to them unto the last. Sensitive men might have broken down under the strain of such a task, but the three or four regulars appointed – including the fabulous Kemp, the boldest of racketeers – were, perhaps, the brawniest and fittest men in the whole camp, not excluding the Japanese, either.

Initially, they had to clear the allotted ground space and then dig the regulation hole, about five feet deep. When one trench had been dug, they did not cease but moved a few feet and commenced another. They could never work too quickly, as the conveyor belt of corpses never ceased. In July, for instance, the rate of death averaged five per day. On one day, twelve men died and, as bodies could not be retained in the small room set aside as a mortuary for more than twenty-four hours, no time could be lost at the graveyard. The grave diggers did not, therefore, stand decorously at the graveside awaiting the arrival of the burial cortege, but kept on working at new graves, only to break off to lower coffins as they arrived on site.

The route to Boot Hill from the sick bay lay around the perimeter of the camp and then across some cleared rubber plantation. It must have been the best part of half a mile and the light duty men were halted once or twice on the way. At least the cemetery was out of view of our compound. I took my turn as bearer more than once and my outstanding memory is the terrible, nauseating smell that often escaped from the makeshift coffins. It was not so much that decomposition had set in after death but before it. Men often died not of, but suffering from, severe tropical ulcers. These, left unbandaged, oozed with pus. On living tissue, the smell was disgusting and death did nothing to improve it. Wrapped in only banana leaves, enclosed in an often used, ill-made, fragile makeshift coffin, the corpses not only exuded nauseating smells but allowed pus to seep through the cracks, between the bottom and sides of the ghastly containers. On such occasions, fatigue was not the only reason to bring a sense of thankfulness when the cemetery was reached.

Our task was not over then. The Japanese were, as of everything else (save brutality), short of wood, so that when the death rate reached high proportions they decreed that 'coffins' should be used only to *convey* the corpses to their resting place. The engineers, therefore, fashioned five body containers with detachable lids, made temporarily secure when the corpses had been placed in position, to be loosened again when the graveside had been reached. Rings had been fixed to both the containers and lids for ease of depositing the bodies. This way, when the cortege reached the cemetery, the grave diggers dropped their digging tools and took over, lowering by means of a rope sling the body boxes to the bottom of the graves, drew forth the slings and then took up their crooks and lifted the covers off the coffins. The crooks were guided through the rings in the boxes, a sudden jerk and out toppled the body to lie uncomfortably on the cold clay. But, the object had been achieved, the receptacles were empty and ready for reuse! Our bugler sounded the last post while a Japanese officer or NCO and the sergeant major who headed us gave the salute – the one cynically, the other matter-of-factly. For a brief moment, bearers and grave diggers bowed their heads and so more of war's victims were disposed of and forgotten. All that remained to be done was the filling in of the graves by the burial party and the carrying of the boxes, sometimes pus-marked, back to the sick quarters for their next victims.

No funeral march was ever accorded the victims of Japanese deprivation but back in our compound we sometimes heard the strumming of a banjo from over the wire between us and the civvies. Never once did I hear a cheerful ditty! The music was always desultory and sad, as if the musician had known nothing but squalor and misery all his life and could interpret nothing else. Hearing this mournful playing after returning one day from Boot Hill, I was struck by the parallel between the fateful poignancy of the music and the fateful cynicism of the Japanese officers' graveside salute. Like the Japanese, we could only now appreciate a predestination that was always unpleasant.

San Mile

When on 1 May 1945, I rejoined the main working party, I found that it had been ordered to dig one metre deep dykes, about seventy metres wide, on each side of a proposed airstrip to be projected through a rubber plantation, off the main road and about halfway from Kuching to the aerodrome. This work was extremely unpleasant because it entailed using a changkol either standing barefooted on the rough scrub as the dyke was excavated or, when the excavation was complete, actually standing in eighteen inches of water that had collected at the bottom of an open drain while the edges were trimmed. Fortunately, as far as I was concerned on rejoining the party, the dykes were already partly complete so that, after a couple of weeks, I was back to more familiar work, that of levelling and shaping the airstrip, with the inevitable changkol and basket, a task which, tedious though it was, possessed certain advantages over ditch-making. Besides which, as time went on, the tempo of the work gradually eased up, due to two causes. Firstly, on nearing completion, the airstrip was bombed by American planes and, although none of us was hurt from our place of refuge in the surrounding rubber plantation, the airstrip itself was heavily damaged. I suspect that it was then that the Japanese realised that it would never receive an incoming Mig, despite their High Command hopes. Secondly, the work dragged on until the end of the war and, as already explained, when it became obvious that the Japanese would not win, their sadism subsided and changkols were wielded at a much slower pace.

As usual, there existed opportunities for business and for scrounging extra food. I soon found that there was as much scope as on special party, though the risks were greater in the absence of the paternal protection of our special party guard. During my initial few weeks on the proposed airstrip, tiffin was taken under the rubber trees near the junction of the strip and the main road. Later, due to the danger of air raids, we marched half a mile along the main road towards the aerodrome to find shelter under less dangerous rubber. The first profitable enterprise that I was introduced to was snail-hunting. Back in camp snails fetched, according to size, as much as twelve to fifteen cents each. Sarawak snails are considerably larger than those of England, but whether their edible qualities are better, I am not qualified to say. I have consumed Sarawak snails, but not English ones. Too squeamish myself to clean and cook them, yet, once eating them as part of a stodge concocted by a friend of mine, I found that they were quite palatable. Rather, I thought at the time, like small lumps of kidney from which most of the taste had been extracted. However, so popular were snails with certain types that a good deal of tiffin time was spent searching for them under the rubber trees. The peculiar advantage of snails was that their possession did not enrage the Japanese guards.

To me the bigger attraction was pineapples. These grew in fair abundance a quarter of a mile from where we ate. The main risk was not to steal them, but to get them back to camp. On site I would not eat more than one with advantage, so I had to rely on sales to make the pineapple racket worthwhile. I succeeded in doing this, on one occasion getting five pineapples back to our lines without being caught. Before the plantation had been stripped, however, there came the order to take tiffin under the rubber trees because of the risk of air raids. Perhaps this was just as well as, because of their bulk, trading in pineapples was a very risky procedure.

I soon learnt, however, that a more paying proposition was to trade in the clothes market. Working on the proposed airstrip were several natives. Far better fed than we were, they thought more in terms of clothes than of food. So it was possible, at various times during the day, to edge near enough to these rag traders to strike a bargain. Prices were fairly stable, say twenty dollars for a pair of shorts, thirty for a shirt, forty for a pair of KD trousers. Few prisoners now possessed these valuable assets, but there still seemed an abundance of them in the civilian camp. To dispose of an article of clothing on behalf of the civilians meant a profit of from five to ten 'bucks', but two risks had to be taken: buying the article of clothing from the civilians over the wire and disposing of it to the natives. The latter operation presented the least risk. I soon found it comparatively easy to wrap a shirt around my waist when working, to strike my bargain with one of the many commercially minded natives on the airstrip and then surreptitiously drop the shirt behind, say on a mound of earth, a skip or branch of a tree while the natives tossed over a roll of notes. There were few accidents in the progress of this operation.

Even finer opportunities for doing business were presented half a mile down the main road during the tiffin adjournment. We ate our meals unsupervised at one end of a clearing in the rubber while the Japanese lunched in lofty isolation at the other. When we had consumed the pint of mixed rice and green stew, the more adventurous slipped through the rubber plantation to make direct contact with a few natives who lurked two or three hundred metres away. There they offered not only dollars for clobber, but salt and sugar, and so we could, if we chose, barter clothes for makan.

To receive food for clothing was very advantageous, as not only could we procure, say twenty dollars worth of salt for a pair of shorts, but resell the salt in camp for double the price, thus making profits two ways. Of course, the risk was greater, for to be found when searched at the entrance of the camp with salt or sugar would most likely entail not only a bashing but confiscation. On the other hand, the Japanese never relieved us of money.

The classical racket, however, was the rice box trick. By now our tiffin was carried out in wooden boxes and reheated on site. At the bottom of the boxes, false bottoms had been fixed so that purchased goods could be safely secreted. A search upon return to camp included an inspection of the boxes, but enough food was always left adhering to the visible uppermost flanks to allay suspicion of any hidden goods.

The trick was never discovered and the participants in this form of smuggling made some very hefty profits. In my opinion, a great opportunity was missed. Had this ruse been organised on a communal basis, far greater good could have been done. Each day, perhaps, four boxes were carried out on working parties and the amount of contraband was enough to have been of real benefit to the sick in our lines. But, although the ruse was well known to our administrative staff, the false bottoms being fashioned by the engineers, the benefit of the spoils accrued mainly to the few sergeants who took advantage of a trick not available to the rank and file. All the poor private got out of it was perhaps a small rake-off for assisting in carrying the boxes to and from the camp. Doubtless, our leaders naturally took advantage of all this. No wonder, therefore, that there was some resentment from the rank and file as they pondered the management's attempt to raid their own profits. If a possible reply to my criticism is that other rackets were being organised in at least as part benefit for the sick, unbeknown to me, then I can only say that our administration made a bad error in not advertising the fact.

Despite these unfair advantages, I managed to maintain a comparatively high standard of living by selling clothes for money and food, and also bringing off an occasional theft. The greatest opportunities still existed in the pineapple plantation. We had, it is true, been forced to take our lunch well removed from the bounds of the plantation, but when an alarm of air raids was given, we were encouraged to shelter in the semi-jungle. Then, the most daring of us, like ferrets for a rabbit hole, nosed for the pineapples. Sergeant Fleming and I were fired with greater ambitions. Foraging further afield one day, we came across an isolated native hut and introduced ourselves to its inhabitant, who not only gave us pineapples, but news. From him we heard that the Allies were now firmly entrenched on the east coast of Borneo. Therefore to make for the hut during an air raid became an obsession with us and one day we chanced it too often. Uncomfortably squatted on the floor of the native hut, we were drinking tea or coffee (I cannot remember which) when, happening to look towards the proposed airstrip, I espied with horror, the top half of a Japanese soldier. My heart pounded fearfully. A ghost could scarcely have been more frightening. Gasping a warning, I dashed out of the hut, with Fleming at my heels, to lie quaking behind some nearby bushes. I had good reason for my fears, for to be caught risked not a charge of illicit purchases, but that of espionage. Kepala katong! (cut off head!) Those two words possessed a nightmarish quality. However, we pulled ourselves together, acquired vulpine cunning and planned a hasty, unseen retreat. Not until we had regained the airstrip did the ex-ferrets cease to be foxes hunted by bloodthirsty hounds. Once there, relief, for there was little risk in joining the rest of the party already working as, peculiarly enough, no tenko was called after an air raid. We never repeated that particular adventure.

I was not entirely deterred, for a week or so later an air raid alarm sounded when we were working at the top of the strip. This time we darted for the country on the other side. Once more our luck was in. A bed of ubi-kayu was discovered. Forgotten was my narrow squeak as, regardless of the Japanese, I frantically pulled at the larger plants.

Such episodes must give an impression of glamorous adventures, but not so. We were fighting for existence, fully aware of the rapidly rising death rate with starvation as its cause. It would have been much easier to have worked free of any worry or responsibility save the evasion of a hiding. To carry on a business entailed, in the first place, a lot of patience and ingenuity in disposing of the article. The bigger test was to come, the smuggling of any edible article into camp. Nearly every night we could expect a search, its thoroughness depending upon not only the searcher, but on his mood. Most of our ruses had been discovered, under hats, water bottles, false bottoms to packs, etc. Indeed, with our wearing apparel reduced to the minimum, there was precious little space about our persons but we took the risk and twice I was caught.

We entered camp about sunset by way of a gate at the corner of the track bounding the ladies' quarters. Just inside the wire at this point, or somewhere between there and the entrance to our lines, we were searched. At one time we could hope to pass any goods to a mate in a rank already examined, but the Japanese were on to this and forced the ranks to stand a few metres apart while the inspection was carried out. We tried to stand in the rear rank, as packages dropped in the vegetation behind might escape notice and be retrieved when the Japanese had passed. Once I was caught in this dodge, but escaped with a few wallops. On the second occasion, I had no chance. I boasted three parcels, two small ones and a large packet of salt and sugar. I decided to secrete one packet under each armpit while the larger reposed, attached to a string and secure about my middle, under a purchased pair of shorts. As ill-luck would have it, however, the Japanese did not search us at the entrance of the camp, but at a spot near the centre of the long side of the ladies' compound, in full view of its inmates. There, the Japanese insisted on us shuffling into single file and passing the 'Customs' officer individually. I sensed that I was for it, but there seemed nothing that I could do. There were ten men between me and the searching hands, five, four, three, two, one: first my pack was checked with no result, then my water bottle; it was empty. My armpits were missed and, for a split second, I thought that the impossible had transpired and I would make it. As I moved off, the bulge in my trunks was spotted and the parcel 'sussed' out! I was motioned towards a small handful of men who had already been caught with goods, but I was not to be so easily dealt with. Why not toss the parcel unseen to a pal already cleared and, on completion of the first of the search, let the bastards spot one only of the parcels tucked under each armpit? So, at a favourable moment, I tossed the large parcel six metres to the receptive arms of my friend and was emboldened to rid myself then of one of the small packages under my armpit, in order to get two out of the three back to the hut. It whizzed, projectile-like, towards my friend.

Just at the critical moment, however, the Japanese turned around to see the parcel in mid-flight. Like a maddened bull he turned on me, whipping out his bayonet. I feared the worse. Slash! It was only the flat end that caught my rump, with two or three more blows, but I did not worry. There was to be no spilling of blood. All that was to be feared now was confiscation and detention in the guard room. Now, luck flew to my aid. The third smuggled item was not discovered. There was no confiscation and no guard room. I could hardly believe it. In retrospect, I know now why I was so lightly punished. A month earlier and I would have spent a weekend in the guardroom for certain frequent bashings, but the writing was on the wall. Some of the guards must have had an inkling of a drastic turn of events: some of them were easing up six weeks before their country's final surrender. It was a mercy that punishment was easing up, for by now I had lost my nerve. No longer could I refrain from flinching as a yellow hand whistled towards my face.

One last thought about this episode. I wonder why Mrs Keith never thought fit to mention the searches and the often brutal punishment of POWs, of which she must have been well aware, being so near to the ladies' quarters. Who knows? She may, as previously suggested, have seen my own maltreatment!

There was also an incident a little earlier at San Mile. Set upon by a Japanese for some alleged slacking, I ducked at the first blow. Enraged at such effrontery, the Japanese drove at me with both hands. Only too well I realised that I must, like the well-armed big game hunter when charged by a wild beast, stand my ground. Despite summoning to my aid all my determination, I found myself quite unable to resist the advancing blows. As a result I suffered probably the biggest hiding, not excepting the 'Gorilla's', that I had so far received. Such bashings sapped not only the energy but the will. Without doubt, similar atrocities shortened the life of many a man. Fortunately, however, by then the Japanese were fighting a losing battle and, although we were unaware of it, the tables were shortly to be turned. San Mile, the last outside working party, would be just an episode of a personal 'Dark Ages'. The Japanese would soon be the underdog.

The Last Days

About six weeks before the end of the war, Dr Yamamoto held a sick parade in our compound. It was no ordinary parade, for every duty man passed in front of him, though he did little more than eye each up and down. My turn came and, as for a moment I lingered in front of him, I had time to observe that he had written on a register against each man's name one of two signs, a cross or a dash. Plainly he was indicating, according to his own standard, whether a man was fit or not. What was the object? If the leer that hovered on his face meant anything, he was up to no good. But what? We could but wonder and worry. Soon, a rumour circulated that we had been categorised fit or unfit to lug Japanese kit to a secret hideout in the mountains of the interior, where a last stand would be made in the event of Kuching being captured. I did not like this one bit. Although we had had no official news for some time, we vaguely trusted that relief would come before the end of 1945 and, despite the heavy death rate, I reckoned that I might hang on for another few months. To be uprooted at this late stage of affairs would mean that all number of untold hazards might confront us, not the least being malaria.

So far, less than half our members had suffered from this disease. I was among the lucky ones and dreaded an attack now that my stamina had decreased. Therefore, despite my having managed very well without a mosquito net for so long, in view of the rumours of moving up-country, I invested the best part of one hundred dollars of hard-earned cash on one of the few remaining nets to be had in the compound. Although we never did move from Kuching, thereafter I used the net, only, however, to contract a sharp but short-lived burst of the disease during the last week of the war. In principle, my investment had been logical, however, for it had indeed been the Japanese intention to remove us into the hills, although the departure date was postponed a month after strong representations had been made to the Japanese, not only by RSM Sunderland but by the officers also, I believe. Even stronger representations would have been made had the full Japanese design been known at the time. Apparently Yamamoto had, indeed, placed us in two categories, those fit enough to hump Japanese equipment to the hills and those not so fit. So would be dashed our cherished hopes over the long years that here would be a return to England, let alone a halfway camp in Lorenco Marques. Doubtless the porters would subsequently have perished, as did those on the ghastly enforced march from San Dakan to Ranau in British North Borneo (now Sabah). Plans had been formulated for the less fit to be exterminated before Allied forces reached the camp. Thus, the Japanese 'final solution' for their cherished Kuching prisoners of war. Colonel Suga's 'shimpashy' would, doubtless, have known no bounds. Perhaps the Japanese had, upon receipt of news from Europe, decided to emulate Auschwitz where the Nazis devised two categories for the Jews, one for *arbeit* (work) and the other for the gas chambers. At Ranau, all of us would have perished.

I had always harboured fears as to what would happen if our friends attempted to capture Kuching. My long association with the Japanese had taught me that they would, if necessary, practise absolute ruthlessness, and the possibility of the turning upon the camps of machine guns, did not escape me. Without mentioning my fears to my comrades, I formulated my own plans. At the first signs of slaughter I must either make a break for it or crawl under a culvert. Either alternative was fraught with danger, yet it was the best that could be hoped for in the absence of guidance from higher up. I think that it was most probable that others, and especially the officers, had also considered the possibility of savagery if the Japanese were attacked from over the land and that they had devised their own plans, but not a whisper of this reached me.

The rank and file had received very little news during the past year. As a result, morale had slumped. The appearance of friendly aircraft tended to raise hopes but, as the weather and the months drifted by with little evidence that bombing had bought the end of the war in sight, a certain depression settled once more over our lines. Most of us began to calculate our expectation of life under the present conditions. Obviously the outlook was bleak unless relief was near at hand. Rumours had reached us of landings in British North Borneo, but this was not enough. We wanted BBC news, so that we could more accurately assess our chances of survival, balancing our health against the days of war yet to come. The radio, that had worked for so long, was of no more use as the batteries had given out. For months, a generator had been under construction but, with none of the ordinary tools or materials available to them, the craftsmen were greatly handicapped. Eventually, largely through the efforts of a Sergeant Miles, a peacetime watch repairer, a hand-generator was at last constructed. What would be the result?

When forming up in our lines, one August morning, before the arrival of the Korean guards on the assembly square, the adjutant CSM Southern, unexpectedly appeared. He was obviously very excited and pleasurably so. Perhaps he had some radio news? For a few days now, there had circulated a rumour that the secret radio would soon be functioning once more. If so, then perhaps a naval victory, perhaps further advances in Burma, or something definite on the European front? There had, for some time, been talk of the end of the war with Germany. We sensed that the CSM had, at least, something extraordinary to tell us but when, in a hushed yet excited voice, he informed us that the war was virtually over, that a request for unconditional surrender by the Japanese was likely to be accepted, we could hardly believe it. There must be some mistake! Before we could query his announcement, he added that the news had come over the radio now back in operation. The initial hush was followed by gasps of wonderment from the hundred men who were still fit enough to gather on the square for working parties. For my own part, I experienced less of a thrill than the sight of the first American plane. I had become too cynical and detached during the last few weeks. The announcement sounded too surreal. It altered suddenly and completely our whole life. What did we do now, shout, sing the national anthem? We did nothing, for Southern quickly warned us not to make a noise or show any elation on our faces as the guards were about to enter our lines. Our captors must have no suspicion that we had wind of the stupendous news item. Certainly, the guards showed little sign that the war was virtually over when they strode into our compound, took charge and marched us out of the main entrance.

It was the last complete day on working party. I did not accompany the main party to the airstrip, having been detailed to weed the square in front of the Japanese offices. This I did without enthusiasm. The only zest that I displayed was in the theft of some ubi-kayu that grew behind a hut occupied by some Indonesian prisoners of war. Was it that I thought some gigantic mistake had been made or that there would be some last minute hitch so that I must still struggle on for that little extra nourishment? Or was it that the habit of theft died hard? I cannot now be certain. All I know is that it was my last adventure of that kind. Casting my memory back to the days when, if nothing else, every day meant a new opportunity to pit wits against the Japanese in an effort to buy or otherwise acquire food illicitly, I experienced some regret that probably never again would I ripple with the excitement of such enterprises. Yes, save one out of spite. It was my last theft as a POW for, although the following morning the main working parties set out as usual while a few of us were sent to complete the weeding, before noon, without a word of explanation, the main working party returned. We were not surprised, for on our square that morning Southern had announced that the Japanese had accepted unconditional surrender. He also told us something of the atomic bomb.

The war was over? It must now be true for did not the return of the working party indicate some stupendous event after three and a half years' of imprisonment? I thought of the papaya tree that had been planted. We had declared that it would never be of any use but it had been for it had fruited twice. I thought of all those who had died, of the agony of Lekas Corner, of the 'Gorilla', of the blows that we had received, of those who had died like Corporal Coventry, Private Fletcher, Private Broughton (tragically as late as July 1945, a month before the war ended), Aircraftsman Clements, Private Attwood and close friends, Norman Williams and Freddie Pafford, but, gradually my thoughts turned towards the future, both immediate and more distant.

Of the immediate future, what would be the Japanese reaction? Would they, like cornered animals, strike out indiscriminately? They did not, but whether because of a newly discovered humanity or because of fear of the consequences, I cannot say. For certain, a terrible vengeance would have been reaped had they committed atrocities.

It soon became obvious too that they would find little chance to do us much more harm. Very few days had elapsed before Allied aircraft, mostly Mosquitos, were almost constantly patrolling our skies. Leaflets showered over the camp, propaganda, enquiries and instructions to the Japanese command. Answers from the Japanese had to be signalled back by the draping of flags in certain patterns on the square in front of their offices. For instance, a certain simple sign was to indicate that food and medical supplies might be dropped. These were parachuted to the ground from Dakotas, christened 'bread baskets'. It would be tedious to recount again the pleasure derived from tasting European food once more but, despite these luxuries, we still consumed large helpings of rice. The Japanese miraculously discovered that they commanded ample supplies to meet all our demands. We still negotiated for extras from outside the wire, with the result that the natives did a roaring trade in duck eggs. A large part of our time was spent crouching over home-made fires which smouldered outside our huts.

The Japanese displayed an amazing interest in our welfare. Toilet soap, tooth brushes, tubes of toothpaste, vests, shorts, shirts and footwear poured into our compound. All these articles must have laid for years dormant in the Japanese QM stores and, the fact they had not been distributed among us before was another indication of our ex-captors' shocking lack of humanity. Short of foodstuffs they had been but, unless they had argued that we only sold our clothes to the natives, there was never any excuse for withholding that which was to hand. Certainly, no such excuse could have been offered for failing to distribute mail. Although as stated previously, we had been handed correspondence from home, for a year practically none had been received. Why? Thousands of letters lay heaped up in piles in the Japanese offices.

Either it had been too much trouble to sort them or it gave further evidence of Japanese callousness. Few would have elected for the first reason.

Yet, we were to listen to another speech from our 'shimpashetic' Suga when summoned to attend upon him over a week after Southern's pronouncement. By then, planes had been over and dropped their leaflets, but Suga did not mention this in his speech. His main theme was the terrible disasters of Nagasaki and Hiroshima: these, and not defeats in the field, had forced Japan to sue for peace. We would soon be returned to our families, but in the meantime, we must stay in the camp. I expressed no 'shimpashy'!

Few of us, indeed, ventured outside, and the Japanese still retained a good deal of administrative control. It was a peculiar position. We, the conquerors, were being governed by the vanquished, but we were also subject to the discipline of our own military police, arguably more stringent than that of the Japanese, within the rankers' compound, as I learnt to my cost. Corporal P, a bullying MP and the one who had taken me into custody for the ubi-kayu theft, mocked me when I passed by as he came striding from the cookhouse, where else? I told him to pipe down, only to have him physically attack me. Despite his superior strength – he was one of the guys who had enjoyed extra rations – we had quite a violent struggle before he forced me to the ground, but was unable to pin me down without the assistance of another MP, one Corporal B. Upon somewhat foolishly complaining to CSM Southern from the detention room the following morning when he made his round, all I gained was an attempted swipe at my face and a threat of being put in irons if I did not buckle down. You can't beat the system, I thought once more, but fortune looked kindly on me because a change in the command of our enclosure resulted in my release from confinement.

I feel that I should report one further unpleasant, perhaps incredible, incident. Although I was still suffering from unhealed ulcerated legs, I was routinely marched, but not as a punishment, with a number of other unfit rankers for duties, into the officers' compound. I was detailed to wash a pile of underclothes. This I much resented, failing to appreciate how officers who had not been called upon for slavery on working parties outside the confines of the camp – working parties that had contributed to the death of so many other ranks' personnel – could have the gall and lack of compassion to require their less fortunate compatriots to perform such menial tasks. Were they 'Lords of the Manor' ordering around people in service to them? Well, indeed, to beat the system is difficult – or it was so in 1945 – but, nevertheless, my laundry skills must have been doubted by the establishment. Perhaps, needless to say, I returned to my hut with a nice supply of stolen peanuts. Was it, I later reflected, that the hidebound nature of the officers had to some extent been a contributory factor to the early defeat of the British in Malaya and Singapore?

In a story of this nature it follows that the last unpleasant incident heralds the end. However, a few further items merit brief reference. A short while after the war ended a concert was staged in our compound. It was well attended and the entertainment was excellent, but what I remember best about it was the tremendous enthusiasm displayed when the national anthem and 'Land of Hope and Glory' were sung. I only hope that the Japanese enjoyed the singing as much as we did. Equally moving was the United Service of Thanksgiving which was well attended by most of the various compounds.

Then, publicly displayed in our lines was the radio set. Cunningly fitted into two army dixies, the marvellous contraption that had enabled us to get authentic news for much of our imprisonment was seen for the first time. What the Japanese thought of all this, I do not know, but their chagrin can be imagined. Not only had they been beaten on an international scale but outwitted on, as it were, a domestic basis.

While these encampment events were taking place, much more was happening both as regards individual compounds and the camp as a whole, of which we rank and file had little knowledge. From a general standpoint, as far as I know, after the commencement of the daily air patrol, the first development was a dramatic parachute drop of food and medical supplies already referred to. After that, came Japanese permission to land aircraft containing Allied officers. As soon as landing space could be improvised, they descended on the badly bombed aerodrome.

When these officers arrived, they arranged with Suga that a detachment of Allied troops should be allowed to pass up the River Sarawak and come ashore. Eventually we witnessed their arrival, Australians and Americans. Long, lean and active supermen they seemed. The administration of the camp was quickly taken over by them. In the meantime, Dr King held a medical parade, in the course of which he decided who, in our lines, should first be moved. Though I had kept working to the end, my tropical ulcers resulted in my being among the first to leave, that is among those fit enough to travel but not considered fit enough to stay to help the chronically sick to move out. Charlie Cleal, my friend for many long years, was detailed for a later batch, as for some months he had acted as medical orderly, and I did not see him again until we were on the high seas bound for England. Although I had looked forward to seeing what befell the Korean and Japanese guards, nevertheless I should have been disappointed to have missed the first detachment to evacuate, in mid-September 1945.

I had done a lot of moving since joining the forces but never, as a free man, had I less packing to do. I just moved out in what I stood in. I had now been fitted up with one decent set of tropical clothes, haversack, letters, papers and a few toilet requisites. The only article that I possessed, which had accompanied me throughout my imprisonment, was my identity disk, retained solely as a souvenir.

On 13 September (two days before the commencement of another Japanese jungle death march, had it not been for the 'A' bomb), we were transported by lorry to the docks and taken direct to a small café near the godowns where we were treated to coffee and biscuits. As I refreshed myself, I caught sight of the woodshed where, while on dock party, I had hidden myself on Sunday afternoons. Overwhelmingly exciting as it was to be on the way home, yet, when reminded of the hardships that we had endured, I could not but think of some of the more satisfying moments. No matter how rough the conditions, all was not bad, just as under the most favourable circumstances, perfect happiness is rarely obtained.

When we had sorted ourselves out in the motor boats, we put

off without any celebration or ceremony. It was all too easy, so easy, in fact that, it seemed a little unreal, or was it that the past three and a half years had been unreal? The transition from abject misery to happiness and hope was too simple, too much like a fairy story to be true, too much like the tale of the Sleeping Princess! The picture of reality was too shadowy, the canvas too flat, too much like reading a novel by the fireside, or the Sunday afternoon walk. Yet, there we were, cruising up the river towards the sea, experiencing what many pay large sums for, passing by the boat-building project, within a few hundred metres of Lekas Corner and Rissole Hill, names that lie engraved in our hearts and imprisoned in the rotting flesh of many a dead ex-comrade.

As I stood with the fine spray gently brushing my face in the bows of the ship, I was little troubled by morbid thoughts. I had made it! Not in vain had I wrestled with death. I had beaten him! I was going home! 'When we sail down the river to the sea.' The strains of this song now rose above the swish of the water, and soon we sped clear of the river and out to sea. A mile offshore we were taken aboard an American ship that took us to Labuan, where, for a month, I was to recuperate in an Australian field hospital. During that time we were thrilled to meet Lady Edwina Mountbatten who went around the hospital wards. An ex-prisoner veteran, who might visit Labuan, would haste to the Imperial War Graves Commission cemetery where the remains of countless fallen military comrades have been reburied, including about five hundred from Kuching.

Both on the ship and at Labuan we learnt again the meaning of hospitality, but this is a story not of my RAF career, but of imprisonment. So, I will revert to where I spent the most of my time with the Japanese.

Back at Kuching, those prisoners who were last to leave learnt something of what befell our former guards. Suga, I was later informed at Labuan, successfully cut his throat with a broken pocket knife and the help of his former batman, an unnecessarily painful method of hara-kiri; Nekata and Yamamoto failed in the attempt. Of the rest, one or two of the more brutal of the guards were, it was whispered, accidentally shot by the Australian troops who had taken over the camp; others were beaten up on the slightest pretext, but Tubby and Moray were looked after, being given cushy jobs in the cookhouse. The rest of the bunch received sentences of imprisonment ranging from one to twenty years. Most of them will thus suffer longer than we did but never, I am sure, with such intensity.

What happened to the worst of the Japanese, the 'Gorilla', I never discovered. He should have been shot out of hand but, unfortunately, he was the type to escape scot-free. Far too capable, he doubtless, not being a camp guard, was nowhere to be found when most wanted. If he did escape punishment, I sincerely hope that to offset such injustice our friend of the special party reached in safety the so-called Land of the Rising Sun, to find his family in good health.

Generally speaking, however, I learnt to abhor the Japanese. Despite the fact that I realised that their methods and culture were fundamentally different from ours, that the best of the Japanese nation could not be found among the personnel of prison camps, I could, after being freed, find little but hate in my heart for this Oriental race. Distasteful as it is to me to kill even a wasp in cold blood yet, as soon as my strength had recovered, I felt I could without a qualm have run a bayonet through the first Japanese encountered. Could I really have done this? Perhaps not! However for years afterwards, as I thought of the toiling bodies at Lekas Corner or of the 'Gorilla' beating up the aerodrome contingent, of the processions to and from Boot Hill, or even of the sight of watching a sadistic Japanese holding a lighted match under an insect, I doubt whether I should have felt a lot of compunction in witnessing the beating up of some of our guards to within an inch of their lives. A few years ago, at Pearl Harbour, a Japanese middle-aged man, seeing my ulcer-scarred legs, apologised for his country's brutality and I can no longer feel revengeful.

Nothing will now bring back the dead, and so I end with a tribute to all those who died in Kuching. A few were rogues, many had sunk to meanness, many before death had caught up with them had lost all self-respect. Yet, I pay tribute to these comrades in misfortune, despite their desperate and despairing struggles because, in their isolation from their families, they died uncared for and unmourned.

May they live for ever!

Nearing the End of the Millennium

For the first time in decades, I have been reading my memoirs and have concluded that I should restate that, throughout my imprisonment, I secretly took written notes which, for accuracy, were invaluable in compiling this account, which was drafted just after the end of the war.

However, it was based on the unvarnished experience of one lowly ranking airman, without the resources which were available to officers and senior NCOs running the camp under the heel of the Japanese. Doubtless, such ranking prisoners would have viewed matters differently. The impressions that I have given were for the most part personal, but then, every survivor of the POW camp at Kuching would have his or her own individual recollection and interpretations, presumably in like manner to Mrs Keith when writing her 1946 book on the adjoining ladies' camp.